Ayurveda Beginner's Guide

Ayurveda Beginner's Guide

Vaishali Verma

ABD PUBLISHERS
Jaipur ■ New Delhi

ABD PUBLISHERS

Regd. Off. "Bony Residency", Gate No. 2
Opp. Tilak Public School, Vishweswariya Nagar,
Gopalpura Road, Jaipur - 302018, India
Ph: 0141 - 2761280, Telefax: 2761381
Email: abdpublishersjpr@gmail.com

Delhi Office: 102, 1st Floor, Satyam House,
4327/3, Ansari Road, Darya Ganj,
New Delhi - 110002, India
Ph: 011-45652440

visit us: www.oxfordbookcompany.com

Distributed By
KEYA INTERNATIONAL PRESS LLP
E-mail: keyainternationalpressllp@gmail.com

Published in India, 2025

ISBN : 978-81-19343-17-1

Typeset by Shivangi Computer, Jaipur

Printed and bound in India by Thomson Press Ltd.,
New Delhi

Contents

Preface

Often viewed as the first system of medicine ever established, Ayurveda is a 5,000-year-old Indian system of care that holistically addresses the mind, body, and spirit. It emphasizes eating right to bring yourself back into balance, exercising, breathing fully, reducing stress, sleeping well, and other basic concepts to keep your body whole, balanced, and healthy. In Ayurveda, food is medicine. When a person eats in a manner that is best for their unique needs, they can improve their health, live longer, and protect themselves from disease. Other Ayurvedic practices further support a strong mind-body constitution. While all of the Ayurvedic practices help you maintain good health, if you do get sick, the thought is that you can heal faster because your body is in better balance. Knowledge of Ayurveda comes from the Vedas, which originated in India, and are some of the oldest written texts in the world. This system of medicine was taught to students who visited the great teachers of India (the rishis) to learn from them. The science of life, which Ayurveda is often called, was originally an oral tradition transmitted through concepts and poetic phrases (sutras, literally meaning "thread") that were used to pass knowledge from one generation to the next. Even today, an Ayurvedic doctor may sing a sutra to explain a treatment or impart wisdom.

Many forms of medicine have roots in Ayurveda. For instance, herbal medicine, energy medicine, traditional Chinese medicine (TCM), polarity therapy, marma therapy, acupuncture, acupressure, and even Reiki and healing touch are either used in Ayurveda or share something in common with this system. That is one reason Ayurveda is so accepting of integrative medicine. It recognizes that there is wisdom to be found in many traditions. Ayurveda is a versatile system of health care because it can be tailored to suit any person's unique needs. Following an Ayurvedic lifestyle can help people stay healthy, recover faster from illness, and hopefully set the stage for a long life.

It can also complement traditional medicine for those who are already unwell or on medications and become an integrative part of their health-care support system.

Many people think of Ayurveda and yoga as Hindu practices, and worry that it will conflict with their religious traditions. You can have a powerful Ayurvedic practice without immersing yourself in Hinduism or learning Sanskrit (the classical language of India) or having statues of Hindu gods and goddesses like Ganesh (the remover of obstacles) around your house. An underlying principle of Ayurveda is that we are both energy and matter combined. Each of us, as well as our environment, is made up of the five great elements (Maha Bhutas): (1) Space, (2) Air, (3) Fire, (4) Water, and (5) Earth. These are the building blocks of our world. They create our foundation and structure (earth); movement and circulation (air and space); transformation, light, and metabolism (fire); and cohesiveness, digestive juices, and secretions (water).

This concise book covers Ayurveda's historical roots, concepts, and various healing methods for beginners. The book will show you how to unlock the transformative powers of Ayurveda and move forward in your journey towards a healthier state of mind, body, and spirit.

— ***Vaishali Verma***

Chapter 1

Ayurveda: An Ancient System of Healing

Introduction to Ayurveda

Often viewed as the first system of medicine ever established, Ayurveda is a 5,000-year-old Indian system of care that holistically addresses the mind, body, and spirit. It emphasizes eating right to bring yourself back into balance, exercising, breathing fully, reducing stress, sleeping well, and other basic concepts to keep your body whole, balanced, and healthy.

In Ayurveda, food is medicine. When a person eats in a manner that is best for their unique needs, they can improve their health, live longer, and protect themselves from disease. Other Ayurvedic practices further support a strong mind-body constitution. While all of the Ayurvedic practices help you maintain good health, if you do get sick, the thought is that you can heal faster because your body is in better balance.

Knowledge of Ayurveda comes from the Vedas, which originated in India, and are some of the oldest written texts in the world. This system of medicine was taught to students who visited the great teachers of India (the rishis) to learn from them.

The science of life, which Ayurveda is often called, was originally an oral tradition transmitted through concepts and poetic phrases (sutras, literally meaning "thread") that were used to pass knowledge from one generation to the next. Even today, an Ayurvedic doctor may sing a sutra to explain a treatment or impart wisdom.

Many forms of medicine have roots in Ayurveda. For instance, herbal medicine, energy medicine, traditional Chinese medicine (TCM), polarity therapy, marma therapy, acupuncture, acupressure, and even Reiki and healing touch are either used in Ayurveda or share something in common with this system. That is one reason Ayurveda is so accepting of integrative medicine. It recognizes that there is wisdom to be found in many traditions.

Who Can Benefit From Ayurveda: Ayurveda is a versatile system of health care because it can be tailored to suit any person's unique needs. Following an Ayurvedic lifestyle can help people stay healthy, recover faster from illness, and hopefully set the stage for a long life. It can also complement traditional medicine for those who are already unwell or on medications and become an integrative part of their health-care support system.

If Ayurveda can do so much for so many people, and has a history of use for over 5,000 years, why isn't it a more common approach to health and wellness? Truth is, people tend to lean toward more modern concepts of health and healing, thinking that if it's newer, it must be superior. This isn't always true. After reading this book and trying out these practices, you may conclude that this ancient understanding of mind-body balance might even be more advanced than today's established health-care system.

Ayurveda and Religion: Many people think of Ayurveda and yoga as Hindu practices, and worry that it will conflict with their religious traditions. I had no idea that Ayurveda had any relationship to Hinduism. I certainly didn't need to be Hindu to incorporate Ayurvedic practices into my life and benefit from them. However, I do find the Hindu religion fascinating, beautiful, and filled with stories and texts like the Bhagavad Gita and the Upanishads that are as relevant today as they were thousands of years ago.

You can have a powerful Ayurvedic practice without immersing yourself in Hinduism or learning Sanskrit (the classical language of India) or having statues of Hindu gods and goddesses like Ganesh (the remover of obstacles) around your house.

The Universe of Ayurveda

An underlying principle of Ayurveda is that we are both energy and matter combined. Each of us, as well as our environment, is made up of the five great elements (Maha Bhutas): (1) Space, (2) Air, (3)

Fire, (4) Water, and (5) Earth. These are the building blocks of our world. They create our foundation and structure (earth); movement and circulation (air and space); transformation, light, and metabolism (fire); and cohesiveness, digestive juices, and secretions (water).

The five great elements are found in varying amounts in every person and the environment. Some people and places will have more of one element than another. Think of the desert as having more fire (heat) and air (dryness), the beach as having more water, and the mountains as having more earth. Likewise, some of us are more "earthy," some us are more "spacey," and others are more "intense" or "hot." Our unique combination of the five elements makes up our predominant body composition, or dosha, of which there are three types: Vata, Pitta, and Kapha. Here are the qualities associated with each of the five great elements:

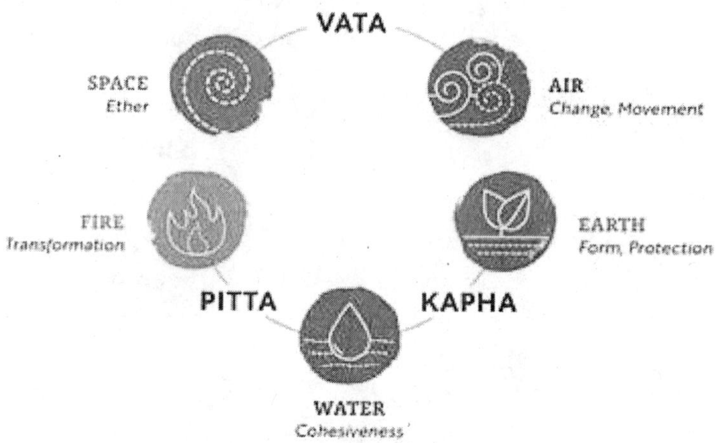

Figure: *Your Unique Body Composition*

(Your Dosha) our unique mind-body constitution, or dosha, comprises the five great elements. The way these elements present themselves at birth depends upon many things, including where you were conceived and born, how the planets were aligned at your birth, the state of mind of your parents when you were conceived, the food they ate prior to conceiving you, and even your past lives. The primary dosha you are born with is known as your prakruti. As we grow, we typically enter into a state of imbalance, or vikruti, due to the influences of our environment, the food we eat, the emotional state of our home, and so on. By adopting the practices of Ayurveda, you can move yourself slowly but surely back toward your natural way of being, your prakruti.

The three doshas are Vata, Pitta, and Kapha. Although one dosha is usually dominant, each of us is made up of all three. In the next section, you will find a simple quiz that can help you identify your dosha, and then you can review the chart here, which includes a brief rundown of the characteristics of each dosha, including signs of balance and imbalance.

When the doshas are disturbed by a person's lifestyle choices and/or environmental conditions, signs of imbalance manifest in both the mind and body. An imbalance can result in a disease or a general feeling of being unwell. The idea isn't to bring all three doshas into equal balance within you. The goal is to be the best unique makeup of yourself that you can be.

Overview of Dosha Characteristics

In addition, Ayurveda has a daily doshic cycle that equally affects all of the doshas. The qualities associated with each dosha are prevalent during certain times of the day. These cycles are the same for all doshas, as follows:

Vata Time: 2 a.m.-6 a.m. and 2 p.m.-6 p.m.

Pitta Time: 10 a.m.-2 p.m. and 10 p.m.-2 a.m.

Kapha Time: 6 a.m.-10 a.m. and 6 p.m.-10 p.m.

With this in mind, here is an ideal daily routine based on the doshic cycle:

Kapha Time 6 a.m.-10 a.m.

- Wake up around 6 a.m., without an alarm.
- Preform your morning routine .
- Exercise: Kapha time is a good time to get moving.
- Meditate facing east (toward the rising sun). At this time, the mind should feel alert and awake; it's perfect for meditation.
- Eat breakfast when you feel hungry.
- Begin your daily activities.

Pitta Time 10 a.m.-2 p.m.

oEat the most nutrient-dense meal of the day (protein is best had at this time of day).

- Rest quietly for a few minutes and allow your food to digest.
- Take a short walk after eating to promote digestion.

Vata Time 2 p.m.-6 p.m.

- The good meal you had during Pitta time will give you plenty of energy that is supported by Vata to be creative, work hard, and perform daily chores.
- Meditate at dusk facing north for cooling, calming energy.

Kapha Time 6 p.m.-10 p.m.

- Begin to wind down, avoiding heavy mental chores.
- Have an easy-to-digest dinner.
- Take a walk. Read spiritual or enjoyable texts. Avoid violent or scary TV and movies.
- Do light, enjoyable activities that promote relaxation.

Pitta Time 10 p.m.-2 a.m.

- Perform your evening routine.
- Be in bed by 10 p.m., as Pitta digestion time begins now.
- This is the time when the body begins the cycle of daily repair and renewal. This is a crucial time of day, as Pitta time works now to digest and transform everything you took in during the day, including all of your experiences, thoughts, emotions, and food. During this process, nutrients and waste are separated. Waste is prepared to be eliminated in the morning. Nutrients are assimilated to heal, repair, and detox the body.

Vata Time 2 a.m.-6 a.m.

- Our most vivid dreams occur once the body has completed the metabolic process.
- If we do not go to sleep before this time, the winds of Vata keep us awake-hence the term "second wind."
- If we wake during this time, it can be hard to fall back to sleep. Use a mantra and breath work to lull yourself back to sleep.
- Awakening before 6 a.m., you will feel the wind and movement of Vata encouraging you to begin your day. You may notice that sometimes you awaken naturally around 5 a.m. or 6 a.m. and feel wide awake. If you decide to go back to sleep, you may wake up at 7 a.m. or 8 a.m. feeling sluggish. This is because you have entered Kapha time. Be aware of the doshic cycle, and use it to your benefit.
- According to the elemental effects on the times of day, our bodies respond accordingly. However, we often fight against it.

Make note of the 24-hour doshic cycle, and see how you can use it to promote balance and harmony in your life. It is better to work with it, rather than against it. The elements and the universe will support you!

Maintaining Balance: One Ayurvedic principle is that "like attracts like." We can be easily thrown off balance if we keep attracting the same things to us. That's why this system employs the law of opposites to help us create balance. Let's say you are feeling dull, heavy, slow, and sluggish. A meal of eggs with cheese and bacon, which is heavy, oily, and slow to digest will just make you feel more of the same. Instead, you would want to eat the opposite of what you are feeling, which would be something light and dry, perhaps puffed cereal with goat's milk or a bowl of beans cooked with detoxifying spices and a light oil, like sunflower oil. And, if you are feeling ungrounded, you would gravitate toward warm, cooked foods and spices such as oatmeal with ginger, cinnamon, and turmeric to ground you.

To help us understand the law of opposites, Ayurvedic texts provide us with a list of 20 common qualities, or attributes, that are experienced in varying degrees throughout nature. The idea is that too much, or too little, of any one quality can throw us off balance, so we would turn to its opposite for healing.

Ayurveda's 20 Qualities

Heavy - Light

Slow - Quick

Cold - Hot

Oily - Dry

Smooth - Rough

Solid - Liquid

Soft - Hard

Stable - Moving

Subtle - Large

Clear - Sticky

The law of opposites is a fairly easy-to-understand concept, but not all of the Ayurvedic concepts are so straightforward. Other concepts include the three universal qualities (gunas), as well as the five layers, or sheaths (koshas). While it's helpful to be at least a little familiar with them, you don't need to delve into it all just yet to start dipping your toes into the dietary recommendations and lifestyle practices found in this book. If you want to know more, I encourage you to turn to appendix B for an overview. Later on, when you start to get into a good routine and begin feeling great, you may choose to further your studies of Ayurvedic concepts.

Mind-Body-Spirit: Before we go too deeply into the everyday practices of Ayurveda, it's important to understand the meaning of mind-body-spirit. Ayurveda teaches that what happens in the physical body is reflected in the mind and spirit, and vice versa. In other words, if the body is suffering from a physical ailment or imbalance, it will negatively affect the other two aspects. Looking at this somewhat vague term from an Ayurvedic perspective can shed some light on its meaning and how it relates to us.

In Ayurveda, the mind-body-spirit can also be viewed as the three dimensions: subtle, gross, and causal.

- The subtle dimension is the mind (consciousness), the intellect (decision-making process), and the ego (power, position, possessions, self-image).
- The gross dimension is the physical body and the environment and the interaction with the environment, such as breathing.
- The causal dimension comprises the personal (soul, memories, and desires); collective (creative desires); and universal (beyond time and space as we know it, where we are all interconnected, one).

The takeaway here is that you need to be aware that whatever you put into your body, you are also feeding to your mind and spirit. And it works the other way, too. When you take care of one, all three benefit.

Concept of Healthy Living in Ayurveda

Ayurveda is an ancient science of life since time immemorial. Ayurveda, apart from providing various therapeutic measures for diseases, emphasizes on maintenance, promotion of health and prevention of diseases through diet and lifestyle regimens. As per Ayurveda, life is sustained by a tripoid of mental, physical and spiritual factors constituted by body (Sharir), senses (Indriyas), mind (Satwa) and spirit (Atma).

The physical world including the human body is derived from the specific combinations of five fundamental entities viz. Akạsh, Vayu,

Teja, Jala and Prithvi which are known as Panchamahabhutas and the soul. Panchamahabhutas form the Tridoshas viz. Vata Dosha, Pitta Dosha and Kapha Dosha, Dhatus (tissues) and Malas (excretory products). Tridoshas carry out the physiological activities and are responsible for the integrity of the human body.

Due to the faulty diet and lifestyle normalcy of the Tridoshas is disturbed and they aggravate in the body. Vitiated Tridoshas disturb the normalcy of Dhatus and Malas causing their vitiation which manifests as various diseases in the body. Thus the health of an individual depends upon the normalcy of the Doshas , Dhatus and Malas.

Health of an individual can be known by following aspects.

- Proper nourishment.
- Proper strength.
- Desire and appetite for intake of food.
- Proper digestion of food ingested at proper time.
- Sleep at proper time.
- Absence of pathological or dreadful dreams.
- Feeling of freshness after waking up in the morning.
- Proper evacuation of faeces, urine, and flatus at the proper time.
- Proper functioning of mental faculties, intelligence and senses in all respect.
- Absence of any kind of pain.

Maintenance of Health and Treatment of Diseases in Ayurveda

Following ways are described in Ayurveda for maintenance of health and treatment of diseases.

1. Diet and Nutrition
2. Regimen of Personal and Social Hygiene :- Daily routine (Dinacharya), Seasonal regimens (Ritucharya), including basic sanitation and healthy living environment.

Our Diet: Diet plays very important role in our physical and mental health status. Many common health problems can be prevented or treated by consumption of a good diet. The following need to be followed.

- Wash vegetables & fruits properly before cooking.

- Use boiling, steaming, grilling etc. as methods of cooking.
- Whole wheat flour (without sieving) may be prepared for making roti. Roti made out of jowar, bajra, ragi, maize (macca) are also having high fibre content. The use of white bread, nan, roomali roti and other maida preparations should be limited.
- It is desirable to take 50-100 gms/day fibre, when whole grain cereals, pulses and vegetables are consumed daily. It is for our advantage to maintain our traditional cooking and eating patterns.
- Increase locally available seasonal fruits and green leafy vegetables in the diet.
- As far as possible eat freshly prepared food. Reheating and refrigerating tends to lose the taste and nourishment.
- Do eat when you feel hungry i.e don't avoid mealtimes. Develop the habit of taking meals at regular intervals.
- Avoid overeating.
- Avoid eating too fast or too slow. Food eaten hurriedly does not get digested properly, it does not give a sense of fulfilment. On the contrary one tends to eat more.
- Don't drink too much or too little water since both hamper the digestion.
- Drinking of luke warm water helps easy passage of motion and urine, enhance digestive power, minimize the diseases related to digestive system and delayed ageing.
- Don't eat when the mind is unstable because you may eat less or in excess.
- Avoid heavy tasks immediately after meals since the blood circulation is diverted towards the site of action rather than towards digestion of food. It also creates pressure on the heart. After meals don't sleep immediately. But do take rest for a while before resuming your work. Dinner should be taken at least two hours before sleep.
- Avoid fried foods, restrict intake of ghee, oils. Cook the vegetables with minimum oil.
- Reduce salt and sugar intake.
- Avoid intake of aerated drinks (cola), fast/junk food (Chips, burger, samosa, pizza etc.).

- Increase intake of milk, butter milk, Lassi, coconut water etc.
- Food should be taken after bathing, washing the hands, legs and face and without any disturbance.
- While taking the food, one should not divert his attention to other things.
- After the meals rinse the mouth and hands thoroughly with water. According to Ayurveda the diet is one of the most important factors which have direct impact on three Doshas/ humors. To keep these Doshas balanced, our diet should contain all Tastes (Rasas) in a balanced way. For healthy person it is advised in Ayurveda to not to fill stomach full, while taking food. Stomach should be divided into three portions and one portion should be filled by food, second by water and third should be kept vacant for movement of Doshas (Humors). The right quantity of food is decided upon the nature of food substances such as heaviness or lightness and digestive power of the person. Food items like flour products, milk products, sugar cane products, pulses like Urad (Phascolus mungo), meat etc. are heavy in nature whereas rice, wheat, pulses like moong dal (green gram) etc. are light in nature and easy to digest. Useful Food Items for Daily Use.
- Edibles prepared with cereals like wheat (Gehun/Godhuma) and Barley (Yava)
- Condiments prepared from meat of animals of arid/dry land,
- Jivanti (Holostemma adakodien), Radish (Muli), Basal (Vastuka - Bathua), Terminalia chebula (Haritaki- Harad) (), Indian gooseberry (Amalaka- Amla), snake gourd (Patola - Parval) and green gram (Mudga - Moong), Pomegranate- (Dadima/ Anaar) and Rock salt- (Saindha Namak) are desirable for regular use.
- Fenugreek (methi) has high fibre content and useful in reducing blood glucose, cholesterol and triglycerides.
- Green vegetables like Bittergourd (karela), Lettuce leaves, Ladies finger (bhindi), Carrot (gajar), Soya Beans, Drumstik, and Jambu (Jamun) seeds are having beneficial effects for people suffering from Diabetes. However, Curd, Kshara like Kanji (Alkaline preparations), Vinegar, uncooked radish, dried meat, pork, meat of sheep, cow, black gram, bean, tuberous roots, the fibres of lotus (Kamalgutta), sweets prepared by

grinding cereals, dried leaves, and molasses are all undesirable for regular use particularly in Diabetes patients.

Personal and Social Hygiene: Personal and social hygiene can be maintained by following Dinacharya (daily routine), Ritucharya (seasonal regimens) and Sadvritta (good conduct) which are described below.

Daily Routine (Dinacharya)

It can be summarized as following.

- Wake up early at least 1 hour before sun rise.
- Attending nature's call (Malotsarg) - bowels, urination etc. Never suppress nor forcefully void the natural urges - Vegavidharan (suppression) can lead to many diseases. For defecation one should always use toilets and it should not be done in open grounds. After defecation, the anal area should be cleaned properly with water and hands should be washed properly with soap.
- Care of Teeth - Usage of fresh stick of Neem (Azadirachta indica), Khadir (Acacia catechu) etc. can clean teeth, and vanish foul smell.
- Nasal drops (Nasya)- Put two drops of sesame oil/ mustard oil/ ghee or Anu Talia (An Ayurvedic medicine if available)- It prevents premature greying of hair, baldness and ensures good sleep.
- Mouth wash (Gandush)- Fill mouth with Triphala decoction or other medicated oils - It prevents excess thirst, improves taste and maintains oral hygiene. It is also useful in managing the mouth ulcers and dryness commonly seen in Diabetes patients.
- Oleation (Abhyanga)- application of oil daily e.g. Tila Taila (Seasame oil) - Keeps skin soft, improves blood circulation and removes waste. This helps in prevention of numbness of extremities due to Diabetes. Apply Tila (Seasame) oil or any suitable oil on head in sufficient quantity which enhances the strength of head and forehead and makes hair black, long and deep-rooted.
- Exercise (Vyayama)- Exercise should be done till sweat rolls down from neck, forehead etc. Exercising early in the morning can help remove stagnation in the body and can help recharge and rejuvenate your body and mind for a productive day.

Regular exercise is an important step for prevention and management of various ailments.

- Hair should be kept properly and should be cut regularly. Similarly, nails should also be kept clear and should be cut regularly.
- Bath (Snana) - Take bath half to one hour after exercise - Prevents premature greying of hair, baldness, ensures good sleep and physical hygiene.
- Food (Bhojan)- The various aspects as mentioned in the topic diet should be followed.
- Sleep (Nidra)- Keep the environment clean and pleasant. Avoid sleeping in day.- Proper sleep provides health and longevity. Improves complexion and glow. One should take proper sleep every night, which should be between 6-8 hours per night. In summer one can take a small nap during day time also. Too much sleep and too little sleep, both are not good for healthy living. Generally day sleeping is not advisable.

Seasonal regimens (Ritucharya): Ayurveda stresses a lot at the role of seasons on the body and advises that we must change our daily routine depending on the seasons. This is known as Ritucharya. It helps in preserving the health as the season changes.

Tips to combat summer heat: There are certain measures that you can take to combat the summer heat and stay cool and comfortable. Follow these guidelines

- Drink plenty of liquids like coconut water, sugarcane juice, buttermilk or atleast 10 glass of water a day.
- Eat light food- avoid hot, spicy, oily meals and opt for foods high in water content including fruits, salads, soups and buttermilk.
- While going out, wear a white handkerchief or use an umbrella to block sunrays.
- Do outdoor work in the early mornings or late evenings.
- Take frequent baths and showers and apply sandal (chandan) paste to body for cooling the body.
- Wear light - coloured, loose-fitting cotton clothes.
- Smoking can constrict blood vessels and impair the ability to acclimatize to heat, so quit it.

- Your lunch should consist of boiled rice or roti with watery decoction of pulses or curries with thin gravy. Always end it with buttermilk or curd. Make it a point to drink some fruit juice in the afternoon after lunch. Similarly, the menu of supper should contain enough onions, mint and coriander leaves, in the form of chutney, made salty and sour by adding salt and lemon juice. The Adverse Effects of Monsoon and How to Combat Them
- The body is weakened during summer, as it is the period of dehydration. The digestive power is also weakened. It is further weakened during the rains. Hence, it is advisable to take moderate diet during the rainy season.
- Avoid sleeping during the day time.
- Use clean drinking water ((boiled and cooled).
- Avoid too much exercise and moving about in the sun after a spell of rain.
- Wear light and clean clothes and try to keep the rooms devoid of humidity.

How to Combat the Winter Cold

- During winter, digestive power becomes stronger and it can effectively digest heavy and large quantities of food. To satiate this, take plenty of food. Consume milk, and new cereals as dietary staples.
- Massaging the skin with mustard oil is good during winter.
- Avoid cold foods.
- Eat plenty of green vegetables and seasonal fruits.
- Cream of milk/ Ghee is good for cracked lips.
- Honey is a good and valuable natural healer. Apply it over cracked lips after diluting it with double the quantity of water.

Activities During Spring (basant) Season

- During spring season food becomes easily digestible, diluted honey, water boiled with extracts of sandalwood, mango juice, barley, bengal gram (chana) etc can be taken in. It is better to avoid heavy, oily, cold, fatty food & sweet and sour stuff.
- Massage, exercise, and fomentation can be used.

Sadvritta (good conduct) - for Conducive Social Life

- Everybody works for his happiness. Happiness should be shared with others. One should strive to have happiness for all. It is characteristic of our culture.

- One should exercise control on sense organs.
- One should keep handkerchief around the nostrils and mouth while sneezing or yawning to avoid spread of infection.
- One should stop work before one is excessively tired.
- One should avoid addiction to alcohol, tobacco etc.
- Hygiene is the most important part of healthy living. One can remain healthy if hygiene is maintained. Selecting the right food are not only choices but also cooking & consuming them in a hygienic way is equally important in preventing many diseases. Adopting hygienic practices and promoting hygiene in the community, schools and workplace prevents innumerable disease.
- Alcohol consumption: It is advisable to avoid any alcoholic beverages. If alcohol is consumed in excess, it will cause burning, intoxication, swelling, liver disorders etc.

Regular Exercise

- Make daily exercise a routine.
- Exercise for a minimum period of 30 min. daily, which can be split into intervals.
- Form a habit of using stairs.
- Include exercise in your routine work, develop a habit of walking e.g. to school, market, friend's house, workplace etc.

Examples of Simple and Comfortable Exercises

- Walking, cycling, jogging, swimming, dancing, playing games/ sports.
- Yogasanas, gardening and household, chores-washing, mopping etc.

Where Should I Find the Time for Exercise

- At home, at work or during leisure.
- Combine shopping, gardening etc. with exercise.
- Take stairs instead of elevator (upto 3 floors).
- Walk to nearby shop rather than drive.

The Path to Healing and Wellness

In Ayurveda, wellness is described as the absence of disease. When you are disease-free, you are healthy, vibrant, and at ease with yourself and others. When disease of mind or body is present, that vibrancy dissipates, and you are uncomfortable with yourself, and perhaps with others. Ayurvedic healing involves customizing a treatment plan that addresses your needs as an individual. Once you have an idea of what your dosha is, and identify your chief concern (e.g., weight, menopause, anger, skin rashes, heartburn, depression, or anxiety), you can begin to create a daily routine that will support you in balancing yourself and addressing the areas where you feel out of balance. The first step, however, is figuring out what is not working in your life. What causes illness in the first place? Let's take a look.

The Source of Illness

In Ayurveda, good digestion is one of the keys to good health. When toxins, or ama, are minimal, your life essence, or ojas, can flow unimpeded in the circulatory channels. When ama is high, ojas is impeded, resulting in a host of issues. What this means is that when your body and mind are not taxed by accumulated toxins, everything in life flows more smoothly.

Ama is caused by low digestive "fire" (agni), which means your food is not being properly digested, the nutrients are not being assimilated, and waste is not being efficiently eliminated. (Other factors can lead to an excess of ama as well, which I'll discuss shortly.) This undigested food accumulates in the stomach and intestines where it can produce gas, bloating, candida overgrowth, and other toxins. It can squash the good bacteria, impeding your metabolic and digestive functions. If we do not move toxins out on a regular basis, we may find ourselves sick, or at least with a general feeling of malaise.

Ama can also be caused by environmental toxins , and it can be caused by mental/spiritual anguish. Remember, what happens in the body on a physical level, can also affect us mentally and spiritually, and vice versa.

Signs of Ama in the System

- Chronic inflammation
- White, yellow, or dark coating on tongue
- Depression
- Difficulty making decisions
- Dull appetite
- Feeling foggy
- Gas, bloating, or heartburn

- Generalized pain and fatigue
- Getting sick often
- Incomplete or "messy" bowel movements
- Joint pain
- Scanty urine
- Sense of pessimism, detachment, impassivity
- Slow-healing wounds
- Sour or foul-smelling breath and body odor
- Weak immune system

Signs of Ojas Flowing in the System

- Body moves with ease regardless of weight
- Breath and body odor smell pleasant and clean
- Clear mind
- Elimination is smooth and regular
- Feeling rested upon awakening
- Focused and clear-headed throughout the day
- Healthy complexion
- Rarely getting sick
- Sense of enthusiasm, optimism, and excitement
- Strong digestion
- Uncoated tongue

As mentioned, when food is only partially digested, toxins accumulate in the body. This occurs when we eat before the previous meal has had time to fully digest; when we eat foods in the wrong combination (e.g., fruit and other foods); and when we eat processed foods, which are filled with preservatives, artificial colours, unnatural flavors, sugars, bulking agents, and so on.

When a chemical-laden food (e.g., Cheez Doodles) hits your system, I imagine the body goes through a thought process something like this: First it looks for the nutrients in the food. After an exhaustive search, it comes up empty and says, "Okay, what else is here that I can use?" Fake cheese flavor, really bad oil, and six different artificial food dyes, as well as a host of preservatives. So the body gives up and says, "Dude, there is nothing even remotely resembling food that I can use to build tissues, supply healthy fats, feed the brain, clean the blood-there is nothing here that is useful." So it gives up. That "food" becomes waste. It is sticky and heavy and sits in your body until it's finally forced out, probably in a very uncomfortable, messy bowel movement.

Toxins can also accumulate when we eat on the run; eat stale or leftover food, microwaved food, and frozen food; and eat while upset or standing up. There is an ancient Ayurvedic proverb that says if you eat while standing up, death is watching over your shoulder. The practical answer is that when you stand, you are not paying proper attention to the act of eating and what you are eating. So sit down in a comfortable setting with little distraction and pay attention and give thanks to your wonderful, healthy, "real" food.

With regard to toxins on a mental and emotional level, when you stew in your emotions and get caught up focusing on and thinking about things that are not going well in your life and in the outside world, you are creating ama-remember, what happens spiritually and mentally will also affect you physically. So think about areas of your life where you feel underserved, misunderstood, sad, and so on. Make a list of these "problems" and next to them, jot down a list of "solutions." By coming up with potential solutions, you are creating a path for ojas to flow. You may be surprised that the solution is easier than you thought.

For example, let's say that you feel that your spouse isn't contributing to the household chores. Here's a solution: Ask your spouse for support in a loving way, clearly and unemotionally laying out your case and your feelings. Together, create a plan to split the chores or look into getting a housekeeper, and be open to the resulting conversation without defensiveness or drama. If you chose to just stew in your emotions and imagine the conversation not going well in your head, you are creating ama. By speaking to your partner in a loving, open way, ojas can begin to flow. Wallowing in ama will eventually lead to feeling unwell (remember, what happens on any level affects the other levels), so it's best to recognize it as soon as possible, come up with a solution, and begin to let it go.

How Toxins Accumulate

Basically, toxins increase when we are not living in a healthy way and in harmony with nature. If you are not expressing yourself and hiding your emotions, toxins are having a field day. If you are staying up late watching scary (anxiety-provoking) movies, and thoughtlessly snacking on chips or ice cream, you probably have a lot of ama in your system. If you work on the computer or other screens up until bedtime, you are also increasing ama. If you don't get out into the sun or surround yourself in nature for at least 30 minutes a day, you are accumulating toxins. If you do not eliminate properly in the morning- yup- you are holding on to toxins, so always follow your natural urges.

Toxins in Everyday Life

It's not just the food we eat or the urges we suppress that introduce toxins to the body. We are surrounded by environmental toxins, too. If you live near conventional (nonorganic) farmland, you may be at risk of exposure to glyphosate and other herbicides and pesticides. So while the food you eat may be organic, the air you breathe isn't. Those in cities are exposed to high levels of toxic gases, fumes, and waste. The simple act of just living in our homes can expose us to chemicals in our furniture, carpets, paint, and even some hardwood and other types of flooring. So what's a person to do? Wrapping ourselves in organic cotton and breathing through a gas mask just isn't feasible, so how can we lessen the burden on the body?

Let's start by looking on our shelves and in the bathroom cabinet. I always ask my clients to tell me what cosmetics and body products they use, including shampoo and conditioner, deodorant, toothpaste, soap, moisturizer, nail polish, mascara, eye shadow, and hair dye. One of the most popular brands of toothpastes has seven potentially toxic ingredients in it: triclosan, sodium lauryl sulfate (SLS), artificial sweeteners, fluoride, propylene glycol, diethanolamine (DEA), and microbeads (tiny plastic pellets that can penetrate the gums, not to mention go into the streams and waterways, and be eaten by fish, for which they prove toxic). This is why most toothpaste labels offer the warning "Do Not Swallow." They know that these ingredients, including fluoride, can be highly toxic when ingested. So why in the world would anyone put that in their mouth? There are several Ayurvedic companies like Auramere and Himalaya that make great, nontoxic toothpaste, but one of my favourite toothpastes is plain baking soda. You can even mix it with a little sea salt and turmeric for a spectacular way to clean your teeth. Add a few drops of organic peppermint or spearmint essential oil if you'd like.

If we are constantly gorging on bad food, slathering our bodies with hazardous chemicals, and colouring our hair with lethal dyes, our body spends all of its time just trying to alleviate the damage we are putting on it and in it. If we reduce the amount of toxins we use, then the body can use its precious energy to do what it's designed to do-repair tissues, clean the blood, assimilate nutrients, eliminate waste, and rejuvenate the mind, body, and spirit. If your energy is being wasted just trying to get rid of what you intentionally added, then you are not efficiently using your vehicle to help yourself move forward in the world and heal yourself and others.

Follow Natural Urges

Ayurveda recommends not suppressing natural urges, which can cause a buildup of toxins in the mind and body.

Here is a list of urges not to suppress:

- Belching
- Bowel movements
- Breathing heavily
- Coughing
- Crying
- Flatulence
- Hunger
- Orgasm, or suppression of genital fluids
- Sleeping
- Sneezing
- Thirst
- Urination
- Vomiting
- Yawning

Suppression of these urges can lead to disease. When "nature calls," attend to the matter at hand immediately. If not, as toxins build in the system, they can bury themselves deep into your tissues until a small problem that could have been easily corrected becomes a serious issue that might require drastic intervention. You can help yourself by letting go and expressing yourself on every level-including these natural urges.

Questions to Ask Yourself: On Your Body: Read the ingredients of everything you put on your body.

- What's in the brand of toothpaste you use?
- What's in the brand of deodorant you use?
- What's in the brand of shampoo/conditioner you use?

- What's in the brand of moisturizer you use?
- What's in the brand of shaving cream you use?
- What's in the brand of mascara you use?
- What's in the brand of lipstick or lip balm you use?
- What's in the brand of hair colour, permanent, or straightening product you use?

Look Before You Flush!

The quality and frequency of your bowel movements can tell you a lot about your current state of health. For each dosha, there are certain characteristics to look for. When your bowel movements are not normal, take steps to eliminate what is not working and to add in food and supplements that promote better digestion, along with more healthy and balancing practices into your lifestyle.

Vata Balanced: Elimination within two to three hours of waking; little to no odor; elimination feels complete; hard stool; dark brown; no gas

Pitta Balanced: Well-formed but soft; breaks up when flushing; mild odor; twice a day, usually upon waking and after a meal

Kapha Unbalanced: Sticky, soft or "mushy"; mucus can be seen; need to wipe several times to clean; incomplete elimination

Vata Unbalanced: No daily bowel movement (or every few days); hard, dark balls; elimination doesn't feel complete; astringent odor; excessive gas

Pitta Unbalanced: Runny, yellowish, or greenish stool or diarrhea; more than twice a day; unpleasant odor; burning sensation

Kapha Balanced: Regular elimination upon waking; once or twice a day; well-formed; brown; large quantity; little odor or even a sweet smell; clean wipe

A Typical Ayurvedic Consultation

As you are beginning your Ayurvedic practice, there is much you can do to heal on your own. Once you start seeing how some simple practices help, you may want to know more and schedule a visit with an Ayurvedic practitioner. So what might happen at a typical visit? Often, a person comes in complaining of one symptom or another as their chief concern-for example, excess weight, trouble sleeping at night, feeling stressed out, or constipation. After a few questions from the practitioner, it may become clear that their initial concern was actually just a symptom of something deeper. There is almost always something else going on that creates these states of imbalance, and this is good to know as you embark on your healing journey. An Ayurvedic consultation uses many tools of detection and observation to discern what the real problem is. Through questions and interpretation of diagnostics tools-examinations of the tongue, skin, sense of smell, eyes, fingernails, and reading the pulses-a trained counselor can determine where you are out of balance and create a sustainable path to wellness. For example, a person complaining of headaches might also have heartburn and a skin rash, and are going prematurely bald or gray. They may also be defensive, impatient, straightforward, and intense.

A practitioner will see right away that this person has a Pitta imbalance. And while addressing the headache symptoms may make the client feel better, what the practitioner is really doing is pacifying Pitta by recommending cooling foods, cooling pranayama (breath work like Cooling Breath), and making other lifestyle recommendations. For a primarily Vata person, complaints to their practitioner often have to do with digestion, gas, and bloating, which can be easily remedied by eating warm cooked foods, using good oils, and decreasing raw and cold foods. Other recommendations would include engaging in grounding and nurturing exercises like yoga and Tai Chi, or swimming in warm water. Dressing warmly and sticking to a schedule of eating can go a long way in balancing Vata. So do you need an Ayurvedic practitioner to begin healing? Not necessarily. If you need more help further down the line, look for a good Ayurvedic practitioner in your area or ask for recommendations.

Nurture Yourself First

As they tell you on an airplane, put your oxygen mask on first, before helping others with theirs! If you don't, you'll start feeling lightheaded very quickly, and you won't be much help to anyone else. Often, people begin to feel unwell because they spend too much time taking care of others, to the detriment of their own health. And they don't really notice it until they fall apart. This is true of both men and women, with each sex trying to fulfill their traditional roles (women as nurturers and keepers of the home front, and men as the money-makers and providers). Those traditional roles are rarely reflective of reality these days, but those old-fashioned expectations are persistent.

Each partner in a relationship, regardless of the demands placed upon them, needs to be sure their own needs are being met. An Ayurvedic routine-a complete system of self-care-is an excellent beginning. There are also many single people who are trying to make it all work on their own, including placing demands on themselves to find a life partner to feel fulfilled. It's only natural to want to partner with someone. That is the way our world is set up, and when the union is right, there is nothing better. But a single person-as I once was-can be equally fulfilled if they value their relationship with themselves enough to practice nurturing self-care.

If you recognize yourself in either scenario, Ayurveda guides you toward putting on your own oxygen mask first. It helps you unravel the conundrums and find your healing path. Ayurveda can help you clear the cobwebs in your mind away, and begin to see clearly that your perfect health and well-being is the key to the well-being of all people. There is a beautiful saying in Hebrew: Tikkun olam. It means "repair the world." But to repair the world, you must repair yourself. Ayurveda holds the key.

An Overview of Ayurvedic Healing Methods

When Ayurvedic practitioners work on healing a doshic imbalance in their patients, they may, in addition to other recommendations and practices, prescribe certain herbs known for balancing the doshas. Depending on the individual's constitution, they can be delivered in the form of tablets or capsules, powders, or a simple mixture that can be licked off a spoon. And depending on the specific doshic imbalance, they may mix the herbal preparations with ghee, aloe, or milk. But you don't need to know how to do this on your own. There are many ways you can begin to heal yourself with the basic Ayurvedic techniques and recipes. Be prepared to make changes, but remember to take it slowly. Small changes can have profound effects. Let's start by looking at some of the basics, including dietary guidelines and other practices you may want to start trying.

Basic Dietary Guidelines

Ayurveda recommends avoiding certain foods that can create toxic residue in the body called ama. The foods to avoid include frozen meals, leftovers (over 36 hours max), processed foods, microwaved foods, and canned soups and sauces with lots of additives. All these foods have a diminished life force, or prana. While it is important to reduce consumption of certain foods, it is just as important to increase and add in other foods. Certain foods are easier to digest, so the body can use its energy for healing and repairing. Also, it is important to follow certain guidelines, such as reducing the consumption of cold foods in winter and hot foods in the summer.

Some basic guidelines to try, which worked wonders for me, include the following:

- Begin your day with hot water and lemon or lime in the morning.
- Sip warm water or tea throughout the day.
- Eat three meals a day. Do not snack between meals. After you eat, your body uses that food for energy and stores what is not needed at that time. Between meals, your body is able to dig deep to use stored pockets of energy to keep you going. Even if you munch on carrots or apple slices throughout the day, you are depriving your body of this natural period of detox-using what is already there. If you are hungry between meals, you are probably not eating enough nutrient-rich food at each meal. (On occasion, the timing may be that there is time for only two meals. That's okay, especially for Kapha who may actually do best with just two meals. There's more on this later.)
- Do not mix fruit with other foods. Eat fruit 45 minutes to one hour before any meal, ideally before breakfast. This is not considered snacking. When you wait that 45 minutes to an hour, your digestive juices will have plenty of time to process the nutrients in the fruit before your main meal.
- Do not eat raw salad veggies or cold fruit or drinks. Avoid ice. Raw food is difficult for the body to process, interfering with digestion. The same is true for cold food.
- Each meal should be about two open handfuls of food, which represents two-thirds of your stomach. (A person with larger hands generally has a larger stomach.) In other words, eat until you are 80 percent full, leaving 20 percent space for the digestive "fires" to metabolize your food.
- Do not overeat. You should feel energized after eating, not wiped out and stuffed. If you feel that way, you ate too much or combined food in a way that made it hard to digest. It's like putting too many logs on the fire-it smothers the flame. Eat just enough to keep your digestion burning bright! Two

handfuls- like a large bowl-should be plenty, if the food you choose is nutrient rich and easy to digest.

- Eat less protein than is typical in a Western diet. In the evening, eat only light amounts of protein, or none at all. Unless you are working the nightshift, in which case your daily cycle is not the norm, you are probably consuming more protein than you need with dinner.
- Don't mix proteins. A buffet can be very confusing with all the offerings. Even if you pile on the "good" foods like beans, tofu, eggs, cottage cheese, and lean meats, you are taxing the body. Each protein digests at a different rate, so stick to one protein per meal.
- Make lunch your most important meal of the day. It should the most densely packed with nutrients, including protein and carbohydrates. This meal is often consumed during work hours, but it is very important to pay attention while you eat. Turn away from the computer, and sit outside if possible.
- Make dinner the easiest-to-digest meal of the day. Easy-to-digest foods include light proteins (if you must have protein with your dinner) such as fish, warm and cooked foods, soups, and sautéed greens (which interestingly have a calming effect). Eat dinner at least three hours before bed.
- Breakfast, while not as important as the most substantial meal of the day between 10 a.m. and 2 p.m., is important, primarily for Pitta and Vata. For these types, it should be warm, nourishing, and easy to digest. Kapha may simply enjoy a bowl of fruit or a light grain porridge.
- Always sit to eat your meals. In general, it is very important to take the time to sit down when eating to be fully present at your meal. Sit and enjoy the process of eating and noticing what is on your plate. Sitting in your car to eat doesn't count.
- Walk after meals. Taking a short walk after lunch and dinner will encourage digestion.
- Sleep on your left side. This will help promote digestion. When you sleep on your left side, your major organs are supported and your digestive juices flow naturally.

You might not be able to make huge shifts and do everything on this list, but even something as simple as avoiding cold water and sipping warm water throughout the day can have a profound effect sipping warm water throughout the day can have a profound effect on the body. The healing benefits of eating at least two to three meals a day (which might be more or less than you are used to), not snacking between meals, and having a light dinner at least three hours before bed can make an enormous difference in your health and well-being. Eating this way allows your body to work most efficiently, stoking your digestive "fires" at meals and digesting your food properly, giving it time to work on detoxing and repairing tissues between meals.

Trying some of these dietary guidelines for a few weeks can shift your awareness to a higher level, preparing you to make further changes and delve more deeply into an Ayurvedic lifestyle. You'll have a chance to start a 21-day routine in chapter 4, and then it's up to you if you want to take this new, health-enhancing lifestyle even further.

Here are a few more recommendations to help you make the shift:

- If you are a coffee drinker, add a pod of cardamom to your unground coffee beans before grinding them, or a pinch of ground cardamom to your brewed coffee. This spice reduces the acid in the coffee, making it easier on the stomach.
- Eat ghee daily. Incidentally, do not combine equal parts ghee and honey in a meal, as this can increase toxins in the body. The ancient texts strongly advise against doing this, so please don't try it!
- Begin your day with the Ayurvedic jam chyawanprash. Chyawanprash has many ingredients that work together to promote optimal health by rejuvenating the tissues and strengthening many functions of the body. A tablespoon of chyawanprash every morning, licked off the spoon while sipping hot water, can benefit everyone. (There are several brands you can purchase; see the resources.)
- End your day by drinking Golden Milk and taking triphala, a toner for the bowels, and the most widely used Ayurvedic supplement. Available in tablets and powder, triphala is made from three detoxifying and tonifying fruits that help you more effectively absorb and assimilate nutrients and get rid of waste through healthy bowel movements. Two tablets should be about right, but an Ayurvedic practitioner may prescribe more or less to maintain health.

- If you like a glass of wine or beer, knowing which dosha you are can help you make a good choice: Vata does best with sweet wines, Pitta does best with beer, and Kapha does best with dry wines. None of the doshas do well with hard alcohol unless it is prescribed by an Ayurvedic practitioner. Ayurvedic concoctions called arishtams or kashayams are highly effective fermented medicines, but they should be used only under guidance.

Using Tastes to Guide Food Choices: In Ayurveda, we divide food into six categories: sweet, sour, salty, pungent, bitter, and astringent. Each taste corresponds to a dosha, and more or less of it can either create balance or imbalance. But we do want some representation of all six tastes in every meal, as that is the most satisfying way to eat. Ayurvedic guidelines aren't intended to make you feel deprived or left out.

The Western diet is composed mostly of sweet, sour, and salty. It's no wonder that we have an obesity epidemic, that irritable bowel syndrome and disorders are prevalent, and many other diseases abound, as these are the heaviest, most addictive foods. When we solely eat from these categories, our bodies have no chance to heal and repair. To help us create balance in the mind and body, it is impeative that we include food from the pungent, bitter, and astringent categories. These three tastes effectively wring out excess toxins from the body.

Interestingly, the word rasa in Sanskrit can mean both taste and emotion. So there is really no such thing as non-emotional eating. It's all tied together-mind and body. Ayurveda also teaches why sweet is the most satisfying of tastes-it's the first thing we taste: Mother's milk, which is naturally sweet. We all crave different tastes at different times, and it's almost always tied to an emotion. A fascinating exploration in Ayurveda leads us to understand why we crave or desire certain foods.

Let's break it down by taste:

Sweet: Sweet foods are the most satisfying of all the tastes, and they are tied to intensely satisfying emotions as well. Sweet foods, in appropriate amounts, can create feelings of deep emotional ties, love and compassion, satisfaction, and a sense of caring and being cared for. When taken in excess, sweetness can promote inertia, dullness, and neediness. Notice how you feel when you just have a bite or two of something sweet, and how it feels when you eat the whole cake.

Ask yourself: "What is it I need? Maybe a hug Perhaps I need to love more, or allow myself to be loved" I advise my clients who have intense sweet cravings to look for new outlets to express their own sweetness. Maybe volunteer at a dog shelter, help out an elderly relative or neighbour, do random acts of kindness, add money to parking meters, pay the toll for the person in the car behind you, or be kind to yourself. All of these actions really can lessen the physical craving for something sweet. What are sweet foods? Sweet is the most densely nutritive of tastes and includes proteins, carbohydrates, fats, grains, dairy, breads, pasta, starchy vegetables, sweet fruits, nuts, oils, sugar, honey, and all animal products, including meat, chicken, and fish. Vata and Pitta both benefit from sweet foods, as they need more water and grounding, and sweetness. Kapha, who is made of the sweet elements of earth and water, should take sweet in moderation, and perhaps avoid it completely during times of too much Kapha.

Sour: Sour foods, when eaten in moderation, can stimulate appetite and digestion, and feel warming and refreshing. In excess, sour foods can feel heavy and hot, and emotions can be negative, pessimistic, and irritable. When a person craves sour foods, they might take a look at how they are viewing the world. Is it you against them? Do you place blame on others and cry "sour grapes" when things don't go your way. Stepping back and assessing the situation can help the "sour" person gain perspective. Cooling off and drying out a bit by eating fewer sour foods and taking a fresh look at the world, situations, and people around you can help balance the sour emotion. What are sour foods? They are refreshing, acidic, and sparkly: Citrus fruits, sour fruits, tomatoes, yogurt, cheese, pickles, most vinegars, and some alcohol. Vata benefits from eating sour as it comprises the elements of earth and fire, which Vata lacks. Pitta and Kapha will be aggravated by sour. It's too hot for Pitta, and too wet for Kapha.

Salty: Salty promotes digestion and, when used in moderation, enhances the flavor of most foods. Emotionally, a balanced "salty behaviour" can help you be more outspoken and address your needs and desires. If you have too much salt, it can lead to feelings of greediness and addiction (try eating just a few kernels of salted popcorn, chips, or French fries-it's hard). Salty personality traits include feeling angry, grouchy, and irritated. If you find yourself craving salt, take a look at your life and see where you may not be expressing yourself. Perhaps you need to speak up more often and express your needs in a balanced way. Salty foods include seafood, seaweed, some meat, salt, and snacks. Check the labels of canned and frozen foods, as they may contain excess salt. Vata benefits from the water and fire elements of salt. Pitta and Kapha, hot and wet respectively, are aggravated by the salty taste.

Pungent: Pungent taste detoxifies, stimulates digestion, and is heating and drying. Emotionally, when taken in small amounts, pungent food can create clarity, purpose, and motivation. It can act to cut through heaviness or fogginess. Too much can promote abrasiveness, anger, and aggression. If you crave pungent foods, you may be looking for a way to express pent-up anger or frustration. Be careful not to "blow up" from too much fire. Look for ways to cool down-take a swim or walk in the evening or early morning when it's cool. Drink some coconut water. Examine the areas in your life where you feel trampled upon, and choose to move aside and rise up with grace. Foods that contain the pungent taste include ginger, hot peppers, tomato salsa, cloves, thyme, basil, cayenne pepper, radishes, mustard, wasabi, chili peppers, garlic, and onions. Kapha should adore pungent foods as they balance their cold, wet nature and it can help them shed extra weight. Pungent, comprising the elements of fire and air, should be limited by Pitta (heat) and Vata (dry).

Bitter: Bitter foods are extremely detoxifying and can reduce inflammation. They are drying and cold, and can be very flavorful. A small amount of bitter can help clear the cobwebs and allow one to see things more clearly. Too much bitter can create a sense of grief and disillusionment. The bitter person is jealous, jaded, and mean. They hold grudges and blame others when things go wrong. When I have clients who feel bitter, they are usually holding on to things that no longer exist or are wishing for a different outcome that will never happen. Visualizing the world as it is, and situations exactly as they are, and learning to accept them can help alleviate feelings of bitterness. Knowing that you are holding it in, and that it's only damaging you, is key to understanding and letting go. Try new things in life. Collect new experiences. Let go of the past. Foods containing the bitter taste include Swedish bitters (an herbal tonic that is added to juice or water); sorrel and other leafy greens; yellow vegetables; bitter herbs like chamomile, mint, and dandelion; and horseradish. Bitter is good for Kapha, who often exudes sweetness and kindness (they can use a touch of bitter to balance these qualities). The cool, lightness of bitter can be balancing for Pitta. Vata should avoid large quantities of bitter for those same reasons; cool and light will increase Vata.

Astringent: stringent foods are detoxifying and have a way of cleansing the palate-emotionally clearing the slate, allowing space to clear the mind and get back to work without any lingering emotions. Too much astringent, because it is so compacting, can lead to a loss of interest in activities and routines. A small amount goes a long way. Astringent is not very common but can be found in beans, lentils, pomegranates, cranberries, unripened bananas, black tea, and dark greens. People with an astringent emotional quality are often filled with bitterness as well. They look contracted, depleted, and dried out. It's hard for them to smile.

The remedy is to add all the qualities of sweet, sour, and salty-in abundance-into their lives. Guided meditation and sweet, floral, and spicy essential oils used daily can help. Getting out into the elements, including walking in the rain, and exposure to early-morning and evening sun, can do wonders. In a nutshell, Vata benefits from sweet, sour, and salty. Pitta benefits from sweet, bitter, and astringent. And Kapha benefits from pungent, bitter, and astringent. Speaking of nuts, they are considered sweet, but they are very hot, making them best for Vata. Pitta and Kapha will want to avoid nuts, but most seeds are great for these two doshas.

Starting an Ayurvedic Kitchen

To start your Ayurvedic kitchen, you won't need to do a complete overhaul-just begin to make shelf and refrigerator space by using up what you have and replacing it with items that will serve you better.

However, before you go out and purchase all of the items mentioned, choose your recipes, see what you need, and begin to make your grocery store purchases as needed.

Daily Practices and Bodywork

The Ayurvedic practices listed here are varied and many. Don't feel as if you need to incorporate them all into your daily routine. Even if you just include one or two, you will begin to feel better. Ayurveda is amazing in that way-subtle changes can have profound effects. Your body will respond because it has been waiting for this!

- Aromatherapy
- Breath work
- Dry brushing
- Foot washing and oil massage

- Head oiling
- Meditation
- Nasya oil
- Neti pot
- Oil massage
- Oil pulling
- Sun gazing
- Tongue Scraping
- Yoga

Dosha-Specific Guidance

Like attracts like. It's a law of the universe. Try to be aware of including food and activities in your day that will satisfy all three doshas, keeping in mind how you are feeling, the weather, your schedule, and which dosha might be aggravated (revealed by signs of imbalance; see here). On any given day, we may feel frustrated and angry (too much Pitta), or we may feel like pulling the covers over our head and not getting out of bed (too much Kapha), or we might be running late for a meeting because we were distracted by so many other things along the way (too much Vata). In Ayurveda, when discussing dosha imbalances, we are always talking about having too much of a doshic quality, not too little.

It's most important when practicing Ayurveda to be aware of your state of being every day. Some people may have an underlying illness or a persistent imbalance that must be constantly pacified, but everyone can change day to day. Stay aware, know yourself, and use the methods in this book to heal yourself subtly, 24 hours a day. That is really what Ayurveda is all about: allowing your body to naturally detox, 24 hours a day, by feeding and caring for yourself in ways that allow the body to easily do the work it was designed to do. All of the doshas can be balanced with food, drink, exercise, meditation, breath work, and more.

As mentioned earlier, each dosha is balanced by eating a combination of all six food categories, but you should limit or favour certain tastes in each meal depending on your needs. Exercise for each dosha is generally a combination of stretching (yoga), aerobics, and weights, with each activity designed to balance the doshas. Meditation can be a challenge for some, and a salvation for others. Nevertheless, it is recommended for each dosha, with time and techniques to help you receive the most benefit. The doshas will also greatly benefit from learning breath work and exercises to enhance or calm imbalances. Chanting a mantra can help calm your thoughts, excite the mind, and open creative and healing channels.

Vata Guidelines: Some of the qualities of Vata are cold, dry, rough, and ungrounded. So we choose to eat, exercise, and breathe in ways that mitigate or reduce those qualities. Vata should eat warm, cooked, easy-todigest foods so that the body can conserve its energy to keep warm and healthy. Vata needs the energy used to digest raw food for other metabolic processes, including repairing the tissues and cleaning the blood. It's also important for Vata to create a schedule and try to stick to a routine-especially with meals. Vata is the only dosha who forgets to eat. They will eat half a candy bar and put the rest in their bag and forget it's there. This would never happen with Pitta or Kapha! In addition, because of Vata's natural inclination toward fear and worry, it's important for Vata to feel safe and secure.

- Food should be well-cooked and easy to digest, and eating should be accompanied by sipping warm liquid throughout the meal, preferably warm water.
- Favour sweet, sour, and salty tastes, which help nourish Vata.
- Reduce pungent, bitter, and astringent tastes, which increase Vata.
- Dress to stay warm. Wear layers even in summer. Wear a scarf in fall, winter, and early spring.
- Ideal exercises for Vata include grounding and slower-paced exercises, such as Tai Chi or Qigong; swimming in warm water; slow, gentle yoga; walking outdoors in warm weather; short hikes; and light bicycling on level ground.

Pitta Guidelines: Pitta attributes include hot, sour, and pungent, so we look to the opposites to balance this fire dosha. Pitta will gravitate toward those things that increase the dosha, as it thrives on hot, vibrant qualities. But when Pitta is out of balance, it can be damaging to oneself and others. Pitta loves spicy food and loves to tell you about it! They will sweat profusely when eating hot chiles and tell you how much they love it. But they will suffer later with heartburn or indigestion. So it's important to calm Pitta with sweet, cooling foods and to encourage less competition and challenges, and more cooperation in either solitary or team sports and activities.

- Favour cool food and drink. Pitta loves cold drinks, so gradually move from iced to chilled to cool to room temperature, if possible.
- Favour sweet, bitter, and astringent tastes, which balance the fiery qualities of Pitta.
- Reduce sour, salty, and pungent tastes, which increase Pitta.
- Avoid overheating when exercising.
- Ideal exercises for Pitta include medium-paced exercises, such as brisk walking or light jogging; swimming in cool water; noncompetitive biking; cross-country skiing; and outdoor activities in cool weather.

Kapha Guidelines: Kapha, made of earth and water, is heavier and sturdier than the other doshas. If left to their own volition, they would eat sweet or heavy, oily, fried foods all day long. Creamy is another favourite texture of Kapha. But that just contributes to that heavy, dull, inert energy.

The tastes of pungent, bitter, and astringent actually act to wring out excess Kapha in the body by drying it up and moving it out. Kapha often has a dull appetite, but if the clock reads 8 a.m. or 12 p.m. or 6 p.m., it must be time for a meal! So they will eat. If Kapha wants to lose weight, they can greatly benefit by having two meals a day. A large meal between 10 a.m. and 2 p.m. and a light meal in the late afternoon or early evening (5 p.m. or 6 p.m.) can be sufficient and can help in reducing excess Kapha.

- Favour a lighter diet of foods that are easy to digest, as Kapha tends to have sluggish digestion.
- Reduce dairy products, because they are cold, sweet, and sour, which are Kapha characteristics.
- Favour warm food and drink, as Kapha is generally cold. Chilled drinks and food increase Kapha, and one needs to expend a lot of energy to create warmth, which could be used for other metabolic processes. o Do not drink copious amounts of water, as it increases Kapha. Just sip warm water throughout the day.
- Eat more pungent, bitter, and astringent tastes, as they wring out excess Kapha from the body.
- Reduce sweet, sour, and salty tastes, so as not to increase these qualities in sweet Kapha, which can cause weight gain and immobility.

- Dress to stay warm so your body can use its energy to rejuvenate and repair the body.
- Ideal exercises for Kapha include vigorous activities and long workouts that promote sweating such as running, aerobics, dance, rowing, active yoga, and weight training

A Gentle 21-Day Introduction to Ayurveda

When trying on anything new, remember to give yourself time and permission to be flexible. Hopefully you will have a lifetime to work these things into your daily practice, so take it one step at a time. Once you begin to see the benefits of Ayurveda, you will likely want to make this a permanent lifestyle, so begin slowly, learn the reasons behind the rituals, and see what makes you feel better. This is an individualized path, so you should take your time, move at your own pace, and add in new elements of Ayurveda when you feel ready. If you move slowly, you are more likely to stick with it.

There's no need to adopt this lifestyle all at once, or commit to it for several months or longer. You can simply dip your toes in for three weeks, using this chapter as your road map. Remember, you can do this on your own, but if you feel it would be helpful to you, go ahead and make an appointment with an Ayurvedic practitioner for further support.

3 Steps to Beginning Ayurveda

Let's take a look at how to prepare the way for your new Ayurvedic lifestyle. First, be certain that this is a good time in your life to begin a transformational project. For example, if you are planning to go on vacation next week or if you are in the middle of a move, you may have difficulty committing to the 21-day plan. If you decide the time is right, begin to formulate your plan using a journal specifically for this purpose-your Ayurvedic journal.

1. Look at Your Current Condition

Define your chief concerns, or the main things in your life you want to change. Take a moment to sit quietly, breathe, and ask yourself the following questions-and remember, the Buddha said, "First thought, best thought." In other words, don't censor yourself. Let it flow. Answer the following questions in your Ayurvedic journal:

- What is not serving me in my life.
- If I could do anything I wanted to, what would it be

- What is stopping me from moving forward

Next, make a list of obstacles that may be interfering with your well-being, or problems currently at play in your life. Next to each one, jot down a simple solution. Don't worry about how the solution could happen, just write it down.

For example:

Problem: At the end of the workday, I don't have the energy to cook a healthy meal.

Solution: Prep your ingredients for your evening meal in the morning so that everything is ready to go when it's time to cook dinner.

Problem: I don't know how to cook. Solution: Take a cooking class and learn one recipe. Have a friend over to cook with you. Problem: I don't have time in the mornings to spend doing a routine. Solution: Wake up 10 minutes earlier and incorporate just one new practice. Don't hit the snooze button. Just get up!

2. Set Your Intention

Think about what you hope to gain by making changes in your life. Most assuredly, these will be positive things, so you will want to set an intention to make those things happen. Spend some quiet time thinking about this first. Then write down whatever occurs to you in your Ayurvedic journal. There's no need to write pages and pages; just a few thoughts or sentences can be enough to set your intention. Be sure to be specific in your needs and desires. And be positive! Once you've written it down, it will feel much more real.

3. Prepare

Your Home Set aside time to go through your home to determine what's not serving you. Start in your kitchen. Look in the cabinets, the refrigerator, and the freezer. Do you have junk food, processed foods, frozen entrées, and other less-than-healthy foods on hand? If so, maybe box up the nonperishables for another time or consider donating them. Finish up any perishables, but be sure to toss old leftovers into the trash or compost bin.

While you're in the kitchen, check to make sure you have some essential cookware. You don't want to cook with anything that has a Teflon coating, as Teflon can be toxic when scratched or overheated. You'll need a variety of pots and pans, but start with at least a 4-quart soup pot, one large pan, and one small pan. Some items that are helpful to have include an immersion blender, a countertop blender, a pressure cooker, a fine-mesh strainer, and a juicer. If you don't have these items, you don't have to run out to purchase them. Spend that money on your Ayurvedic-friendly supplies instead. Next, take a look at the items in your bathroom, on your vanity, and in your cleaning-supply cabinet. Anything that contains harsh chemicals is not conducive to an Ayurvedic practice.

You don't need to toss everything in the garbage, but do be aware of what you are running low on and make a plan to choose their healthier counterparts in the future. If you can afford to, buy some Ayurvedic-friendly items. And for home-cleaning products I especially like Seventh Generation. (You can also make your own multi-surface cleaner with white vinegar, lemon juice, borax, and baking soda.)

Your 21-day Ayurvedic Self-care Plan: Think in terms of weeks, rather than days. Week One will begin by getting your supplies together, learning a few recipes, and thinking about how you can begin implementing your daily routine, called dinacharya. Week Two will have you applying more Ayurvedic rituals into your day and more Ayurvedic meals into your plan. By week 3, you may find yourself inspired to keep learning new recipes, creating space and time for your morning routine, and beginning to implement your evening routine, which is part of your dinacharya. Each week in the 21-Day Plan is divided into mind, body, and spirit. The following entries provide guidance on how you can nurture those parts of yourself.

Week One: Mind: Focus on the changes you would like to see occur, and visualize the steps it will take to make them happen. In your Ayurvedic journal, write one step you will take each day to move toward feeling more balanced. List one thing that you can do for yourself to make you feel good, and list one thing you can let go of that no longer serves you. In addition, commit each day to work on making this happen, or at least to set a plan in motion.

Body: Prepare for the week by reading through the recipes in chapter 5. Choose three new recipes to try, making sure Kitchari is among them . You can have kitchari for any meal of the day. Make a pot of Everyday CCF Tea each morning and sip it throughout the day. Alternatively, you can prepare ginger tea by adding a few slices of fresh ginger to hot water. Sip it throughout the day. Purchase a tongue scraper, a dry brush, nasya oil, and abhyanga oil for the purposes of beginning your daily routine. Organic sesame seed oil is good to have on hand for oil pulling and other practices (not toasted sesame seed oil, which is only used in cooking!).

Spirit: Set up a time and space to meditate and do your breath work for at least five minutes. Download a supportive app on your smartphone or tablet, such as Insight Timer or Headspace. Log your meditation time in your Ayurveda journal or on your app. Increase the time by a few minutes each day throughout the week. Notice how you feel, and jot down a few words after you meditate to remind yourself of any insights or observations.

Week Two: Mind: Notice your feelings during this 21-day process. Do you feel resistance, acceptance, excitement, boredom, or something else? Whatever it is, write it down in your Ayurveda journal. Let all these emotions come up and out, and focus on what is making you feel better. If you find yourself creating obstacles on your path, write them down, ball them up, throw them away, and get back on the plan. Remind yourself that you are not your thoughts. Give yourself a pep talk. And remember baby steps-one thing at a time. There's no need to create blockages to making a few simple changes. Let it go, and come back to your enthusiasm.

Body: Review the sample routine here, and begin your daily routine (dinacharya). Set out your tongue scraper, abhyanga oil, and dry brush. Make time in the mornings to put each practice into your morning routine. Make two new recipes this week. Find new breakfast foods. Learn to make ghee.

Spirit: Practice silent walking meditation outside in the elements. Notice how your body feels outside: moving, breathing, being connected. Immerse yourself in the elements. Practice Sun Gazing at dawn and dusk. Continue your meditation and breath work from the week before, extending the time a few minutes each day as you did in week one.

Week Three: Mind: Check in with yourself to see what is working and what is not working. Allow yourself to make adjustments until it feels right. Do not force anything. There's no need to be rigid. Go easy on yourself and allow change to take place naturally, at a slow pace.

Body: Every day or two, create a new meal. Pay attention to the seasons and learn which fruits and vegetables are in season, and when shopping, choose those fruits and vegetables. Make smaller portions of your meals to avoid having leftovers.

Practice yoga every day for at least 10 minutes. Choose a few poses that feel good to you, and work through them. If you can, sign up for a yoga class with a good teacher. Just once a week for a class is fine, but continue your daily yoga practice at home. Start incorporating your evening routine into your dinacharya. Oil your feet and scalp. Before bed, take triphala and drink Golden Milk.

Spirit: Lengthen your meditation time, working toward 30 minutes a day. Be easy on yourself and others. Lower your expectations and accept things as they are, but with a vision of how they could be. Begin to practice self-inquiry meditation and continue your breath work.

Your Custom Self-Care Plan Worksheet

With the guidance you've received in this chapter, use the following worksheet to create your own customized Ayurvedic daily practices.

Week 1

	Sun	Mon	Tue	Wed	Thu	Fri	Sat
MIND							
BODY							
SPIRIT							
NOTES							

Week 2

	Sun	Mon	Tue	Wed	Thu	Fri	Sat
MIND							
BODY							
SPIRIT							
NOTES							

Week 3

	Sun	Mon	Tue	Wed	Thu	Fri	Sat
MIND							
BODY							
SPIRIT							
NOTES							

Sample Daily Routine (Dinacharya): As mentioned earlier, in Ayurveda, we call our daily routine dinacharya. I have a pretty standard routine, but it changes according to the season, the amount of time I have, and how I'm feeling that day. Dinacharya will look a little different for everyone, but let's see one example of what a typical Ayurvedic-style day looks like.

Morning

- Wake up sometime between 6 a.m. and 7 a.m., preferably without an alarm. Sleeping with the shades open, if appropriate for your living situation, is a wonderful way to allow natural light to wake you up.
- Before getting out of bed, set your intention for the day. Take a few deep breaths into your belly and focus on what is important for you on this day. Take a moment to express gratitude, and name one thing that you will do just for yourself today.
- Sit up in bed. Do some gentle twisting and stretching to get your blood flowing. Stand and allow yourself to do a few Forward Bends, inhaling up and exhaling down. Feel your heart beating. Give thanks.
- Move to the bathroom and take your time for complete elimination of the waste that was separated from the nutrients during the night. Urinate and give yourself time for a complete bowel movement. A Squatty Potty-a stool that fits around the toilet bowl on which you can rest your feet-is a great investment. You can use it to raise your knees to just above your hips to promote an easier bowel movement. Don't strain. Breathe deeply. The bowels evacuate best on the out breath. Relax. Notice the quality of your bowel movement, as this is a clear indication of your health.
- After washing your hands, scrape your tongue with a tongue scraper or spoon. Notice if there is a coating on your tongue and what colour it is.
- Brush your teeth with a natural or Ayurvedic toothpaste or with baking soda.
- Do oil pulling with either coconut oil or sesame seed oil. Spit the oil into a trash can after 10 to 20 minutes. Do not spit the oil in the sink; it will clog your pipes.
- Rinse your mouth with ¼ teaspoon of baking soda mixed into some warm water.
- Drink a small glass of warm water with lemon or lime. Do not drink your warm water until you have cleaned the bacteria out of your mouth, or you will just be ingesting what your body worked hard to expel during the night.

- If you live in a humid climate, have seasonal allergies, or are doing a cleanse, use a neti pot.
- If you did not use a neti pot, use nasya oil in your nostrils. If you did use a neti pot, wait at least one hour before applying oil to the nasal passages.
- Meditate for 20 to 30 minutes.
- Exercise appropriately for your dosha. Ayurveda encourages exercising during Kapha time of day, so it's best anytime between 6 a.m. and 10 a.m. and 6 p.m. and 10 p.m.
- Use your dry brush and/or perform your oil massage.
- Shower or bathe using natural soaps and shampoo. If you performed an oil massage, you can leave a thin sheen of oil on your skin to block environmental toxins when you venture out; you don't have to scrub off all the oil.
- Eat a warm, nourishing breakfast. Remember not to mix fruit with other food, because fruit digests at a different rate. One good idea is to eat your fruit before or after you meditate. This will give the fruit time to digest (it needs 45 minutes), so your body has more digestive juices ready for your main meal, after you shower. To save time and keep your routine flowing, consider keeping an electric kettle in your bathroom to heat water for drinking and other routines. I have an Ayurvedic bench in my bathroom to make my routine easier. What's on my bench? A kettle, apple cider vinegar, coconut oil, abhyanga oil, Ayurvedic herbal powders and tablets, essential oils, a dry brush, a neti pot, nasya oil, measuring spoons, ramekins for mixing powders, a small glass, and baking soda.
- Eat the largest meal of the day sometime between 10 a.m. and 2 p.m., Pitta time of day. If your morning routine takes you past 10 a.m., try to make this your most nutrient-dense meal of the day. Think of it as a late breakfast or early lunch. Allow 4 to 5 hours before your next meal. That might mean you eat two meals on some days, and three on others, depending on when you eat breakfast. It's okay to occasionally eat only two meals on some days, especially for Kapha.

Midday

- The best time to perform concentrated work that requires either mental or physical attention is Pitta time, 10 a.m. to 2 p.m.

- Eat lunch mindfully-your largest meal of the day. This is a good time of day to eat protein.
- Walk for 5 or 10 minutes after your meal to promote digestion.
- A great time for creative work is between 2 p.m. and 6 p.m., Vata time of day.

Evening Routine

- A quick rinse or shower before dinner, if necessary, is a nice way to "wash off the day."
- Eat a light meal for dinner, between 5 p.m. and 7 p.m. (Kapha time of day is 6 p.m. to 10 p.m.) o Walk for 5 or 10 minutes after your meal to promote digestion.
- Perform calming activities, like folding laundry, reading a book, or listening to music.
- Take your triphala and drink Golden Milk before bed.
- Floss and brush your teeth.
- Be in bed by 9 p.m. or 10 p.m. This is also the best time of day for sex.
- Journal any thoughts running through your head so they won't disturb your sleep.
- Oil your ears, head, and feet to calm the nervous system and promote deep sleep.
- Apply essential oils such as nutmeg or lavender (good for all doshas) to help with sleep.
    - Practice a calming pranayama with mantras before falling asleep.
    - Try to be asleep by 10 p.m. or 11 p.m. (Pitta time of night is 10 p.m. to 2 a.m.)
    - If you wake during the night, do some breath work or chant a mantra to help you fall back asleep.

Chapter 2

A Wide Range of Ayurvedic Healing Methods

Introduction

Ayurveda, a natural system of medicine, originated in India more than 3,000 years ago. The term Ayurveda is derived from the Sanskrit words ayur (life) and veda (science or knowledge). Thus, Ayurveda translates to knowledge of life. Based on the idea that disease is due to an imbalance or stress in a person's consciousness, Ayurveda encourages certain lifestyle interventions and natural therapies to regain a balance between the body, mind, spirit, and the environment.

Ayurveda treatment starts with an internal purification process, followed by a special diet, herbal remedies, massage therapy, yoga, and meditation. The concepts of universal interconnectedness, the body's constitution (prakriti), and life forces (doshas) are the primary basis of ayurvedic medicine. Goals of treatment aid the person by eliminating impurities, reducing symptoms, increasing resistance to disease, reducing worry, and increasing harmony in life. Herbs and other plants, including oils and common spices, are used extensively in Ayurvedic treatment.

In India, Ayurveda is considered a form of medical care, equal to conventional Western medicine, traditional Chinese medicine, naturopathic medicine, and homeopathic medicine. Practitioners of Ayurveda in India undergo state-recognized, institutionalized training. Currently, Ayurvedic practitioners are not licensed in the United States, and there is no national standard for Ayurvedic training or certification. However, Ayurvedic schools have gained approval as educational institutions in some states.

Ayurveda can have positive effects when used as a complementary therapy in combination with standard, conventional medical care. Many Ayurvedic materials have not been thoroughly studied in either Western or Indian research.

Some of the products used in Ayurvedic medicine contain herbs, metals, minerals, or other materials that may be harmful if used improperly or without the direction of a trained practitioner. Ayurvedic medicines are regulated as dietary supplements rather than as drugs in the United States, so they are not required to meet the safety and efficacy standards for conventional medicines. These medicines can interact, or work against, the effects of Western medicines. Investigate the training and background of Ayurvedic practitioners whom you intend to use.

It's important to discuss any Ayurvedic treatments that you use with your doctor. Women who are pregnant or nursing, or people who are thinking of using Ayurvedic therapy to treat a child, should consult their healthcare provider. It is important to make sure that any diagnosis of a disease or condition has been made by a healthcare provider who has substantial conventional medical training and experience with managing that disease or condition. While Ayurveda can have positive effects when used as a complementary therapy in combination with standard, conventional medical care, it should not replace standard, conventional medical care, especially when treating serious conditions.

Origins and Principles of Ayurveda

Ayurveda has its roots in ancient Indian texts known as the Vedas. The principles of Ayurveda revolve around the concept of three doshas: Vata, Pitta, and Kapha. These doshas represent different qualities and elements within the body and determine an individual's physical and mental characteristics.

Best Ayurvedic treatments in India are deeply rooted in these foundational principles, leveraging the wisdom of Ayurvedic techniques to bring about holistic well-being. Ayurvedic treatment methods encompass a wide array of therapies, including herbal remedies, dietary adjustments, and lifestyle practices, all tailored to balance and harmonize the doshas. Ayurveda solutions are renowned for their personalized approach, recognizing the unique constitution of each individual and addressing imbalances through natural means. The diverse range of Ayurvedic treatments available in India spans from rejuvenating therapies to therapeutic interventions, showcasing the effectiveness and versatility of Ayurveda in promoting health and vitality. With different types of Ayurvedic treatments gaining popularity, individuals seeking a holistic and natural approach to wellness can explore the rich heritage of Ayurveda in India, discovering the time-tested methods that have been passed down through generations.

A Range of Ayurvedic Therapies

Ayurvedic techniques include:

- dietary changes
- herbal medicine, including combining herbs with metals, minerals or gems (known as rasha shastra medicines) that can take the form of pellets, tablets and powders of various colours and scents)
- acupuncture (practiced by some practitioners)
- massage
- meditation
- breathing exercises
- panchakarma ('5 actions') - a specialised treatment consisting of 5 therapies including emesis (vomiting), enemas and blood-letting, which are meant to detoxify the body and balance the doshas (in Ayurveda, the body's 3 vital energies)
- sound therapy, including the use of mantras
- yoga.

Ayurveda Claims to Treat a Range of Disorders

Ayurveda practitioners believe their approach is effective in treating a range of disorders, including:

- anxiety
- asthma
- arthritis
- digestive problems
- eczema
- high blood pressure
- high cholesterol levels
- rheumatoid arthritis
- stress.

Special Considerations- Herbs and Rasa Shastra Medicines

Alongside diet, herbal medicine is central to Ayurveda treatment. Safety issues to consider include:

- Herbal medicines can be as potent as pharmaceutical drugs and should be treated with the same caution and respect. The belief that herbs are safe and harmless may encourage inappropriate use or overdose.
- Before buying or taking a complementary medicine, check the label for an 'AUST L' (listed) or 'AUST R' (registered) code. This means they meet Australian safety standards designed to protect your health.
- Ayurvedic medicines that do not have an 'AUST L' (listed) or 'AUST R' (registered) code on the label are not registered with the TGA. There have been reports of some unlisted and unregistered Ayurvedic medicines being sold in Victoria that contain ingredients classed as poisons in Australia. These ingredients may cause serious side-effects.
- Avoid purchasing or using complementary medicines not registered with the TGA, including those obtained from overseas.
- Most complementary medicines have not been tested on pregnant women, breastfeeding mothers or children and may be harmful.
- Complementary medicines such as herbs can be bought without prescription. However, they may still have side effects, interact with other drugs or treatments, or contain harmful ingredients not shown on the label.
- Products from other countries that are sold over the Internet or brought into Australia from overseas are not subject to the same laws or regulations as those sold in Australia. Please note that Ayurvedic practitioners may consider some toxic ingredients to be safe. Ask for a full list of ingredients of all herbal medicines. If in doubt, check with your doctor. Cases of lead poisoning as a result of taking Ayurvedic treatments imported from India have been reported in Victoria.
- If you are given a preparation by a friend or relative and you cannot identify the origin or ingredients, it is safer not to take it.

- Tell your doctor about the Ayurvedic treatments you are having. This will help to reduce the risk of adverse reactions.
- Never stop taking your conventional medicine or alter the dose without the knowledge and approval of your doctor.

Benefits of Ayurvedic Treatments

Ayurvedic treatments offer a wide range of benefits for both physical health and mental well-being.

1. Physical Health Ayurveda employs various techniques to promote physical health. These treatments can help alleviate chronic conditions, boost the immune system, improve digestion, enhance sleep quality, and promote overall vitality.
2. Mental Well-being:Ayurvedic treatments also focus on mental well-being by addressing stress, anxiety, and imbalances in the mind. Through practices such as meditation, yoga, and specific herbal remedies, Ayurveda aims to restore mental clarity, emotional stability, and a sense of inner peace. Techniques Used in Ayurvedic Treatments Ayurveda encompasses a range of techniques to restore balance and promote healing.

1. Panchakarma Panchakarma is a comprehensive detoxification and rejuvenation treatment. It involves a series of therapeutic procedures that aim to remove toxins, balance the doshas, and restore optimal health.
2. Abhyanga and Swedana Abhyanga is a massage technique that uses warm herbal oils to nourish the body and relax the muscles. Swedana, on the other hand, involves steam therapy to induce sweating and promote toxin elimination.
3. Shirodhara Shirodhara is a deeply relaxing treatment where a continuous flow of warm herbal oil is poured onto the forehead. It helps calm the mind, relieve stress, and improve sleep quality.
4. Ayurvedic Diet Ayurveda emphasizes the importance of proper nutrition. An Ayurvedic diet is tailored to individual doshas and focuses on fresh, whole foods, herbs, and spices that support digestion and overall well-being. Mechanisms of Ayurvedic Treatments Ayurvedic treatments work through various mechanisms to restore balance and promote healing.

1. Balancing Doshas By identifying and addressing imbalances in the doshas, Ayurvedic treatments help restore harmony

within the body. This balance is essential for optimal health and well-being.

2. Detoxification and Cleansing Panchakarma and other detoxification techniques help remove toxins from the body, allowing it to function more efficiently and improving overall health.
3. Rejuvenation and Restoration Ayurvedic treatments aim to rejuvenate the body and mind, promoting vitality and slowing down the aging process. These treatments nourish the tissues, strengthen the body, and enhance overall resilience.
4. Strengthening the Immune System Ayurvedic therapies and herbal remedies can help strengthen the immune system, making the body more resistant to diseases and promoting overall wellness. Integrating Ayurvedic Treatments into Daily Life Incorporating Ayurvedic principles into daily life can have profound effects on overall well-being. Simple practices like mindful eating, self-care rituals, and following a daily routine according to your dosha can support balance and health.

Ayurvedic treatments, rooted in ancient Indian traditions, further enhance the holistic approach to wellness. Ayurveda, which means "knowledge of life" in Sanskrit, encompasses a diverse range of therapies that aim to harmonize the mind, body, and spirit.

A list of Ayurvedic treatments includes Panchakarma, an intensive detoxification process, Abhyanga, a therapeutic massage using herbal oils, and Shirodhara, a technique involving a continuous flow of warm oil on the forehead to promote relaxation.

What are Ayurvedic treatments, you might ask? Well, they are time-tested remedies that seek to restore balance by addressing the root causes of imbalances within the body. Explore the vibrant array of Ayurvedic therapies available in India, and embark on a journey toward optimal well-being through these time-honored practices.

1. Morning Routine (Dinacharya)

A key aspect of Ayurveda is the emphasis on daily routines, known as Dinacharya. This morning routine is designed to align your body with the natural rhythms of the day, promoting optimal health and vitality. Begin your day by rising with the sun, as Ayurveda places great importance on syncing your internal clock with the external environment.

- Oil Pulling (Gandusha): Kickstart your morning by practising oil pulling, known as Gandusha. Swish a tablespoon of warm sesame or coconut oil in your mouth for 15-20 minutes. This ancient technique not only promotes oral health but is believed to detoxify the entire body by pulling out harmful toxins.
- Tongue Scraping (Jihwa Prakshalana): Follow up with tongue scraping using a copper or stainless-steel scraper. This helps remove toxins that accumulate on the tongue overnight, supporting digestive health and preventing bad breath.
- Hydration with Warm Water: Hydrate your body with a glass of warm water to stimulate digestion and flush out toxins. Adding a squeeze of lemon can enhance the detoxifying effects.
- Self-Massage (Abhyanga): Treat yourself to a daily self-massage with warm oil, such as sesame or almond oil. This Ayurvedic practice, known as Abhyanga, not only nourishes the skin but also promotes relaxation, improves circulation and supports the elimination of toxins.

2. Balanced Diet

Ayurveda emphasizes the importance of maintaining a balanced diet to support overall well-being. The concept of "Doshas" forms the basis of Ayurvedic nutrition, categorizing individuals into three predominant body types: Vata, Pitta, and Kapha. Understanding your Dosha can guide you in making food choices that promote balance and harmony.

- Vata-Pacifying Foods: If you are predominantly Vata, focus on warm, nourishing, and grounding foods. Incorporate cooked vegetables, whole grains, and warm spices like ginger and cumin into your meals.
- Pitta-Balancing Diet: Pitta individuals benefit from cooling foods that balance their fiery nature. Include sweet and bitter tastes, such as fresh fruits, leafy greens, and cooling herbs like mint and coriander.
- Kapha-Soothing Choices: Kapha types should opt for foods that are warm, light, and stimulating. Include a variety of colourful vegetables, legumes, and spices like black pepper and ginger to enhance digestion.

3. Mindful Eating

Ayurveda places equal importance on how you eat, not just what you eat. Mindful eating involves being present and attentive during meals, promoting better digestion and nutrient absorption.

- Eat in a Calm Environment: Create a peaceful and calm eating environment. Avoid distractions like TV or electronic devices, allowing yourself to fully focus on the flavours and textures of your food.
- Chew Your Food Thoroughly: Digestion begins in the mouth, so chew your food thoroughly. This not only aids digestion but also allows you to savour the taste of each bite.

4. Daily Exercise

Ayurveda emphasizes the importance of regular exercise to maintain physical health and balance the Doshas. However, the type and intensity of exercise should align with your unique constitution.

- Vata-Predominant Individuals: Gentle and grounding exercises such as yoga, tai chi, or walking are beneficial for balancing Vata.
- Pitta-Dominant Individuals: Pitta types benefit from moderate, cooling activities like swimming, biking, or hiking to release excess heat.
- Kapha-Dominant Individuals: Engage in more vigorous and stimulating exercises such as jogging, aerobics, or strength training to counteract Kapha's tendency towards stagnation.

5. Stress Management

In the fast-paced modern world, stress has become a prevalent health concern. Ayurveda offers a range of practices to manage stress and promote mental well-being.

- Yoga and Meditation: Incorporate daily yoga and meditation practices to calm the mind and reduce stress. These ancient techniques have been shown to lower cortisol levels and enhance overall mental resilience.
- Herbal Remedies: Ayurvedic herbs such as ashwagandha, Brahmi, and holy basil are renowned for their adaptogenic properties, helping the body adapt to stress and promoting balance.
- Pranayama (Breath Control): Practice pranayama techniques to regulate your breath and activate the parasympathetic nervous system. Deep, slow breathing can induce a state of relaxation and counteract the effects of chronic stress.

Healing Ayurvedic Recipes

Most of the recipes mentioned here are one-pot meals that are usually complete meals on their own. The combination of oils, spices, beans, grains, and greens creates wholesome, hearty, and nutritionally complete dishes. All of these recipes are vegetarian, but in Ayurveda, we do take into account that some people need meat on occasion. If you are not used to vegetarian dishes, just try these out for a few meals a week. You will notice that no raw-food recipes are included. In Ayurveda, we prefer food to be at least slightly cooked or steamed, to make the digestive process easier. When we eat raw food, the body uses an enormous amount of energy to break it down and digest it. By cooking our food (and chewing it well), we help our body begin the digestive process. That way, we can immediately use the nutrients and conserve energy for other parts of our body and mind that need healing and restoration. Try eating this way for a few weeks and notice how good you feel.

Everyday Ccf Tea

Vata, Pitta & Kapha pacifying

YIELD: 5 servings PREP: 3 minutes COOK: 5 minutes

This easy-to-make tea is profoundly healing. The mix of cumin, coriander, and fennel helps kindle your digestive "fire" (agni), improve digestion, nourish the tissues, and keep cravings at bay. At Ayurvedic conferences and lectures, they often serve this tea for attendees to sip all day long.

5 cups water

1 teaspoon cumin seeds

1 teaspoon coriander seeds

1 teaspoon fennel seeds

½ teaspoon ajwain seeds (optional)

1. In a small pot, add the water and seeds. Stir.
2. Bring to a boil, and let it simmer for 5 minutes. Remove from the heat and strain.
3. Pour the tea into a mug, and enjoy.

I often make a pot of tea in the morning, adjusting the amount of seeds to the amount of water I use. I mix the seeds together beforehand in equal amounts and use 1 teaspoon of the seed mixture per cup of water

Ghee

Vata & Pitta pacifying, Kapha use in moderation YIELD: about 10 ounces COOK: 15 to 25 minutes (varies) This magical elixir is the base of so many Ayurvedic recipes, medicines, and healing practices. Ghee is believed to be the only oil that carries the nutrients in food and spices through all seven layers of our tissues: plasma, blood, bones, muscles, fat, nervous system, and reproductive system. Ghee is also a high-heat cooking oil. It activates many healing qualities in spices, which is why spices are sautéed in ghee as one of the first steps in many recipes.

Once you master making ghee, you can try it with different spices and herbs, such as clove buds, garlic, or cilantro. Some people find making ghee intimidating, but by staying present, using all your senses, and preparing ghee in a loving, caring way, your ghee will be delicious, nutritious, and healing.

1 Pound (4 sticks) of Organic, Unsalted Butter

1. Place the butter in a saucepan, preferably one with a heavy bottom. Turn the heat to medium, and watch the butter as it melts. Ghee requires all of your senses, so do not step away.
2. As the butter begins to melt, lower the heat to medium-low, and stir occasionally, or even not at all. White foam will form on the top as the milk solids separate from the butter, and fine steam will rise as the water evaporates. The butter will begin to sputter, the sounds becoming loud and rapid.
3. Ghee cooking time varies depending on your altitude, the type of butter, and the stove and pot being used, but after about 10 to 15 minutes, you will notice the ghee beginning to quiet down. The colour will change to a deep golden hue, and the milk solids will settle at the bottom of the pan and begin to turn brown, and become very aromatic. As soon as the ghee quiets down and only a few bubbles are present, it is done. At this point, remove the pot from the heat. The milk solids burn quickly, so pay attention.
4. Allow the very hot ghee to cool off for a few minutes in the pot.
5. Carefully pour the ghee through a fine mesh sieve into a Pyrex glass or stainless-steel ghee container, if you have one, to cool off even further. Do not pour the ghee directly into a glass jar

until it has cooled off significantly, or the jar will crack. If you must pour it into a jar immediately, place a metal spoon in the jar to absorb the heat.

6. The curds at the bottom of the pot can be given to your pet as a treat in small amounts, or you can add a bit of Indian boiled sugarcane solids, called jaggery, to them for a delightful treat.

Do not refrigerate ghee, and do not get it wet. Ghee has an incredibly long shelf life when kept covered and dry. Never use a wet knife or spoon to scoop out your ghee, as it will spoil it. Ghee that has been aged 100 years is sold in India as medicine, but yours doesn't need to age to have incredible health benefits.

Golden Milk

Vata, Pitta & Kapha pacifying

YIELD: 1 serving

PREP: 2 minutes

COOK: 5 minutes

Golden milk is an age-old recipe that nourishes the body on many levels. Turmeric helps reduce inflammation, ghee distributes the healing properties throughout the body, and tryptophan in the milk will help you sleep.

It is calmative, restorative, and delicious. You can make this a vegan drink by substituting milk and ghee with almond oil and a dairy alternative (such as almond milk, hemp milk, or coconut milk made without zinc oxide). 6 to 8 ounces whole-fat goat's milk (for Kapha and Pitta) or cow's milk (Vata)

½ teaspoon ghee

½ teaspoon turmeric powder

½ teaspoon ginger powder

1 pinch ground black pepper

1 pinch ground cinnamon

1 pinch ground nutmeg (to promote sleep)

1 small piece jaggery (optional)

1. Add all the ingredients to a small pot. Over mediumhigh heat, bring the mixture to a boil, then lower the heat and simmer for a minute or two.

2. Pour into a mug, and drink before bed. If you want to enjoy this drink during the day, leave out the nutmeg.

TIP: If you are experiencing constipation, adding more ghee to the milk will help you be good to go!

Vata Kitchari

Vata pacifying

YIELD: 4 servings

PREP: 10 minutes (plus soaking time)

COOK: 20 to 30 minutes

The first Ayurvedic dish I made was kitchari from Amadea Morningstar's Ayurvedic Cookbook. I bought all the exotic ingredients. I had no idea what I was doing, but I was determined to begin living an Ayurvedic lifestyle. When I sat down to eat it and took my first spoonful, my entire body said "mmmmm." It felt like my gut and brain finally found something that was thoroughly filling on every level-emotionally, spiritually, and physically. I truly felt complete, and I hope you will, too. This recipe is good for seasonal cleanses as well as just calming down the mind and body. It's good to eat for breakfast, lunch, and dinner.

½ cup dried split yellow mung beans (dal)

½ cup uncooked white basmati rice

2 cups chopped vegetables (one or two types, see choices on next page)

2 tablespoons ghee

1 teaspoon black mustard seeds

1pinch hing

½ teaspoon cumin seeds

½ teaspoon ajwain seeds

½ teaspoon ground coriander

1 teaspoon turmeric powder

1 small yellow onion, chopped

1 clove garlic, chopped

1 (2-inch) piece fresh ginger, peeled, and grated or minced

4 to 6 cups water 1 teaspoon sea salt

½ teaspoon pepper

1 additional teaspoon ghee (optional)

1 teaspoon Bragg's Liquid Aminos (optional)

1 small handful chopped fresh cilantro (for garnish)

1. Place the beans and rice in a bowl of water, and rinse until the water runs relatively clear. Fill the bowl with water, and allow the beans and rice to soak while you prepare the recipe, for up to an hour.
2. Wash and chop the vegetables.
3. Before starting the vagar (oil-spice mixture), turn on the exhaust fan over the stove, as spices can give off a strong aroma. Then in a 6-quart soup pot over medium-high heat, heat the ghee. Add the black mustard seeds. When they pop, add the hing, cumin seeds, ajwain seeds, coriander, and turmeric. Cook for about 1 minute, or until aromatic. Spices burn quickly; do not allow them to smoke.
4. Stir the onion, garlic, and ginger into the vagar.
5. Drain the rice and beans, and add them to the vagar. Stir until the rice and beans are coated. Allow to sit for 1 to 2 minutes, stirring occasionally.
6. Add the water to the pot, and stir. Add the vegetables, and stir again. Cover the pot, and bring to a boil over medium-high heat.
7. Lower the heat to a simmer. Place the lid askew to let out steam (which lets out excess Vata). Simmer until the water is absorbed, about 15 minutes, or until the kitchari is the consistency you desire.
8. Add the salt and pepper toward the end of cooking.
9. Remove from the heat. Divide into four portions. If using, add more ghee and Bragg's Liquid Aminos to the portion you will eat right away. Then garnish the single portion with cilantro, if using.

Use less water for a stew-like consistency or more water for a soupier consistency. It is important to use sea salt for the extra moisture provided. Do not use Himalayan salt in this recipe.

Ideal vegetables for this dish include squash, green beans, beets, okra, daikon radish, carrots, peas, and sweet potatoes. To reheat uneaten portions, add some water to the pot and heat over a medium heat. Never microwave or freeze.

Pitta Kitchari

Pitta pacifying

Yield: 4 Servings

Prep: 10 Minutes (Plus Soaking Time)

Cook: 20 To 30 Minutes

Much like the Vata version, in the sense that it's completely nourishing and satisfying, this Pitta-pacifying recipe includes cooling herbs and spices to help balance Pitta on every level. By removing the heating spices like black mustard seeds and hing, and adding in some cooling elements like garnishing with cilantro and coconut, Pitta can enjoy this feel-good comfort food without overheating. Pitta can even allow the dish to cool down a bit before eating.

½ cup dried split yellow mung beans (dal)

½ cup dried white basmati rice

2 cups chopped vegetables (one or two types)

2 tablespoons ghee

½ teaspoon cumin seeds

½ teaspoon ground coriander

½ teaspoon fennel seeds

1 teaspoon turmeric powder

1 small yellow onion, chopped

1 (1-inch) piece fresh ginger, peeled, and grated or minced

4 to 6 cups water

1 teaspoon sea salt

1 additional teaspoon ghee (optional)

1 teaspoon Bragg's Liquid Aminos (optional)

1 small handful chopped fresh cilantro (optional)

1 to 2 tablespoons unsweetened shredded coconut (optional)

1. Place the beans and rice in a bowl of water, and rinse until the water runs relatively clear. Fill the bowl with water, and allow the beans and rice to soak while you prepare the recipe, for up to an hour.
2. Wash and chop the vegetables.
3. Before starting the vagar (oil-spice mixture), turn on the exhaust fan over the stove, as spices can give off a strong aroma. Then

in a 6-quart soup pot over medium-high heat, heat the ghee. Add the cumin, coriander, fennel, and turmeric. Cook for about 1 minute, or until aromatic. Spices burn quickly; do not allow them to smoke.

4. Stir in the onion and ginger. Allow the onion to become tender to sweeten it up for Pitta.
5. Drain the rice and beans, and add them to the vagar. Stir until the rice and beans are coated. Allow to sit for 1 to 2 minutes, stirring occasionally.
6. Add the water to the pot, and stir. Add the vegetables, and stir again. Cover the pot, and bring to a boil over medium-high heat.
7. Lower the heat to a simmer. Simmer until the water is absorbed, about 15 minutes, or until the kitchari is the consistency you desire.
8. Add the salt toward the end of cooking.
9. Remove from the heat. Divide into four portions. If using, add ghee and Bragg's Liquid Aminos to the portion you will eat right away. Garnish the single portion with cilantro and/or coconut, if desired.

Use less water for a stew-like consistency or more water for a soupier consistency. It is important to use sea salt for the extra moisture provided. Do not use Himalayan salt in this recipe.

Ideal vegetable choices for this dish include burdock root, zucchini, green beans, asparagus, carrots, and celery. To reheat uneaten portions, add some water to the pot and heat over a medium heat. Never microwave or freeze.

Kapha Kitchari

Kapha pacifying

Yield: 4 Servings Prep: 10 Minutes Cook: 20 to 30 minutes

This extremely nourishing meal can be eaten for breakfast, lunch, and dinner. It is ideal for a mono-fast during a cleanse. In Kapha kitchari, we use less ghee than for the other two doshas, but it is still an important ingredient for a satisfying meal, as the ghee deposits nutrients deep down into all seven layers of your tissues. A little bit of ghee goes a long way! Kapha can also speed up the cooking process by preparing over a higher heat. Just stay present and stir more frequently. The fast cooking time may translate into helping Kapha speed up a bit!

½ cup dried split yellow mung beans (dal)

½ cup dried white basmati rice or

½ cup uncooked quinoa

2 cups chopped vegetables and/or leafy greens (two or three types)

3 carrots, chopped

2 celery stalks, chopped

1 teaspoon ghee

1 teaspoon black mustard seeds

½ teaspoon cumin seeds

½ teaspoon ground coriander

½ teaspoon ajwain seeds

½ teaspoon ground cinnamon

½ teaspoon ground cloves, or 2 to 3 whole clove buds

1 pinch hing

1 teaspoon turmeric powder

1 to 2 cloves garlic, chopped

1 (2-inch) piece fresh ginger, peeled and grated or minced

1 small yellow onion, chopped

4 to 6 cups water

1 to 2 teaspoons Himalayan salt

1 teaspoon pepper

1. teaspoon Bragg's Liquid Aminos (optional) 1 small handful chopped fresh cilantro (for garnish) 1. Place the beans and rice or quinoa in a bowl of water, and rinse until the water runs relatively clear. Fill the bowl with water, and allow the beans and rice or quinoa to soak while you prepare the recipe, for up to an hour.
2. Wash and chop the vegetables, carrots, and celery.
3. Before starting the vagar (oil-spice mixture), turn on the exhaust fan over the stove, as spices can give off a strong aroma. Then in a 6-quart soup pot over medium-high heat, heat the ghee.

Add the black mustard seeds. When they pop, add the cumin, coriander, ajwain, cinnamon, cloves, hing, and turmeric. Cook for about 1 minute, or until aromatic. Spices burn quickly; do not allow them to smoke.

4. Stir in the garlic, ginger, and onion.
5. Drain the rice or quinoa and beans, and add them to the vagar. Stir until the rice or quinoa and beans are coated. Allow to sit for 1 to 2 minutes, stirring occasionally.
6. Add the water to the pot, and stir. Add the vegetables, carrots, and celery, and stir again. Cover the pot, and bring to a boil over medium-high heat. (If using leafy greens, add them in step 7.)
7. Lower the heat to a simmer. Simmer until the water is absorbed, about 15 minutes, or until the kitchari is the consistency you desire. Just before removing the pot from the heat, add the greens and stir until wilted.
8. Add the salt and pepper toward the end of cooking.
9. Remove from the heat. Divide into four portions. If using, add Bragg's Liquid Aminos to the portion you will eat right away. Garnish the single portion with cilantro, if desired.

Use less water for a stew-like consistency or more water for a soupier consistency. It is important to use Himalayan salt in this recipe; sea salt will add more water to already watery Kapha, which is undesired.

Ideal vegetable choices for this dish include burdock root, cauliflower, broccoli, white potato, daikon radish, green beans, spinach, kale, mustard greens, and chard. To reheat uneaten portions, add some water to the pot and heat over a medium heat. Never microwave or freeze.

How to Eat Warm Kitchari at Work: How do you eat a hearty warm lunch at the office? Instead of using the microwave, which destroys the nutrients in food, buy a Thermos. Heat your food up on the stove in the morning, put it in the Thermos, and leave it on your desk until lunchtime.

Your food will be piping hot. You can also use an Indian Tiffin. This stackable container unit is ubiquitous in India. Made of stainless steel, three, four, five or more compartments can be stacked on top of each other. Typically one contains rice, dal, chapatti (unleavened flat bread), vegetables, and maybe a sweet. To help keep the food warm, wrap the tiffin in a towel before packing it in your bag. It won't keep your food as hot as a Thermos will, but the food won't get too cold, either.

Winter-warming Whole Mung Bean Soup

Vata, Pitta & Kapha nourishing

YIELD: 4 servings PREP: 15 minutes (plus soaking time overnight) COOK: 60 minutes

There is something indescribably satisfying about mung beans, so it is no wonder that many cultures call them their own. Whole mung beans are green, unlike the split version, which are yellow. Mung, which packs a nutritious punch, is called the "mighty mung bean" for good reason:

The little green bean and its yellow counterpart contain a host of minerals, including folate, manganese, magnesium, iron, thiamine, copper, zinc, and potassium. It also includes vitamins A, C, B6 , B12 , E, and K. How can they not be delicious? When the body recognizes how good a food is for it, it embraces the food.

1 cup dried green whole mung beans

6 to 8 cups water (depending on desired consistency)

1 strip kombu

2 tablespoons ghee

½ teaspoon black mustard seeds

1 teaspoon cumin seeds

1 teaspoon ajwain seeds, or celery seeds

1 teaspoon ground cumin

1 teaspoon turmeric powder

4 to 6 fresh or frozen curry leaves (optional)

1 small yellow onion, chopped

2 to 3 garlic cloves, chopped (for Vata and Kapha), or

2 garlic cloves chopped (for Pitta)

1 tablespoon roughly chopped fresh ginger

1 to 2 cups organic vegetable broth (optional)

2 carrots, chopped 2 celery stalks, chopped

1 to 2 yellow potatoes, cubed

1 small green jalapeño, deveined, seeds removed, and chopped

½ lemon Fresh parsley or cilantro, chopped, for garnish (optional)

1 teaspoon ghee (optional for Vata and Pitta, less for Kapha)

1. Soak the mung beans in water overnight.
2. Rinse the beans and place them in a 6-quart pot. Add the water and kombu. Bring to a boil over medium-high heat. This will take about 45 minutes. Discard the kombu, and set the pot aside.
3. In a small sauce pan, add the olive oil, or avocado oil or ghee. Heat the pan to medium heat.
4. Add the black mustard seeds. When the mustard seeds pop, add the cumin seeds, ajwain, cumin powder, turmeric, and curry leaves, if using. Stir quickly.
5. Add the onion, garlic, and ginger. Over medium heat, being careful not to let anything burn, cook for about 5 to 10 minutes, or until the onion becomes translucent. Then add the mixture to the pot of beans.
6. Add a few more cups of water or organic vegetable broth, if desired, to increase the liquid content. Add the carrots, celery, potatoes, and jalapeño. Bring to a boil over medium-high heat, and then lower to a simmer. Simmer for about 15 minutes, and remove from the heat.
7. Use an immersion blender to roughly blend the soup, or transfer in small batches to a countertop blender, being careful to allow steam to escape between pulses. Just a few pulses will do.
8. Before serving, squeeze in the juice of half a lemon. Garnish with chopped parsley or cilantro, if desired, and a teaspoon of ghee (less for Kapha), if using, before serving.

Urad Dal Porridge: Vata pacifying; Vata, Pitta & Kapha benefit after travel YIELD: 4 servings PREP: 10 minutes COOK: 30 minutes

Urad dal, also known as black gram, is a heavy type of dal that is great for calming Vata.

This recipe is perfect to make after traveling-whether it's a 13-hour trip to India or a 5-hour coast-to-coast flight-all travelers can benefit from the grounding, heating qualities of urad dal. As airplane travel dries you out, urad dal counteracts that with its moist, unctuous, heating qualities.

While those qualities tend to increase Pitta and Kapha, I find that using this recipe just after travel can benefit all doshas. Vata can also add another spoonful of ghee before eating.

1 cup uncooked white basmati rice

1 cup dried split urad dal

2 tablespoons white, brown, or red miso paste

3 cups vegetable broth, mushroom broth, or a combination

1 to 2 cups water (depending on desired consistency)

1 tablespoon ghee ½ medium yellow onion, chopped

1 teaspoon garlic powder

1 teaspoon turmeric powder

½ teaspoon ground cumin

½ teaspoon ground coriander

4 to 5 leaves Swiss chard, rainbow chard, kale, or mustard greens, chopped

½ teaspoon sea salt Freshly ground black or white pepper

½ teaspoon Bragg's Liquid Aminos (optional)

2 tablespoons raw, unsalted pumpkin seeds, or sunflower seeds, for garnish (optional)

1. In a bowl, mix the rice and dal together and rinse well. Fill the bowl with water and allow the dal and rice to soak while you prepare the other ingredients.
2. Boil ½ cup of hot water, pour into a small bowl, and stir in the miso paste until it dissolves.
3. In an 8-quart soup pot, add the miso broth, vegetable broth, and water, and heat over medium heat.
4. Add the ghee, onion, garlic powder, turmeric, cumin, and coriander to the broth.
5. Bring to a boil, and add the soaked rice and dal. Allow the mixture to come to a boil again, and then lower to a simmer and cover the pot. Stir occasionally until all the liquid is absorbed.
6. Toward the end of cooking, add the greens and stir well. Cover the pot and allow the greens to wilt over very low heat or no heat.

7. Add the salt and pepper. Let the porridge sit for about 5 minutes. Divide into four servings and, if desired, top each serving with the Bragg's Liquid Aminos and the pumpkin or sunflower seeds.

To make this recipe vegan, use avocado oil instead of ghee. Refrigerate remaining portions and reconstitute it by adding more water or broth the next day before reheating over medium heat.

Easy Breakfast Bowl

Vata, Pitta & Kapha pacifying (with dosha-specific ingredients)

Yield: 2 Servings Prep: 5 Minutes Cook: 15 minutes

One of the most popular questions I hear is, "What should I eat for breakfast?" Since Ayurveda doesn't like mixing fruit with other foods, because they digest at different rates, people can be confused over things like yogurt with fruit, oatmeal with berries, or cold cereal with sliced fruit.

So here is a recommendation: Eat your fruit about 45 minutes before your main meal so that it does not disturb your digestion. Try this porridge anytime of year. It's deeply satisfying and should give you long-lasting energy throughout the morning.

1 cup quinoa (for Pitta or Kapha), or

1 cup millet (for Kapha), or

1 cup rice (for Vata)

2 cups water

½ cup goat's milk (for Pitta, Kapha, and Vata), or almond milk (for Vata)

1 teaspoon ground cinnamon

¼ teaspoon ground nutmeg ¼ teaspoon ginger powder

½ teaspoon pea protein powder, chia seeds, or ground flaxseeds (optional for power boost)

1 tablespoon maple syrup or honey

1 teaspoon ghee (optional for Vata and Pitta) or

½ teaspoon ghee (optional for Kapha)

1. Rinse the quinoa, millet, or rice well. In a 4-quart sauce pan, combine the grain and water, and bring to a boil over medium heat. Lower the heat to a simmer and cover. Simmer until all the water is absorbed.

2. In a separate 2-quart saucepan, add the milk, cinnamon, nutmeg, and ginger, and heat gently over low heat.
3. Divide the grain into two servings, and pour an even amount of the hot milk and spices on top.
4. If using the optional power boost, stir half the pea protein powder, chia seeds, or flaxseeds into each bowl.
5 .Add the maple syrup or honey and the ghee, if using. Either stick with the grain or seed recommended for your dosha or choose your grain or seed seasonally. In the winter, use millet or rice, and in the spring and summer, use quinoa.

Crunchy Chickpeas: Pitta & Kapha pacifying YIELD: 5 cups PREP: 20 minutes Cooking: 30 minutes

While we don't promote snacking in Ayurveda, sometimes we just need a little something to peck on now and then. Crunchy garbanzo beans make a satisfying and supremely healthy choice for Pitta and Kapha.

As witnessed by the many packaged chickpea snacks now commonly seen in stores, chickpeas are popular these days. You can make this snack yourself for a quarter of the price. You can also customize the flavors to satisfy your dosha, and your palate, by getting creative with the spices.

2 cups precooked chickpeas, or

2 (8-ounce) cans chickpeas, drained and rinsed

1 teaspoon sea salt (for Pitta), or Himalayan salt (for Kapha)

½ teaspoon smoked paprika, or

½ teaspoon ground cumin, or

½ teaspoon garam masala powder (optional)

1 tablespoon sunflower or safflower oil (optional for crunchiness; no oil for Kapha)

1. Spread the rinsed chickpeas on a baking sheet to dry, about 20 minutes.
2. Preheat the oven to 450°F.
3. In a mixing bowl, add the chickpeas; salt; paprika, cumin, or garam masala (if using); and the oil (if using). Toss well to coat, and spread on a baking sheet in a single layer.

4. Place the baking sheet in the oven and bake for 20 minutes. Remove from the oven, and use a spatula to turn the chickpeas over. Place back in the oven and roast for an additional 10 minutes, or until the chickpeas are slightly browned. Roast a little longer, if desired, for crunchier chickpeas.

Store the crunchy chickpeas in an airtight container. Do not refrigerate. These are great to sprinkle on salads and rice dishes. Don't make more than you can eat in three days. To cook your Crunchy Chickpeas, soak overnight, drain, and place into a large soup pot. Cover with water, at least double the amount of beans. Bring to a boil, then cover and simmer for at least 30 to 45 minutes. Check on the beans during cooking. When they are soft, they are done.

Chapter 3

Universal Attributes and Doshic Theory

The Five Elements and their Attributes

Dr. Frawley explains the relationship between the 5 elements in the following manner, "All elements originate from ether. Ether moves to become air, air causes friction to become fire, fire becomes water as it becomes denser, water becomes earth as it coagulates.

And all five elements are contained in the Earth." Consciousness is Ether because they both have the qualities which are clear, subtle, light, expansive, and omnipresent.

The 5 elements are the different manifestations of Awareness/ Consciousness.

The Sanskrit words for the 5 elements are as follows:

- Akasha (Ether, space)
- Vayu (Air)
- Tejas or Agni (Fire)
- Apas (Water)
- Prthivi (Earth)

The 5 elements and their associated organs and Chakras

- Ether (ears, hearing) (throat)
- Air (skin, touch) (heart)
- Fire (eyes, seeing) (navel)
- Water (tongue, taste buds, taste) (sacral)
- Earth (nose, smell) (root)

The 5 elements and the Doshas

- Vata - Air and Ether
- Pitta - Fire and Water
- Kapha - Water and Earth

The Doshas and their associated attributes (gunas)

- Vata - Dry, Light, Cold, Rough, Subtle, Mobile, Clear
- Pitta - Hot, Sharp, Light, Liquid, Mobile, Oily
- Kapha - Heavy, slow/dull, cold, oily, liquid, slimy/smooth, dense, soft, static, sticky/cloudy, hard, gross

How we use the properties of 5 elements for healing in Ayurveda:

- Heavy (Guru) - decreases Vata & Pitta, and increases Kapha; examples of substances with the heavy quality include meat, cheese, yogurt, sugar, sleeping for long periods of time, insufficient exercise. It is necessary for stability, increased grounding, and nourishment.
- Light (Laghu) - decreases Kapha and increases Vata & Pitta; examples include Panchakarma, cleanses, heat, saunas lighten the body, mint leaves & cardamom seeds are light. It moves us to alertness, clarity, and attentiveness.
- Slow/Dull (Manda) - decreases Vata & Pitta, increases Kapha; examples are rich fatty foods. It induces calmness, quietude and silence. Think of how heavy snow dulls traffic sounds and creates silence.
- Sharp (Tikshna) - decrease Kapha and increases Vata & Pitta; spicy foods, cayenne pepper, and fire are examples. It aids learning, concentration, understanding and comprehension.
- Cold (Shita) - decreases Pitta and increases Kapha & Vata; It aids the cooling down of burning sensations on the skin and in the body and an overactive mind. Examples would be cucumbers, cucumber water, aloe, plant juice, and lunar breath.
- Hot (Ushna) - decreases Vata & Kapha and increases Pitta; It stimulates digestion, improves assimilation and circulation, promotes cleansing. Examples include: hot curry, hot chilies, cayenne pepper, horseradish, spicy mustard
- Oily or Unctuous (Snigdha) - decrease Vata, increases Pitta & Kapha; Sesame oil and avocados are oily. We need this property for relaxation and creating moisture, lubrication, smoothness,

and vigor. Oil represents love and compassion and nourishment. If we have problems with digesting oils on a physical level, there may be difficulties with expressing self-love on an emotional and spiritual level.

- Dry (Ruksha) - decreases Pitta and Kapha, and increases Vata; the tannins in red wines, vinegars, and walnuts are examples. This quality stimulates fire. On a emotional and spiritual level, dryness is seen as loneliness or rejection or separation.
- Slimy/Smooth (shlakshna) - decreases Vata and increases Pitta and Kapha; Cheeses, oils, avocado, tapioca, heavy sesame oil are examples; this quality makes the body flexible and lubricates the body which is very helpful in osteoporosis and arthritis.
- Rough (Khara) - this quality decreases Kapha, increases Vata, and can both increase and decrease Pitta; examples include raw vegetables and beans; It facilitates the drying out of Kapha's excess water; Fear is dry and rough.
- Dense (Sandra) - decreases Vata & Pitta, and increases Kapha; examples are meat and cheese; it helps to create stability, a more grounded nature, strength, solidity.
- Liquid/Flowing (Drava) - decreases Vata, increases Kapha, and mostly increases pitta; an example is water; this promotes salivation, cohesiveness, and compassion.
- Soft (Mrudu) - decreases Vata & decreases imbalanced hard Pitta, increases Kapha, is a strong component of balanced Pitta; examples include ghee, water, bamboo; it creates softness, relaxations, tenderness, love, care.
- Hard (Kathina) - decreases Kapha, increases Vata, can both increase imbalanced hard Pitta; examples include metals, insensitivity, selfishness, callousness; It aids the development of strength.
- Static (Sthira) - decreases the mobility of Vata, and the fluidity of Pitta; it increase Kapha; examples include ayurvedic yoga therapy with static poses, sitting quietly, meditation, quieting the senses and the mind; it is needed for creating stability, security, confidence, more grounding, and healing.
- Mobile (Chala) - decreases Kapha and increases Vata & Pitta; examples include ayurvedic yoga therapy with dynamic and flowing poses, exercise and physical activity; It is needed to

loosen stagnation, stuckness, lethargy, excess weight, and heaviness symptoms like congestion.

- Subtle (Sukshma) - decreases Kapha, and increases Vata & Pitta; examples are drugs, herbs, marijuana, alcohol; This aids the lightening of a dense and heavy nature. So herbal cigarettes made with Ayurvedic herbs help to lighten both heaviness in the body and mind.
- Gross (Sthula) - decreases Vata & Pitta and increases Kapha; examples include meat and cheese; this is helpful for increasing strength in the body especially for Vata types.
- Clear (Vishada/Visada) - decreases Kapha, increases Vata & Pitta; examples include water, fire, mind clearing herbs like vacha, cleansing with purgatives, and enemas. This property helps with the lightening process.
- Sticky (Picchila) or Cloudy/Turbid (avila) - decreases Vata & Pitta, and increases Kapha; examples include dairy products. This aids the strengthening and stabilizing process.

The rishis perceived that in the beginning the world existed in an unmanifested state of Consciousness, avyakta-meaning unmanifest. From that state the subtle vibrations of the cosmic, soundless sound Aum manifested. From the subtle vibration of Aum came the Ether or Space element. This ethereal element then began to move and through its subtle movements created the Air element, which is Ether in action. The movement of Air produced friction and through friction heat was generated.

Particles of this heat combined to form intense light and from this light the Fire element emerged. Thus, Ether produced Air and it was Air that further manifested into Fire. The heat of Fire dissolved and liquefied certain ethereal elements, forming Water that then solidified to form the molecules of Earth. In this way, Ether manifested into the four elements of Air, Fire, Water, and Earth.

From Earth, all physical bodies for organic living beings were created, including both the plant and animal kingdoms. Earth was also the origin of all inorganic substances that comprise the mineral kingdom. Thus, out of the womb of the Five Elements all matter was born.

The five basic elements exist in all matter. Water provides the classic example: the solid state of water, ice, is a manifestation of the Earth principle. Latent heat (Fire) in the ice liquefies it, revealing the

Water principle. Eventually water turns into steam, expressing the Air principle. The steam disappears into Ether or Space. Thus the five basic elements-Ether, Air, Fire, Water, and Earth-are all present in one substance. All five originated from the energy within Cosmic Consciousness and all five are present in all matter in the universe. Thus, energy and matter are one.

Man is a microcosm of the universe and, therefore, the five basic elements present in all matter also exist within each individual. In the human body, many spaces are aspects of the Ether or Space element. The spaces in the mouth, nose, gastrointestinal tract, respiratory tract, abdomen, thorax, capillaries, and tissues are all examples of Space.

Air is the element of movement. All movements involve Air as an element, because it alone moves everything. Any time there is motion, it means Air is present. The nature of the elements themselves determines the nature of physiology. Within the human body, Air is present in the pulsations of the heart and the expansion and contraction of the lungs. Under a microscope, even a single cell can be seen to move. Response to a stimulus is the movement of afferent and efferent nerve impulses, which are sensory and motor movements respectively. Movements of the nervous system are also governed by the Air principle present in the body.

The third element is Fire. The source of Fire and light in the solar system is the sun. In the human body, the source of Fire is metabolism. Fire works in the digestive system as well as in the gray matter of the brain, where Fire manifests as intelligence. Fire also activates the retina to perceive light.

Therefore, body temperature, digestion, thinking processes, and vision are all functions of bodily Fire. All metabolism and enzyme systems are controlled by this element. Water, the fourth element, manifests in the body as the secretions of digestive juices, in the mucous membranes and in plasma and cytoplasm. Water is vital for the functioning of all the systems of the body.

For example, dehydration resulting from diarrhea and vomiting must be treated immediately to protect the patient's life. Earth, the fifth element, is also present in the microcosm of the human being. Life is possible on this planet because the Earth holds all living and non-living substances to its solid surface. In the body, all solid structures are derived from Earth.

Table: The Senses and the Elements

Jñānendriya (Sensory Faculties)	**Sensory Organs**	**Karmendriya** (Faculties of Action)	**Motor Organs**	**Tanmātrās** (Objects of the Senses)	**Maha Bhūtas** (Elements)
Hearing	Ears	Speech	Vocal Cords	Shabda (Sound)	Ether
Tactile perception	Skin	Giving and receiving	Hands	Sparsha (Touch)	Air
Vision	Eyes	Walking	Legs	Rūpa (Form)	Fire
Taste	Tongue	Procreation	Genitals	Rasa (Taste)	Water
Smell	Nose	Excretion	Excretory organs	Gandha (Odor or Smell)	Earth

The Five Elements and Tanmatras: The five elements manifest in the functioning of the five senses as well as in certain functions of human physiology. Tan means subtle and matra means elements. The Tanmatras, the subtle elements, are the objects of the five senses. The five Tanmatras are sound, touch, form, taste, and odor or smell; the five senses are hearing, tactile perception, vision, taste, and smell. The Tanmatras are the ways in which the objective world is sensed. The five elements have functional integrity with the five sensory organs, which allows us to perceive the external environment. Their presence is the reason for the existence of the senses themselves. The Tanmatras form the Common Ground for the expression of the objective world and the entire world exists on this Ground.

These five elements-Ether, Air, Fire, Water, and Earth-are also related to the five organs of action-mouth, hands, feet, genitals and excretory organs-which allow us to respond to the input we receive from the objective world. Ether is the medium through which sound is transmitted and is thus related to the function of hearing. The sensory organ of hearing is the ear. The organ of action associated with the sense of hearing is the mouth and vocal cords, which produce sound. Air is related to the sense of touch and the sensory organ of touch is the skin.

The organ of action related to the sense of touch is the hand. The skin of the hand is especially sensitive and the hand is responsible for the actions of holding, giving, and receiving. Fire, which manifests as light, heat, and colour is related to vision. The sensory organ of vision is the eye. The organ of action related to the sense of vision is the feet. A blind man can walk but his walking has no direction. Eyes give direction to the action of walking. Water is related to taste.

The sensory organ of taste is the tongue. Without water the tongue cannot perceive the different tastes. The related organ of action is the reproductive system.

The tongue is closely related in function to the action of the genitals (penis and clitoris). In Ayurveda, the penis and clitoris are considered the lower tongue and the tongue in the mouth is the upper tongue. The person who controls the upper tongue has control over the lower tongue and vice versa.

Panchmahabhoota -5 Elements

The Panchamahabhuta concept of Indian philosophy states that the fundamental structural basis of all living beings (including all plants, animals and humans) is composed of 5 elements or 'Panchmahabhutas.' Panch means five; maha means supreme and bhootas means powers, so panch bhootas means five supreme powers. The 5 elements form the subtle essence or tanmatra. (Tanmatra is a Sanskrit word which means subtle essence.) These tanmatras embodied the panch mahabhutas as follows.

The 5 tanmatras are Sound (Shabda), Touch (Sparsha), Vision (Roopa), Taste (Rasa), Smell (Gandha). These tanmatras are related to each sense organ.

These Five Basic Elements Include

Ether or Universal Space (Aakash)- The first of the panchmahabutas is akasha or space. That is, having space/ freedom to move. The qualities of the akasa element include- light: subtle and immeasurable. It is related to actions such as expansion, vibration, non-resistance. The ear is the sensory organ related to this element. The tanmatra of the ether element is Sound or Shabda.

Air (Vayu)- The next of the panch bhootas is the Air element. This is related to movement or a sense of constant motion. The qualities of air element include sensitivity, motion, cool and subtle presence. Skin is the sensory organ related to air element. The tanmatra of the air element is Touch or Sparsha.

Divine Fire (Agni)- The air element performs movements and whenever there is movement, it causes friction and this leads to the formation of fire, the third of the panchmahabhutas. The qualities of fire element are related to various functions such as penetration, digestion of food, conversion of thoughts, intellect and perception of light. The tanmatra of the fire element is Vision or Rupa.

Water (Jala)- The qualities of the water element, the fourth of the panch bhootas, is liquidity or fluidity. Water imparts the vital quality of binding - e.g. when we add water to soil, then only we can easily mould the mud into a shape we desire like mud pot or balls etc. Thus, this important element is constructive in nature and exhibits qualities such as adhesion, cooling, binding and liquidity. The tanmatra of the water element is Taste or Rasa.

Earth (Pruthvi)- The earth element, is the ultimate element of the panch bootas. It is solid, gross, hard and dense. Earth element gives form, shape, structure and strength. For e.g. teeth, nails, bones and muscles. Nose is the sense organ related to the earth element. The tanmatra of the Earth element is Smell or Gandha.

Imbalances in these panch bhootas create imbalances or "tridoshas."

- 'tri' means three
- 'doshas' means basic components which constitute every human body.

Every individual's constitution is created by these three doshas at the time of fertilization during garbhdharana (when the embryo is formed.) The proportions of these 3 doshas' are determined at this time and remain unchanged during his/her life. These doshas together determine our prakruti (body organization).

Each human being is either of

1. Vaat prakruti (prakruti dominated by vaat dosh) or
2. Pitta prakruti (prakruti dominated by pitta dosh) or
3. Kapha prakruti (prakruti dominated by kapha dosh)

Vaat dosh is formed by Aakash (Universal Space) and Vayu (air) elements; Pitta dosh is caused by Agni (Divine Fire) elements and Kafa dosh is produced by Jala (Water) and Pruthvi (Earth) elements.

Every human body is a well-adjusted mixture of the vaat, pitta and kafa. These doshas when in an ideal balance state gives healthy status to the individual. But when there is an imbalanced, it results in disease. Pivotal is our attitude and behaviour that help in upholding health or conversely, bring on an array of diseases.

Thus, the balanced sattvic diet or food intake, regular yoga exercise and timely medication (which changes according to the dominant dosh) are advocated to avoid health problems.

Doshic Theory

Ayurvedic principles teach us that every living and non-living being in Nature is a combination of five basic eternal elements, called Panchamahabhootas. The five basic eternal elements (the 'Panchamahabhootas') that comprise the Universe are Prithvi (Earth), Jala (Water), Agni (Fire), Vayu (Air), Akash (Space or Ether).

As the human body is an integral part of Nature it is also created from these elements in various compositions and, in essence, every cell of the body has all the properties of life. The only difference between the human body and the external world is the expression of Chaithanya, also known as consciousness, life spark, spirit or the soul.

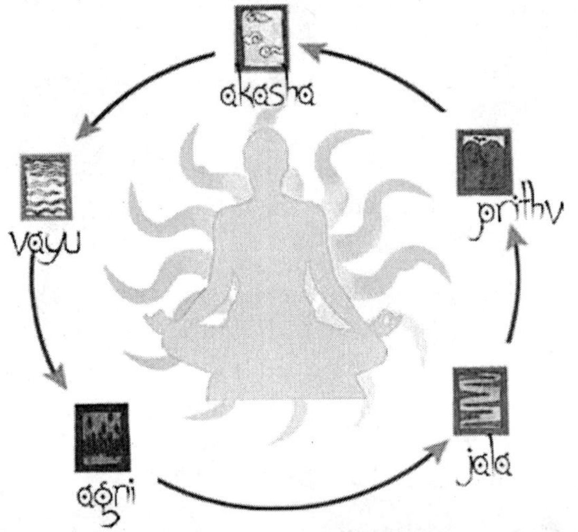

Some Concepts to Take Into Consideration.

Ayurveda is a holistic science of health and life involved in the prevention and cure of disease, balancing the forces in action in a person. Ayurveda considers the physical, mental, and spiritual health of human beings, but also the well-being of animals and plants:

The physical aspect consists in regulating and balancing the forces supporting the physiological integrity of the tissues and organs forming the anatomical structure.

The mental aspect consists in searching for a healthy lifestyle, without toxins; to identify and eliminate tensions and hostile elements leading you to a happy life in harmony with the environment. The spiritual aspect consists in raising one's consciousness to the universal dimension, realizing one's position as a tiny piece of a bigger entity to access inner peace.

The Tri-Doshas

Figure: *The eternal elements manifest in the human body as three subtle life energies known in Sanskrit as Vatha, Pitha and Kapha (collectively known as 'Tridosha' in Sanskrit). The word Dosha literally means 'the humors which maintain and control the body'. The air and space elements combine to form Vatha. The fire and water elements combine to form Pitha. Earth and water elements combine to form Kapha.*

These subtle energies govern all biological, physiological and physio-pathological functions of the body, mind and spirit. Every individual has a unique combination of these three Doshas. Ayurveda understands the uniqueness of every individual, where each of the Doshas combine in different proportions.

Generally, the occurrence of seven body types can be observed:

Mono: Either Vata, pitha or kapha

Dual: Either Vata-pitha, pitha-kapha or kapha-vata

Equal: Vata, pitha and kapha are in equal proportions

For each of the elements, there is a state of balance and imbalance. An important goal of Ayurveda is to identify a person's ideal state of balance, determine where they are in or out of balance, and offer interventions using various Ayurvedic treatments to restore the natural balance to the body.

The Main Actions of DOSHAS on the Body

Vata: A force that controls the central nervous system, the skull, and the spine; the sympathetic system, heart rate and muscle contractions; the parasympathetic system, organs, glands, and blood vessels. A very active force on the sensory level, influencing the perception of the world and the environment. It increases creativity and concentration. It helps reduce fatigue, anxiety, and fear. It promotes firmness and flexibility of the skin.

Pitta: A force that controls thermogenesis, metabolic activity, and neurotransmitter hormones. It is responsible for digestion, blood colouring, secretions, molecular and energy transformations in the body. very active force on the emotional level, typifying the relationship to oneself and the relationship to others. It increases intelligence and helps assimilate ideas. It regulates anger and jealousy. It promotes digestion and cell regeneration.

Kapha: A force that controls the fluids, the mechanical and joint activity of the body. It acts on the biological activity of the body. It contributes to physical resistance. A very active force on the functional level, increasing the flexibility and natural immunity of the body. It helps to overcome resentments and disappointments. It promotes microvascularization and good skin's hydration.

According to Ayurveda, these three forces are inseparable and essential for a body to function properly and must be balanced for good health and well-being. The 3 doshas are active in everyone, in greater or lesser proportion. To determine which is your dominant dosha and to adjust the possible imbalances that can result from it.

Chapter 4

Ayurvedic Texts

Sushruta Samhita

The Sushruta Samhita ('Su?ruta's Compendium') is an ancient Sanskrit text on medicine and surgery, and one of the most important such treatises on this subject to survive from the ancient world. The Compendium of Su?ruta is one of the foundational texts of Ayurveda (Indian traditional medicine), alongside the Charaka-Samhit?, the Bhela-Sa?hit?, and the medical portions of the Bower Manuscript. It is one of the two foundational Hindu texts on the medical profession that have survived from ancient India.

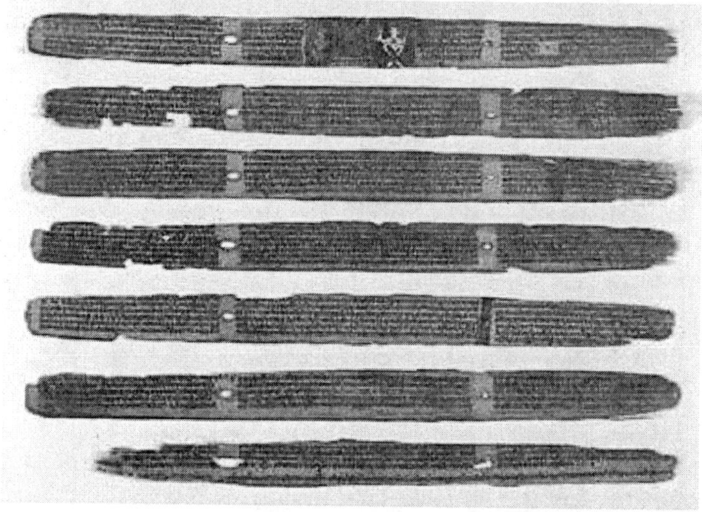

Figure: *Palm leaves of the Sushruta Samhita or Sahottara-Tantra from Nepal, stored at Los Angeles County Museum of Art. The text is dated 12th-13th century while the art is dated 18th-19th century.*

The Sumrutasamhita is of great historical importance because it includes historically unique chapters describing surgical training, instruments and procedures which is still followed by modern science of surgery. One of the oldest Sushruta Samhita palm-leaf manuscripts is preserved at the Kaiser Library, Nepal.

History

Date: The most detailed and extensive consideration of the date of the Su?rutasamhit? is that published by Meulenbeld in his History of Indian Medical Literature (1999-2002). Meulenbeld stated that the Su?rutasamhit? is likely a work that includes several historical layers, whose composition may have begun in the last centuries BCE and was completed in its presently surviving form by another author who redacted its first five sections and added the long, final section, the "Uttaratantra." It is likely that the Su?ruta-samhit? was known to the scholar D??habala (fl. 300-500 CE), which gives the latest date for the version of the work that has survived into the modern era.

In Sumrutasamhita- A Scientific Synopsis, the historians of Indian science Ray, Gupta and Roy noted the following view, which is broadly the same as Meulenbeld's: "The Chronology Committee of the National Institute of Sciences of India (Proceedings, 1952), was of the opinion that third to fourth centuries A. D. may be accepted as the date of the recension of the Suruta Samhita by Nagarjuna, which formed the basis of Dallana's commentary."The above view remains the consensus amongst university scholars of the history of Indian medicine and Sanskrit literature.

Hoernle's view: Regrettably, given its subsequent influence, a century ago, the scholar Rudolf Hoernle (1841 - 1918) proposed that because the author of Satapatha Brahmana, a Vedic text from the mid-first-millennium BCE, was aware of Sushruta's doctrines, Sushruta's doctrines should be dated based on the composition date of Satapatha Brahmana. The composition date of the Brahmana was itself unclear, added Hoernle, but he estimated it to be about the sixth century BCE.

Unfortunately, Hoernle's date of 600 BCE for the Su?rutasa?hit? continues to be widely and uncritically cited in spite of much intervening scholarship over the last century. Yet because of further research, scores of scholars have subsequently published more considered opinions on the date of the work, and these many views have been summarized by Meulenbeld in his History of Indian Medical Literature.

Central to the problem of chronology is the fact that the Su?rutasa?hit? is the work of several hands. The internal tradition recorded in manuscript colophons and by medieval commentators makes clear that an old version of the Susrutasamhita consisted of sections 1-5, with the sixth part having been added by a later author. However, the oldest manuscripts we have of the work already include the sixth section, called the Uttara-tantra. Manuscript colophons routinely call the whole work "The Su?rutasa?hit? together with the Uttara-tantra," reinforcing the idea that this was perceived as a five+one composition.

Selected Views on Chronology

As mentioned above, scores of scholars have proposed hypotheses on the formation and dating of the Su?rutasa?hit?. The following are some of these views that broadly follow Hoernle's old 1907 publication.

Rao in 1985 suggested that the original layer to the Sushruta Samhita was composed in 1st millennium BCE by "elder Sushruta" consisting of five books and 120 chapters, which was redacted and expanded with Uttara-tantra as the last layer of text in 1st millennium CE, bringing the text size to six books and 184 chapters. Walton et al., in 1994, traced the origins of the text to 1st millennium BCE.

Tipton in a 2008 historical perspectives review, states that uncertainty remains on dating the text, how many authors contributed to it and when. Estimates range from 1000 BCE, 800-600 BCE, 600 BCE, 600-200 BCE, 200 BCE, 1-100 CE, and 500 CE.

Partial resolution of these uncertainties, states Tipton, has come from a comparison of the Sushruta Samhita text with several Vedic hymns particularly the Atharvaveda such as the hymn on the creation of man in its 10th book, the chapters of Atreya Samhita which describe the human skeleton, better dating of ancient texts that mention Sushruta's name, and critical studies on the ancient Bower Manuscript by Hoernle. The first Sushruta Samhita was likely composed by the mid-1st millennium BCE.

Authorship

Sushruta or Su?ruta (Su?ruta, lit.?'well heard', an adjective meaning "renowned") is named in the text as the author, who is presented in later manuscripts and printed editions a narrating the teaching of his guru, Divod?sa. A person of this name is said in early texts such as the Buddhist Jatakas to have been a physician who taught in a school in Kashi (Varanasi) and lived in Varanasi too, sometime between 1200 BCE and 600 BCE. The earliest known mentions of the name Sushruta firmly associated with the tradition of the Su?rutasa?hit? is in the Bower Manuscript (4th or 5th century CE), where Sushruta is listed as one of the ten sages residing in the Himalayas.

Figure: *A statue of Sushruta (600 BCE) at Royal Australasian College of Surgeons (RACS) in Melbourne, Australia.*

Rao in 1985 suggested that the author of the original "layer" was "elder Sushruta" (Vrddha Sushruta), although this name appears nowhere in the early Sanskrit literature. The text, states Rao, was redacted centuries later "by another Sushruta, then by Nagarjuna, and thereafter Uttara-tantra was added as a supplement". It is generally accepted by scholars that there were several ancient authors called "Su?ruta" who contributed to this text.

Affiliation

The text has been called a Hindu text by many scholars. The text discusses surgery with the same terminology found in more ancient Hindu texts, mentions Hindu gods such as Narayana, Hari, Brahma, Rudra, Indra and others in its chapters, refers to the scriptures of Hinduism namely the Vedas, and in some cases, recommends exercise, walking and "constant study of the Vedas" as part of the patient's treatment and recovery process. The text also uses terminology of Samkhya and other schools of Hindu philosophy.

The Sushruta Samhita and Caraka Samhita have religious ideas throughout, states Steven Engler, who then concludes "Vedic elements are too central to be discounted as marginal". These ideas include the use of terms and same metaphors that are pervasive in the Hindu scriptures - the Vedas, and the inclusion of theory of Karma, self (Atman) and Brahman (metaphysical reality) along the lines of those found in ancient Hindu texts. However, adds Engler, the text also includes another layer of ideas, where empirical rational ideas flourish in competition or cooperation with religious ideas. Following Engler's study, contemporary scholars have abandoned the distinction "religious" vs. "empirico-rational" as no longer being a useful analytical distinction.

The text may have Buddhist influences, since a redactor named Nagarjuna has raised many historical questions, whether he was the same person of Mahayana Buddhism fame. Zysk states that the ancient Buddhist medical texts are significantly different from both Sushruta and Caraka Samhita.

For example, both Caraka and Sushruta recommend Dhupana (fumigation) in some cases, the use of cauterization with fire and alkali in a class of treatments, and the letting out of blood as the first step in treatment of wounds. Nowhere in the Buddhist Pali texts, states Zysk, are these types of medical procedures mentioned. Similarly, medicinal resins (Laksha) lists vary between Sushruta and the Pali texts, with some sets not mentioned at all. While Sushruta and Caraka are close, many afflictions and their treatments found in these texts are not found in Pali texts.

In general, states Zysk, Buddhist medical texts are closer to Sushruta than to Caraka, and in his study suggests that the Sushruta Samhita probably underwent a "Hinduization process" around the end of 1st millennium BCE and the early centuries of the common era after the Hindu orthodox identity had formed. Clifford states that the influence was probably mutual, with Buddhist medical practice in its ancient tradition prohibited outside of the Buddhist monastic order by a precedent set by Buddha, and Buddhist text praise Buddha instead of Hindu gods in their prelude. The mutual influence between the medical traditions between the various Indian religions, the history of the layers of the Sumruta-samhita remains unclear, a large and difficult research problem.

Sushruta is reverentially held in Hindu tradition to be a descendant of Dhanvantari, the mythical god of medicine, or as one who received the knowledge from a discourse from Dhanvantari in Varanasi.

Manuscripts and Transmission

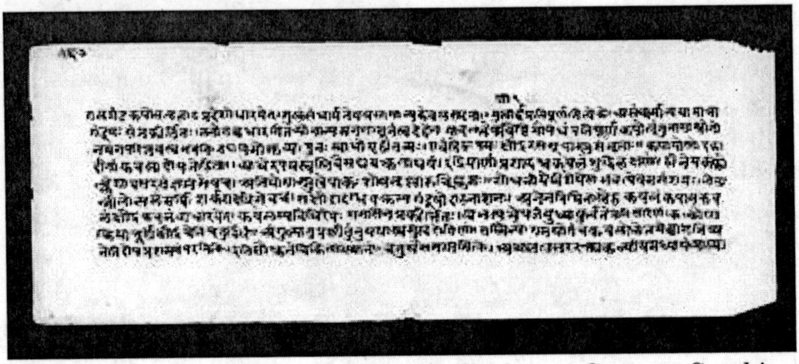

***Figure:** A page from the ancient medical text, Susruta Samhita.*

One of the oldest palm-leaf manuscripts of Sushruta Samhita has been discovered in Nepal. It is preserved at the Kaiser Library, Nepal as manuscript KL-699, with its digital copy archived by Nepal-German Manuscript Preservation Project (NGMCP C 80/7). The partially damaged manuscript consists of 152 folios, written on both sides, with 6 to 8 lines in transitional Gupta script. The manuscript has been verifiably dated to have been completed by the scribe on Sunday, April 13, 878 CE (Manadeva Samvat 301). The first book to publish an edition and translation of part of this manuscript appeared in 2023.

Much of the scholarship on the Sumruta-samhita is based on editions of the text that were published during the nineteenth and early twentieth centuries. This includes the important edition by Vaidya Y?dava?arman Trivikram?tmaja ?c?rya that also includes the commentary of the scholar Dalha?a.

The printed editions are based on the small subset of surviving manuscripts that was available in the major publishing centers of Bombay, Calcutta and elsewhere when the editions were being prepared - sometimes as few as three or four manuscripts. But these do not adequately represent the large number of manuscript versions of the Sumruta-samhita that have survived into the modern era. Taken together, all printed versions of the Su?rutasa?hit? are based on no more than ten percent of the more than 230 manuscripts of the work that exist today. These manuscripts exist in the libraries in India and abroad today. More than two hundred manuscripts of the work exist, and a critical edition of the Sumruta-samhita is yet to be prepared.

Contents

The Sushruta Samhita is among the most important ancient medical treatises. It is one of the foundational texts of the medical tradition in India, alongside the Caraka-Samhita, the Bhema-Samhita, and the medical portions of the Bower Manuscript.

Scope: The Sushruta Samhita was composed after Charaka Samhita, and except for some topics and their emphasis, both discuss many similar subjects such as General Principles, Pathology, Diagnosis, Anatomy, Sensorial Prognosis, Therapeutics, Pharmaceutics and Toxicology. The Sushruta and Charaka texts differ in one major aspect, with Sushruta Samhita providing the foundation of surgery, while Charaka Samhita being primarily a foundation of medicine.

Chapters: The Sushruta Samhita, in its extant form, is divided into 186 chapters and contains descriptions of 1,120 illnesses, 700 medicinal plants, 64 preparations from mineral sources and 57 preparations based on animal sources. The Sumruta-Sa?hit? is divided into two parts: the first five books (Skt. Sthanas) are considered to be the oldest part of the text, and the "Later Section" (Skt. Uttaratantra) that was added by the author Nagarjuna. The content of these chapters is diverse, some topics are covered in multiple chapters in different books, and a summary according to the Bhishagratna's translation is as follows:

Prevention versus cure: Sushruta, states Tipton, asserts that a physician should invest the effort to prevent diseases as much as curative remedial procedures. An important means for prevention, states Sushruta, is physical exercise and hygienic practices. The text adds that excessive strenuous exercise can be injurious and make one more susceptible to diseases, cautioning against such excess. Regular moderate exercise, suggests Sushruta, improves resistance to disease and physical decay. Sushruta has written Shlokas on the prevention of diseases.

Human skeleton: The Sushruta Samhita states, per Hoernle's translation, that "the professors of Ayurveda speak of three hundred and sixty bones, but books on Shalya-Shastra (surgical science) know of only three hundred". The text then lists the total of 300 as follows: 120 in the extremities (e.g. hands, legs), 117 in the pelvic area, sides, back, abdomen and breast, and 63 in the neck and upwards. The text then explains how these subtotals were empirically verified. The discussion shows that the Indian tradition nurtured diversity of thought, with Sushruta school reaching its own conclusions and differing from the Atreya-Caraka tradition.

The osteological system of Sushruta, states Hoernle, follows the principle of homology, where the body and organs are viewed as self-mirroring and corresponding across various axes of symmetry. The differences in the count of bones in the two schools is partly because Charaka Samhita includes thirty two teeth sockets in its count, and their difference of opinions on how and when to count a cartilage as bone (both count cartilages as bones, unlike current medical practice).

Surgery: The Sushruta Samhita is best known in non-specialist sources on medical history for its approach and discussions of surgery. It is amongst the first medical treatises in history to suggest that a student of surgery should learn about human body and its organs by systematically examining a dead body.

A student should practice, states the text, on objects resembling the diseased or body part. Incision studies, for example, are recommended on Pushpaphala (squash, Cucurbita maxima), Alabu (bottle gourd, Lagenaria vulgaris), Trapusha (cucumber, Cucumis pubescens), leather bags filled with fluids and bladders of dead animals.

The ancient text, state Menon and Haberman, describes haemorrhoidectomy, amputations, plastic, rhinoplastic, ophthalmic, lithotomic and obstetrical procedures.

The Sushruta Samhita mentions various methods including sliding graft, rotation graft and pedicle graft. Reconstruction of a nose (rhinoplasty) which has been cut off, using a flap of skin from the cheek is also described. Labioplasty too has received attention in the samahita.

Medicinal Herbs: The Sushruta Samhita, along with the Sanskrit medicine-related classics Atharvaveda and Charak Samhita, together describe more than 700 medicinal herbs. The description, states Padma, includes their taste, appearance and digestive effects to safety, efficacy, dosage and benefits.

Rhinoplasty: Rhinoplasty, surgery to repair the flesh of the nose, is performed to achieve two results:

- To improve the breathing function of the nose
- To improve the cosmetic appearance of the nose

Sushruta's treatise provides the first written record of a cheek flap rhinoplasty, a technique still used today to reconstruct a nose.

The text mentions more than 15 methods to repair it. These include using a flap of skin from the cheek, which is akin to the most modern technique today.

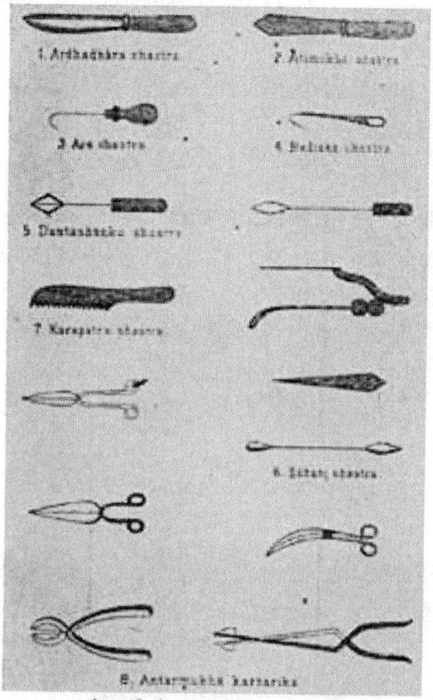

Figure: *Some shastras (tools) and kartarika (scissors and forceps) mentioned in Sushruta Samhita*

The nose in Indian society has remained a symbol of dignity and respect throughout antiquity. Rhinoplasty was an especially important development in India because of the long-standing tradition of rhinotomy (amputation of the nose) as a form of punishment. Convicted criminals would often have their noses amputated to mark them as untrustworthy, but amputation was also frequently practiced on women accused of adultery - even if they were not proven guilty. Once branded in this fashion, an individual had to live with the stigma for the rest of his or her life. Reconstructive surgery, therefore, offered a hope of redemption and normalcy.

Reception

Transmission outside South Asia: The text was translated to Arabic as Kitab Shah Shun al-Hindi' in Arabic, also known as Kitab i-Susurud, in Baghdad during the early 8th century at the instructions of a member of the Barmakid family of Baghdad. Yahya ibn Barmak facilitated a major effort at collecting and translating Sanskrit texts such as Vagbhata's Astangahrdaya Samhita, Ravigupta's Siddhasara and Sushruta Samhita. The Arabic translation reached Europe by the end of the medieval period. There is disputed evidence that in Renaissance Italy, the Branca family of Sicily and Gasparo Tagliacozzi (Bologna) were familiar with the rhinoplastic techniques mentioned in the Sushruta Samhita.

The text was known to the Khmer king Ya?ovarman I (fl. 889-900) of Cambodia. Su?ruta was also known as a medical authority in Tibetan literature.

Commentaries: The earliest surviving commentary on the whole text, known as Nibandha-samgraha, was written by Dalhana in ca. 1200 CE. Earlier commentaries existed but have only been transmitted to modern times in fragmentary form. These include lost or partially-lost commentaries by Jejja?a (ca. 700 CE), Gayad?sa (ca. 1000 CE), and Cakrap??idatta (ca. 1025 CE). Commentaries continued to be written on the work into the nineteenth century, e.g., the Su?rut?rthasand?pan? by Haranachandra written in 19th century AD.

Modern reception: A number of Sushruta's contributions have been discussed in modern literature. Some of these include Hritshoola (heart pain), circulation of vital body fluids (such as blood (rakta dhatu) and lymph (rasa dhatu), Diabetes (Madhumeha), obesity, and hypertension. Kearns & Nash (2008) state that the first mention of leprosy is described in Sushruta Samhita. The text discusses kidney stones and its surgical removal.

Editions and Translations

The first printed edition of the text was prepared by Madhusudan Gupta (2 vols, Calcutta 1835, 1836). A partial English translation by U. C. Datta appeared in 1883. The first complete English translation of the Sushruta Samhita was by Kaviraj Kunjalal Bhishagratna, who published it in three volumes between 1907 and 1916 (reprinted 1963, 2006).

An English translation of both the Sushruta Samhita and Dalhana's commentary was published in three volumes by P. V. Sharma in 1999. Scholars of Ayurveda generally consider this to be the most accurate and scholarly translation of the complete work to date.

Charaka Samhita

The Charaka Samhita (IAST: Caraka-Sa?hit?, "Compendium of Charaka") is a Sanskrit text on Ayurveda (Indian traditional medicine).

Along with the Sushruta Samhita, it is one of the two foundational texts of this field that have survived from ancient India. It is one of the three works that constitute the Brhat Trayi.

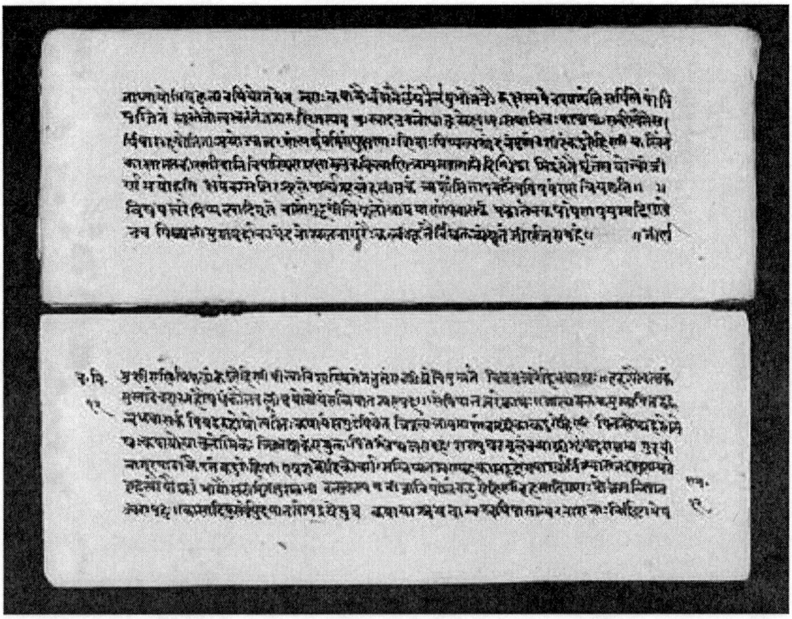

Figure: *A section of the A section of the Charaka Samhita.*

The text is based on the Agnivesha Samhit?, an older encyclopedic medical compendium by Agnive?a. It was revised by Charaka between 100 BCE and 200 CE and renamed Charaka Samhit?. The pre-2nd century CE text consists of eight books and one hundred and twenty chapters. It describes ancient theories on human body, etiology, symptomology and therapeutics for a wide range of diseases. The Charaka Samhita also includes sections on the importance of diet, hygiene, prevention, medical education, and the teamwork of a physician, nurse and patient necessary for recovery to health.

Authorship

The Charaka Samhita states that the content of the book was first taught by Atreya, and then subsequently codified by Agnive?a, revised by Charaka, and the manuscripts that survive into the modern era are based on one completed by D??habala. D??habala stated in the Charaka Samhita that he had to write one third of the book himself because this portion had been lost, and that he also re-wrote the last part of the book.

Based on textual analysis, and the literal meaning of the Sanskrit word charaka, Chattopadhyay speculated that charaka does not refer to one person but a lineage or sect of people. Vishwakarma and Goswami state that the text exists in many versions and entire chapters are missing in some versions.

Date: Dates of composition of the Charaka Samhita are uncertain. Meulenbeld's History of Indian Medical Literature dates it to be between fourth century BCE to the second century CE, with Charaka's compilation likely between 100 BCE and 200 CE. The D??habala revision and completion, the source of current texts, is dated to the 6th century CE.

Roots: In Sanskrit, charaka is a term for a wanderer, sannyasi (ascetic), and sometimes used in the context of the ancient tradition of wandering physicians who brought their medical expertise and magico-religious rites from village to village.

Surendranath Dasgupta states that the medical tradition of wandering physicians are traceable to the Atharvaveda, particularly the Caranavaidya shakha - one of the nine known shakha of Atharvaveda-based Vedic schools. The name of this school literally means "wandering physicians". Their texts have not survived into the modern era, but manuscripts from two competing schools - Paippalada and Saunakiya, have.

The Atharvaveda contains chapters relating to medicine, surgery and magico-religious rites. This Atharvaveda layer of text was likely compiled contemporaneously with Samaveda and Yajurveda, in about 1200 BCE-1000 BCE. Dasgupta and other scholars state that the Atreya-Charaka school and its texts may have emerged from this older tradition, and he cites a series of Atharvaveda hymns to show that almost all organs and nomenclature found in Charaka Samhita are also found in the Vedic hymns.

Contents

The extant text has eight sth?na (books), totalling 120 chapters. The text includes a table of contents embedded in its verses, stating the names and describing the nature of the eight books, followed by a listing of the 120 chapters. These eight books are

1. Sutra Sthana (General principles) - 30 chapters deal with general principles, philosophy, definitions, prevention through healthy living, and the goals of the text. It is divided into quadruplets of 7, making it 28 with 2 concluding chapters.

2. Nidana Sthana (Pathology) - 8 chapters on causes of diseases.
3. Vimana Sthana (Specific determination) 8 chapters contain training of a physician, ethics of medical practice, pathology, diet and nourishment, taste of medicines.
4. ?arira Sthana (Anatomy) - 8 chapters describe embryology & anatomy of a human body (with a section on other living beings).
5. Indriya Sthana (Sensory organ based prognosis) - 12 chapters elaborate on diagnosis & prognosis, mostly based on sensory response of the patient.
6. Cikitsa Sthana (Therapeutics) - 30 chapters deal with medicines and treatment of diseases.
7. Kalpa Sthana (Pharmaceutics and toxicology) - 12 chapters describe pharmacy, the preparation and dosage of medicine, signs of their abuse, and dealing with poisons.
8. Siddhi Sthana (Success in treatment) - 12 chapters describe signs of cure, hygiene and healthier living.

Seventeen chapters of Cikits? sth?na and complete Kalpa sth?na and Siddhi sth?na were added later by D??habala. The text starts with S?tra sth?na which deals with fundamentals and basic principles of Ayurveda practice. Unique scientific contributions credited to the Caraka Sa?hit? include:

- a rational approach to the causation and cure of disease
- introduction of objective methods of clinical examination

Physician, nurse, patient and medicines: The text asserts that there are four important parts to medical practice - the patient, the physician, the nurse and the medicines. All four are essential to recovery and return to health, states the text. The physician provides knowledge and coordinates the treatment, he is who can "explore the dark interior of the body with the lamp of knowledge", according to the text and Valiathan's translation. The physician must express joy and cheer towards those who can respond to treatment, masterfully avoid and save time in cases where the patient suffers from incurable disease, while compassionate towards all. The nurse must be knowledgeable, skilled at preparing formulations and dosage, sympathetic towards everyone and clean. The patient is responsible for being positive, have the ability to describe how he or she feels, remember and respectfully follow the physician instructions.

The Charaka Samhita, states Curtin, was among the earliest texts that set a code of ethics on physicians and nurses, attributing "moral as well as scientific authority to the healer". The text, in chapters 8 and 9 of the Vimana Sthana dedicates numerous verses to discussing the code. It mandates that the physician must seek consent before entering a patient's quarters, must be accompanied by a male member of the family if he is attending a woman or minor, must inform and gain consent from patient or the guardians if the patient is a minor, must never resort to extortion for his service, never involve himself in any other activities with the patient or patient's family (such as negotiating loans, arranging marriage, buying or selling property), speak with soft words and never use cruel words, only do "what is calculated to do good to the patient", and maintain the patient's privacy.

There is no end in the knowledge of medical science, claims verse 3.8.12 of the Charaka Samhita, and the physician must constantly learn and devote himself to it. The text asserts that a physician should discuss his findings and questions with other physicians because "when one discusses with another that is possessed of a knowledge of the same science, such discussion leads to increase of knowledge and happiness". The verses that follow outline that discussions can be hostile or peaceful, the former are unproductive, the latter useful; even if one faces hostile criticism, one must persuade with gentle words and manner, asserts the text.

Religious ideas: The Charaka Samhita, like many ancient Hindu literature, reveres and attributes Hindu gods as the ultimate source of its knowledge. The Charaka Samhita mentions Bharadvaja learning from god Indra, after pleading that "poor health was disrupting the ability of human beings from pursuing their spiritual journey", and then Indra provides both the method and specifics of medical knowledge. The method, asserts the text, revolves around three principles: etiology, symptomology and therapeutics. Thus, states Glucklich, the text presumes proper goals to include both spiritual and physical health.

The Charaka Samhita, in addition to initial recitations, uses the foundational assumptions and values embedded in various layers of the Vedas. These assumptions include the Vedic doctrine that a human being is a microcosmic replica of the universe, and the ancient Hindu theory of six elements (five Prakriti and one Brahman), three humors (Vata, Pitta, Kapha), three Gu?as (Sattva, Rajas and Tamas) as constituent forces innate in a human body, and others.

The Charaka Samhita is premised on the Hindu assumption that Atman (soul) exists, it is immutable, and thereafter the text defines physical and mental diseases as caused by a lack of correlation and imbalance in body, or mind, or both, because of external factors (Prakriti, objects of senses), age or a want of correlation (appropriate harmony, equilibrium) between the three humors or the three Gunas.

The Sushruta Samhita and Charaka Samhita have religious ideas throughout, states Steven Engler, who then concludes "Vedic elements are too central to be discounted as marginal".

These ideas appear, for example, in the theoretical foundations and Vedic metaphors used in these texts. In addition, states Engler, the text includes another layer of ideas, where empirical rational ideas flourish in competition or cooperation with religious ideas, as well as the evidence of later additions of some Brahminic ideas.

There is a close relationship between the philosophic presuppositions and the approach to medicine in Caraka Samhita.

Nutrition and diet: Charaka Samhita dedicates Chapters 5, 6, 25, 26 and 27 to "Aharatattva" (dietetics), stating that wholesome diet is essential for good health and to prevent diseases, while unwholesome food is an important cause of diseases.

The tastes are six. They are sweet, sour, saline, pungent, bitter and astringent. Properly used, they nourish the body.

Improperly used (excess or deficient), they verily lead to the provocation of the Dosha. The Dosha are three: Vata, Pitta and Kapha.

When they are in their normal state, they are beneficial to the body. When, however, they become disorganized, verily they afflict the body with diseases of diverse kinds. -Charaka Samhita, 3.I.3-4

The text suggests that foods are source of heat, nutritive value as well as physiological substances that act like drugs inside human body. Furthermore, along with medicine, Caraka Samhita in Chapters 26 and 27, states that proper nutrition is essential for expedient recovery from sickness or surgery.

Meat for dietetics and medicine: The Charaka Samhita suggests a regimen of Mamsa Rasa (meat soup) during pregnancy from 6th month onwards. Freshly cut meat is also recommended by the text for treatment of poison: the cut meat is pressed against the affected part or spot of insect or reptile bite to absorb the poison.

Ray et al. list medicinal substances from over one hundred fifty animal origins that are described in Charaka Samhita, and the chapters these are found in. These range from meat of wild animals such as fox and crocodile, to that of freshly cut fish, fish oil, eggs of birds, bee's wax. Additionally, the text describes hundreds of formulations (gruel) it asserts to be of medicinal value from a mixtures of animal products and herb or plant products, as well as inert minerals such as various salts, soots and alkalis.

Ancient Pharmacy

Numerous chapters in the Charaka Samhita are dedicated to identifying and classifying seeds, roots, flowers, fruits, stems, aromatic leaves, barks of different trees, plants juices, mountain herbs, animal products ranging from their milk to their excretory waste after the animals eat certain diet or grasses, different types of honey, stones, salts and others. The text also describes numerous recipes, detailing how a particular formulation should be prepared. A typical recipe appears in the Cikitsa Sthana book of the Caraka Samhita as follows:

Anu Taila recipe

Take a measure of sesame seeds.

Macerate them in goat's milk.

Then pound them in goat's milk.

Place the pounded product on a piece of clean cloth.

Place the product and cloth over a vessel filled with goat's milk.

Apply mild heat to the vessel. Let vapors from heated milk slightly boil the sesame paste.

Mix the boiled paste with pulverized liquorice, adding an equal measure of goat's milk.

Press the oil out of the mixed product.

Add this oil to the (standard) decoction of ten roots in the ratio of one to four.

To this oil mix, add paste of Rasna, Madhuka and Saindhava salt in the ratio of four to one.

Boil all these together. Filter. Extract and collect the oil.

Repeat the root-paste-salt-oil combining and boiling process ten times.

The resulting oil is called Anu-taila.- Charaka Samhita 6.XXVI

The text, thereafter, asserts that this Anu-taila is to be used as a rubbing oil and as nasal drop for a certain class of ailments. Glucklich mentions other medical texts from ancient India which include the use of Anu-taila in skin therapy.

Sexual Health

The Charaka Samhita discusses sexual diseases as well as its theory of treatment of sexual dysfunctions and virility (Vajikarana). The text emphasizes methods of body cleansing, sexual health promoting conduct, behaviour and diet. Certain herb and mineral combinations are part of its regimen. The text asserts that obesity and a lifestyle lacking exercise is linked to sexual dysfunctions (K?cchra Vyav?ya), dedicating many verses to this.

The text, states Arnold, contains many verses relating to women's sexual health, suggesting "great antiquity of certain methods and therapeutic agents used in the treatment of gynecological cases", for example the cautery, pessaries, and astringent washes.

Medical education: Chapter VIII of the Charaka Samhita's Vimana Sthana book includes a section for the student aiming to become a physician. The text asserts that any intelligent man who knows the challenge and patience necessary to become a physician must first decide on his guru (teacher) and the books he must study.

The Charaka Samhita claims, according to Kaviratna and Sharma translation, that "diverse treatises on medicine are in circulation", and the student must select one by reputed scholar known for his wisdom, is free from tautology, ascribed to a Rishi, well compiled and has bhasya (commentaries), which treats nothing but the professed subject, is devoid of slang and unfamiliar words, explain its inferences, is non-contradictory, and is well illustrated.

The teacher for apprenticeship should be one who knows the field, has experience gained from successfully treating diseases, who is compassionate towards who approach him, who lives a life of inner and outer Shaucha, is well equipped, who knows the characteristics of health and disease, one who is without malice towards anyone, is free of anger, who respects privacy and pain of his patients, is willing to teach, and is a good communicator. When one finds such a teacher, asserts the Caraka Samhita, the student must revere the teacher like a deity or one's own father, because it is by his grace that one becomes educated.

When the teacher accepts a student as his apprentice, asserts the Charaka Samhita, he should in the presence of fire initiate the student with the following mandates during the period of apprenticeship - "thou shalt be a brahmacharin, wear beard and mustache, thou shalt be always truthful, abstain from meat and unclean diet, never harbor envy, never bear weapons, thou shalt do anything I say except if that may lead to another person's death or to great harm or to a sin, thou shalt behave like my son, never be impatient, always be attentive, behave with humility, act after reflection, and always seek whether sitting or standing the good of all living creatures".

Commentaries

The most celebrated commentary on this text is the Carakatatparya-tika "Commentary on the Meaning of the Caraka" or the Ayurveda Dipika, "The Lamp to Ayurveda" written by Chakrapani Datta (1066). Other notable commentaries are Bhattaraka Harichandra's Carakanyasa (c. 4th-6th century), Jejjats Nirantarapadavyakhya (c.875), Shivadasa Sena's CarakatattvapraDipika (c.1460). Among the more recent commentaries are Narasimha Kaviraja's Carakatattvaprakasa, Ga?g?dhara Kaviratna's Jalpakalpataru (1879) and Yogindra Nath Sen's Charakopaskara (1920).

The earliest scholarly bhasya (review, commentary) in Sanskrit may be of Bhattar Harichandra's Carakanyasa on the redaction by D??habala. Two manuscripts of this bhasya have survived into the modern era, and currently stored as number 9290 in Asiatic Society of Kolkata and number 13092 manuscript at the Government East Library, Chennai.

Comparison with Sushruta Samhita

The Charaka Samhita is among the most important ancient medical treatises. It is one of the foundational texts of the medical tradition in India, alongside the Susruta Samhita, the Bhema-Samhita, and the medical portions of the Bower Manuscript.

The Charaka Samhita is the oldest known Hindu text on Ayurveda (life sciences), followed by the Sushruta Samhita and Ashtanga Hrdaya. Except for some topics and their emphasis, they discuss many similar subjects such as General Principles, Pathology, Diagnosis, Anatomy, Sensorial Prognosis, Therapeutics, Pharmaceutics and Toxicology. The Sushruta and Caraka texts differ in one major aspect, with Sushruta Samhita providing the foundation of surgery, while Caraka Samhita being primarily a foundation of medicine.

A source for socio-cultural and ecological history of ancient India

The text is not only an interesting source of ancient medical practices, it also may be a source of valuable information on ecological, social, and economic conditions in ancient India. The text describes physical geography with words such as Jangala, Aanoopa, and Sadharana, then lists the trees, vegetables, lakes and rivers, bird life and animals found in each of these regions. Many of the drugs mentioned, they state, are linked to region of their origin (e.g. Maghadi from Maghada and Kashmarya from Kashmir). Ray et al. list the numerous mammals, reptiles, insects, fishes, amphibians, arthropods and birds and the respective chapters of Caraka Samhita these are mentioned in.

The text also states that the food habits of ancient Indians varied by regions. Mamsa (meat) was popular with people who lived in Bahlika, Pahlava, Cheena, Shoolika, Yavana and Shaka. People of Prachya preferred Matsya (fish), according to Bhavana and Shreevathsa translation. Those living in Sindhu Desha (now Gujarat and south Pakistan) were habituated to milk, according to Caraka Samhita, while people of Ashmaka and Avantika consumed more oily and sour food. The people of Dakshina Desha (South India) preferred Peya (thin gruel), whereas those of Uttara (North) and Pashchima (West) liked Mantha. Residents of Madhya Desha (Central India) preferred barley, wheat and milk products according to the text.

Chapter 5

Ayurvedic Healing and Treatments

Introduction

Ayurveda (a Sanskrit word that means "science of life" or "knowledge of life") is one of the world's oldest whole-body healing systems. It was developed more than 5,000 years ago in India.

Ayurveda is based on the belief that health and wellness depend on a delicate balance between the mind, body, spirit, and environment. The main goal of ayurvedic medicine is to promote good health and prevent, not fight, disease. But treatments may be geared toward specific health problems.

Ayurveda and Your Life Energy

Ayurveda is based on the theory that everything in the universe - dead or alive - is connected. If your mind, body, and spirit are in harmony with the universe, you have good health. When something disrupts this balance, you get sick. Among the things that can upset this balance are genetic or birth defects, injuries, climate and seasonal change, age, and your emotions. Those who practice ayurveda believe every person is made of five basic elements found in the universe: space, air, fire, water, and earth.

These combine in the human body to form three life forces, or energies, called doshas. They control how your body works. They are vata dosha (space and air); pitta dosha (fire and water); and kapha dosha (water and earth).

Everyone inherits a unique mix of the three doshas. But one is usually stronger than the others. Each one controls a different body function. It's believed that your chances of getting sick - and the health issues you develop - are linked to the balance of your doshas.

The Three Doshas in Ayurveda

Vata dosha: Those who practice ayurveda believe this is the most powerful of all three doshas. It controls very basic body functions, like how cells divide. It also controls your mind, breathing, blood flow, heart function, and ability to get rid of waste through your intestines. Things that can disrupt it include eating again too soon after a meal, fear, grief, and staying up too late.

If vata is your dominant dosha, you may be smart, creative, vibrant, and your moods change quickly. Physically, you may be thin and lose weight easily, and are usually cold. When you are out of balance, you can get overstimulated and have anxiety , phobias, and be forgetful. You can also be more likely to have conditions like asthma, heart disease, skin problems, and rheumatoid arthritis. In ayurveda, like increases like. For this dosha (space and air), you can balance out too much vata by doing things that are grounding like meditation, massage, keeping a regular sleep and wake schedule, and eating warm, mild foods.

Pitta dosha: This energy controls your digestion, metabolism (how well you break down foods), and certain hormones that are linked to your appetite. Things that can disrupt pitta are eating sour or spicy foods, spending too much time in the sun, and missing meals. If you are pitta dominant, then you may be goal-oriented, competitive, confident, and a natural leader. Physically, you may have a medium-sized, muscular build and tend to be hot most of the time. When out of balance, you can be too competitive, cranky, quick to anger, and impulsive. If pitta is your main dosha, you're thought to be more likely to have conditions like Crohn's disease, heart disease, high blood pressure, indigestion, and fever when you are out of balance. To bring pitta (fire and water) back into balance, you can focus on things that are cooling and light, like salads, cucumbers, and practicing moderation and slow or restorative yoga.

Kapha dosha: Kapha dosha is thought to control muscle growth, body strength and stability, weight, and your immune system. Things that can disrupt kapha include daytime naps, eating too many sweet foods, and eating or drinking things that contain too much salt or water. If kapha is your main dosha, you may like routine, stick to expectations, and be accepting, calm, and patient. Physically, you are more likely to have a broad frame and easily gain weight.

When out of balance, you can easily get fatigued, avoid taking on new projects, and be possessive, stubborn, and depressed. If you are kapha dominant, you may be more likely to develop asthma and other breathing disorders, cancer, diabetes, nausea after eating, and obesity.

To reduce excess kapha (earth and water) and be more balanced, you can increase the amount of fruits and vegetables in your diet, and do exercise that gets the blood flowing like jogging or sun salutations in yoga.

Ayurvedic Treatment

An ayurvedic practitioner will create a treatment plan specifically designed for you. They'll take into account your unique physical and emotional makeup, and your primary and secondary doshas. They will use that information to work toward the goal of treatment, which is to bring your mind and body into balance.

There are several tools used in ayurvedic medicine to help you create harmony, avoid disease, and treat conditions you may have. These include:

- Herbal medicine. A key component of ayurveda, it's used in different combinations, depending on your dosha, and includes licorice, red clover, ginger, and turmeric.
- Yoga
- Meditation
- Purification programs. Also known as panchakarma, these are used to cleanse your body of undigested food through practices like blood purification, massage, medical oils, herbs, enemas, and laxatives.
- Counseling. Your practitioner will help you understand your dosha, how it impacts your life, and how you can change your lifestyle to create more balance and harmony.

Other treatments used in ayurveda include oil massage, breathing exercises (known as pranayama), and repeating mantras, or phrases.

Benefits of Ayurveda

As with many alternative therapies, not as much clinical research has been done on ayurveda as on Western medicine. But many practices of ayurveda have been shown to improve health and well-being.

- If you have conditions like rheumatoid arthritis, ayurveda treatments may improve symptoms.
- Ayurveda has also been shown to lower blood pressure and cholesterol.

- An ayurvedic diet focuses on an increase in eating fruits, vegetables, and whole grains and decreasing meat intake, particularly red meat. This could reduce the risk of heart disease.
- Practicing yoga can reduce chronic pain and anxiety and improve circulation and digestion.
- Fenugreek has been shown to lower bad cholesterol (LDL) and increase good cholesterol (HDL).
- Meditation may reduce anxiety, increase focus, help you better manage stress, and improve the quality of your sleep. It may also help you manage symptoms of conditions like chronic pain, cancer, depression, and irritable bowel syndrome.

It is important to note that the FDA doesn't review or approve ayurvedic products. In fact, it has banned certain ones from entering the country since 2007. What's more, the FDA has warned that 1 in 5 ayurvedic medicines contain toxic metals, like lead, mercury, and arsenic. These heavy metals can cause life-threatening illnesses, especially in children.

Always talk to your doctor before you try ayurveda or any other alternative medical treatment.

Finding an Ayurveda Practitioner

There is no exact data on the number of people who use ayurvedic medicine, but an estimated 80% of people in India are thought to use at least some ayurvedic treatments.

In India, ayurveda is considered a traditional medical system, and some practitioners can perform surgery. In the U.S., it's considered a form of complementary and alternative medicine.

If you'd like to try ayurvedic medicine, talk with an integrative medicine specialist or functional medicine doctor to make sure any herbal medicines you want to take have been tested for contaminants and approved by an independent laboratory. These doctors can also help integrate Western medicine and ayurveda.

There are a few state-approved ayurvedic schools in the U.S. But there's no national standard training or certification program for those who practice ayurveda. You can find a practitioner near you at the National Ayurvedic Medical Association.

Ayurvedic Lifestyle

If you have only used Western medicine, ayurveda may sound exotic. If you're not ready to visit an ayurvedic practitioner for a consultation, there are many simple ayurvedic practices you can do at home to help balance your mental, physical, and spiritual health.

For sleep/stress relief: Try keeping a regular sleep/wake schedule and adopting better sleep hygiene. (Keep your bedroom quiet, at a comfortable temperature, and dark at bedtime. Keep laptops and phones out of the bedroom at night.) Set aside time (daily, if possible) for meditation. Practice deep breathing techniques like box breathing - breathe in for four counts, hold your breath for four counts, breathe out for four counts and hold again for four. Repeat this three or four times.

Exercise: Try a yoga class. You can go to a local studio, take online classes, or find free ones on YouTube. Increase the amount you move during the day. Listen to your body - maybe you need a long, slow walk one day and a brisk run another.

Ayurvedic food: Eat fresh, homemade food instead of processed products. Enjoy your food and eat when you are calm, instead of stressed or angry, for good digestion. Eat your biggest meal at lunch when your digestion is best. This may also help you sleep at night if you aren't trying to digest a heavy dinner. Focus on foods that balance all of the doshas, including fruits, vegetables, rice, nuts, and honey as a sweetener.

Herbs: You can incorporate many herbs used in ayurveda when cooking food. Before taking herbal supplements, check with your doctor to make sure they are safe and won't interact with any medications you are taking. Some of the most commonly used, and easy-to-access, herbs in ayurveda include:

- Ashwagandha, which reduces stress and helps with sleep
- Turmeric, an anti-inflammatory
- Ginger, a root that can reduce nausea
- Cumin, a spice that helps with digestion
- Black pepper, which can be a decongestant

Takeaways: Ayurveda is a complex system that takes into account nearly all parts of your physical, spiritual, and mental health. But there are easy practices you can do at home as well. If you want to find out which dosha is your dominant one, The Ayurvedic Institute has a dosha quiz. Using this can help you understand your dominant energy, or constitution, and follow simple treatments to reach the goal of Ayurveda - to bring balance to your life.

Ayurvedic Treatments

The ideology of Ayurveda views the human body as part of its environment, which means any changes in the environment will manifest in the physical, mental, emotional, and spiritual faculties of the human body.

This holistic ideology furthermore extends to how Ayurveda treatments are performed. Ayurvedic treatments target the root cause of the problem rather than merely suppressing the symptoms. It focuses on achieving the perfect harmony between the mind, body, and soul to live a disease-free, active life.

What is Ayurvedic Treatment/Therapy?

Ayurvedic therapy or treatment is administered as a combination of herbal concoctions and lifestyle changes that help balance the three principal energies of the body: Vata, Pitta, and Kapha. These principle energies or doshas are present in every individual with varying strength and magnitude. The one dosha that is predominant among the rest determines the overall constitution of the individual, also known as Prakriti.

According to Ayurveda, diseases arise when these doshas become vitiated because of an external or internal stimulus linked to eating habits and the amount of physical exercise you get in a day.

Ayurvedic treatments ensure all three doshas are at their optimum levels. The duration and method of the treatment may vary depending on the Prakriti or inherent constitution of the individual.

Contrary to the modern medicine system, Ayurvedic treatments harness the power of nature and the body's inherent qualities to heal itself. The treatments are performed in a certified Ayurveda center under the supervision of experienced practitioners and nurses. As far as oral medications go, it is recommended to seek the advice of your Ayurveda practitioner to avoid major side effects and disappointment because of poor results.

Diagnosis: The most common techniques of diagnosing an illness in the Ayurvedic system are Naadi Pariksha and Ashtavidha Pariksha. Naadi Pariksha translates to checking the pulse, whereas Ashtavidha

Pariksha is more elaborate and involves checking the pulse, urine, faeces, tongue, voice, skin, eyes, and overall body appearance.

A knowledgeable and well-trained Ayurveda practitioner can determine the underlying condition using these methods. It helps understand an individual's basic physiological and psychological makeup, providing insight into the dosha imbalance.

Treatment: Your Ayurveda practitioner will consider your symptoms, Nadi pariksha, dominant dosha and overall constitution to create a tailored treatment for you.

Then, the practitioner will prescribe herbal remedies, diet, exercise, and certain lifestyle adjustments to start the healing process and effect positive changes in your body.

It's a misconception that Ayurvedic treatments cannot work alongside modern therapies. If your doctor allows, you can seek Ayurvedic treatments in a supplementary manner to expedite healing and recovery.

List of Ayurvedic Treatments

We have described some popular Ayurvedic treatments that work holistically to balance doshas and ensure perfect harmony between your mind, body, and soul to start self-healing.

Abhyanga Massage: Abhyanga is a traditional full-body massage performed by oneself using medicated oil.

The oil is slightly heated before applying to the entire body, from head to toe, followed by gentle strokes to release stress, improve circulation and relieve inflammation. The oil is infused with specific herbs, and the ingredients may vary depending on the target ailment. Let's look at some of the variations of Abhyanga and Swedana therapies.

Kati Vasti Treatment: raditional treatment for back pain and inflammation in the lumbosacral region, Kati Vasti, is performed by retaining warm medicated oil over the lower back for a specific duration. Think of it as a small frame or a well made of gram dough to keep the oil-the heated oil puddles over the target region to provide external stimulation for a soothing effect.

Elakizhi Treatment: Perspiration is good for you. It helps open up skin pores and eliminate toxins as sweat. If your day-to-day routine doesn't involve -physical activity, you might need this treatment to break a sweat. Elakizhi therapy induces perspiration by massaging the body with a bundle of herbs packed in a muslin cloth and soaked in warm oil. The treatment helps relieve stress, sore muscles, and body ache.

Njavara Kizhi Treatment: It's a traditional Ayurvedic massage therapy using boluses of cooked rice, milk and herbal extracts to induce perspiration. This massage therapy benefits arthritis patients or anyone suffering from acute or chronic musculoskeletal discomfort.

Panchakarma Treatment: It's a holistic treatment performed over a week to naturally send the body into overdrive to get rid of toxins. Panchakarma treatment has been around for centuries, designed and prescribed by ancient sages to nurture healthy living. Let's understand the five therapies that makeup panchakarma treatment.

Vamana Therapy: This therapy involves administering medicated oil or ghee for a few days to agitate doshas and eventually induce vomiting. Vamana is performed to treat illnesses caused by elevated Kapha doshas by eliminating toxins from the tissues.

Virechana Treatment: This therapy involves administering herbal laxatives to evacuate the bowel, eliminate toxins from the GI tract and treat the ailments caused by elevated Pitta dosha.

Basti Treatment: This therapy involves administering a herbal enema into the rectum to clear the colon. Although this technique is used to treat vitiated vata dosha, it's an essential step in panchakarma treatment for gut cleansing and detox. The therapy is minimally invasive and mostly painless.

Nasyam Treatment: This therapy involves administering herbal nasal drops into the nostrils to help the recipient find relief from Kapha affiliations above the head.

Raktamokshana Treatment: This traditional therapy removes blood impurities by letting a leech suck up blood from key areas or letting the blood out by making a minor cut using a metal instrument.

Varicose Veins Treatment: Varicose Veins are a common condition among middle-aged women but can also affect young women. Varicose Veins Treatment in Ayurveda uses a combination of herbs and massage oils, such as Sahacharadi thailam, Pinda thailam, etc. The treatment can be performed at home or by an Ayurveda practitioner.

Psoriasis Treatment: Psoriasis is an autoimmune syndrome that causes itchy, dry, and flaky skin. The patches may appear on the scalp, neck, or body. Psoriasis treatment in Ayurveda is usually performed by a certified practitioner using a variety of herbal pastes.

Ayurvedic Foods

The Ayurveda-Digestion Connection

According to Ayurveda, one of the most important factors in health is good digestion. When your agni (digestive fire) is strong, ojas (life essence) is abundant in your mind and body. On the other hand, when your digestion is poor, ama (toxins) are deposited in the digestive tract. Over time, when ama accumulates it can give rise to all manner of discomforts in the mind and body, ranging from acid stomach, constipation, and/or diarrhea, to skin issues, allergies, brain fog, hampered immunity, and a host of other problems.

How does it work: The Ayurvedic diet is a type of eating plan that sets guidelines for when, how, and what you should eat based on your dosha, or body type.

Here are some of the main characteristics for each dosha to help you determine which type matches you best:

- Pitta (fire + water). Intelligent, hard-working, and decisive. This dosha generally has a medium physical build, short temper, and may suffer from conditions like indigestion, heart disease, or high blood pressure.
- Vata (air + space). Creative, energetic, and lively. People with this dosha are usually thin with a light frame and may struggle with digestive issues, fatigue, or anxiety when out of balance.
- Kapha (earth + water). Naturally calm, grounded, and loyal. Those with a kapha dosha often have a sturdier frame and may have issues with weight gain, asthma, depression, or diabetes.

According to this diet, your dosha determines which foods you should eat to promote inner balance. For example, the pitta dosha focuses on cooling, energizing foods and limits spices, nuts, and seeds.

Meanwhile, the vata dosha favours warm, moist, and grounding foods while restricting dried fruits, bitter herbs, and raw veggies.

Finally, the kapha dosha limits heavy foods like nuts, seeds, and oils in favour of fruits, veggies, and legumes. Red meat, artificial sweeteners, and processed ingredients are limited for all three doshas. Instead, the Ayurvedic diet encourages eating healthy whole foods.

The Ayurvedic diet is an eating pattern focused on promoting balance within your body by following guidelines for your specific dosha, or body type.

Benefits: Here are a few of the potential benefits of the Ayurvedic Diet.

Encourages whole foods: Although the Ayurvedic diet has specific guidelines for each dosha, the diet as a whole encourages eating whole foods like fruits, vegetables, grains, and legumes.

This can benefit your health greatly, as these foods are rich in many essential nutrients.

The diet also minimizes processed foods, which often lack fibre and important vitamins and minerals. Studies show that eating higher amounts of processed foods may be associated with a higher risk of heart disease, cancer, and even death. Thus, the Ayurvedic diet may help protect against chronic disease and promote better health. However, more studies are needed.

Could promote weight loss: Given that the Ayurvedic diet emphasizes nutrient-rich whole foods, it might boost weight loss. While limited research is available on the Ayurvedic diet and weight loss, some studies have found that it may be effective in this regard. For example, one study in 200 people with pitta or kapha doshas showed that following the Ayurvedic diet for three months led to significant weight loss. These people supposedly tend to be heavier than those with vata doshas. Another small study found that following an Ayurveda-based lifestyle modification program, which included dietary changes and yoga classes, resulted in an average weight loss of 13 pounds (6 kg) over 9 months.

A small 2019 study found that people who followed an an Ayurvedic diet and practiced yoga three times per week for 3 months experienced an average weight loss of 5.6 kg and continued to lose weight afterward.

That said, large, high-quality studies are needed to evaluate the effectiveness of the Ayurvedic diet for weight loss in the general population.

Promotes mindfulness: In addition to what foods you eat, mindfulness is another major part of the Ayurvedic diet. Mindfulness is a practice that involves paying close attention to how you feel in the present. In particular, mindful eating emphasizes minimizing distractions during meals to focus on the taste, texture, and smell of your food. According to one small study in 10 people, practicing mindful eating reduced body weight, depression, stress, and binge eating. Mindful eating may also enhance self-control and promote a healthy relationship with food. The Ayurvedic diet emphasizes eating whole foods, which can improve your overall health and boost weight loss. The diet also encourages mindful eating, a practice that may promote a healthy relationship with food.

Downsides: Although there are several benefits associated with the Ayurvedic diet, there are drawbacks to consider. Here are a few of the potential downsides of the Ayurvedic diet.

Can be confusing:Benefits One of the major issues with the Ayurvedic diet is that it can be confusing and difficult to follow.

Not only are there specific food lists for each dosha but also many additional rules to follow. For example, the recommendations regarding which foods you should eat and avoid change throughout the year based on the season. There are also suggestions for when, how often, and how much you should eat, which can be challenging - especially for those just getting started on the diet.

May feel overly restrictive: On the Ayurvedic diet, there are extensive lists of foods that you are advised to eat or avoid depending on your dosha. This can mean cutting out healthy, whole foods or entire food groups that are thought to aggravate specific doshas.

Other ingredients like red meat or processed foods are also left out, which may require you to make significant modifications to your current diet. This can feel overly restrictive and less flexible than other meal plans and may make it difficult to stick to the diet long term.

Often subjective: Another issue with the Ayurvedic diet is that it's subjective. The diet is centered around determining your dominant dosha, which is based on a set of physical and mental traits. Although there are plenty of guidelines and online quizzes available to help ease the process, figuring out your dosha is not foolproof.

As the recommendations for the diet are tailored to each dosha, choosing the incorrect dosha could negatively impact your results.

Furthermore, no evidence currently supports the concept of doshas or the claim that your personality traits determine which foods you should eat and avoid. Therefore, it's unclear how beneficial the diet is, even if you correctly determine your dosha. The Ayurvedic diet can be confusing and may feel overly restrictive, especially as you start out. Also, the theory of doshas is subjective and not based on scientific evidence.

Foods to eat: In Ayurveda, foods are categorized based on their physical qualities and the way they are said to affect your body. This helps determine which ingredients work best for different doshas. Below are some of the foods you should eat based on your specific dosha.

Pitta

- Protein: poultry in small amounts, egg whites, tofu
- Dairy: milk, ghee, butter
- Fruits: sweet, fully ripe fruits like oranges, pears, pineapples, bananas, melons, and mangoes
- Vegetables: sweet and bitter veggies, including cabbage, cauliflower, celery, cucumber, zucchini, leafy greens, sweet potatoes, carrots, squash, and Brussels sprouts
- Legumes: chickpeas, lentils, mung beans, lima beans, black beans, kidney beans
- Grains: barley, oats, basmati rice, wheat
- Nuts and seeds: small amounts of pumpkin seeds, flax seeds, sunflower seeds, coconut
- Herbs and spices: small amounts of black pepper, cumin, cinnamon, cilantro, dill, turmeric

Vata

- Protein: small amounts of poultry, seafood, tofu
- Dairy: milk, butter, yogurt, cheese, ghee
- Fruits: fully ripe, sweet, and heavy fruits, such as bananas, blueberries, strawberries, grapefruit, mangoes, peaches, and plums
- Vegetables: cooked vegetables, including beets, sweet potatoes, onions, radishes, turnips, carrots, and green beans
- Legumes: chickpeas, lentils, mung beans
- Grains: cooked oats, cooked rice
- Nuts and seeds: any, including almonds, walnuts, pistachios, chia seeds, flax seeds, and sunflower seeds
- Herbs and spices: cardamom, ginger, cumin, basil, cloves, oregano, thyme, black pepper

Kapha

- Protein: poultry in small amounts, seafood, egg whites

- Dairy: skim milk, goat milk, soy milk
- Fruits: apples, blueberries, pears, pomegranates, cherries, and dried fruit like raisins, figs, and prunes
- Vegetables: asparagus, leafy greens, onions, potatoes, mushrooms, radishes, okra
- Legumes: any, including black beans, chickpeas, lentils, and navy beans
- Grains: oats, rye, buckwheat, barley, corn, millet
- Nuts and seeds: small amounts of pumpkin seeds, sunflower ***seeds, flax seeds***
- Herbs and spices: any, including cumin, black pepper, turmeric, ginger, cinnamon, basil, oregano, and thyme

Depending on your dosha, there are specific guidelines regarding which foods to eat as part of an Ayurvedic diet.

Foods to avoid: Here are some of the foods you should limit or avoid based on your dosha.

Pitta

- Proteins: red meat, seafood, egg yolks
- Dairy: sour cream, cheese, buttermilk
- Fruits: sour or unripe fruits, such as grapes, apricots, papaya, grapefruit, and sour cherries
- Vegetables: chili peppers, beets, tomatoes, onions, eggplant
- Grains: brown rice, millet, corn, rye
- Nuts and seeds: almonds, cashews, peanuts, pine nuts, pistachios, walnuts, sesame seeds
- Herbs and spices: any spices not included in the list above

Vata

- Proteins: red meat
- Fruits: dried, unripe, or light fruits, such as raisins, cranberries, pomegranates, and pears
- Vegetables: any raw vegetables, as well as cooked broccoli, cabbage, cauliflower, mushrooms, potatoes, and tomatoes
- Legumes: beans, such as black beans, kidney beans, and navy beans
- Grains: buckwheat, barley, rye, wheat, corn, quinoa, millet

- Herbs and spices: bitter or astringent herbs like parsley, thyme, and coriander seed

Kapha

- Proteins: red meat, shrimp, egg yolks
- Fruits: bananas, coconuts, mangoes, fresh figs
- Vegetables: sweet potatoes, tomatoes, zucchini, cucumbers
- Legumes: soybeans, kidney beans, miso
- Grains: rice, wheat, cooked cereal
- Nuts and seeds: cashews, pecans, pine nuts, Brazil nuts, sesame ***seeds, walnuts***

Based on your dosha, the Ayurvedic diet recommends that you limit or avoid certain foods.

The Ayurvedic Diet: Eat According to Your Dosha Type

One of the key tenets of Ayurveda is that no two people are alike, so no two people's dietary needs are exactly the same. For this reason, there is no "one-size-fits-all" Ayurvedic diet. In Ayurveda, the ideal diet is based on an individual's constitution, also known as their "dosha type" or "mind-body type." The three dosha types are VATA, PITTA, and KAPHA.

The doshas are mind-body elements that govern all facets of our bodies' functioning-from the size and shape of our body to the power of our digestion, the way our thoughts move, and the way we speak.

10 Ayurvedic Dietary Dos and Don'ts

Knowing your dosha (mind-body) type is the first step toward finding the perfect diet for you. That being said, there are some basic Ayurvedic dietary foods and practices that apply to everyone. They are as follows:

Favour a Vegetarian Diet

The Ayurvedic diet is, generally speaking, a whole foods diet rich in plenty of fresh, organic produce, whole grains, legumes, nuts, seeds, herbs, spices, and-if tolerated-dairy foods like milk, yogurt, and soft cheeses like panir.

Fruits and vegetables (largely cooked) are valued in Ayurveda not only for their nutritional value, but also because they are good natural internal cleansers. The specific food guidelines for Vata, Pitta, and Kapha dosha diets will help you choose a variety of fruits and vegetables suited to your physiology and the season. If meat is currently part of your daily diet-don't worry! Simply aim to reduce the quantity you eat and favour lighter proteins like fish and chicken, over heavier, harder-to-digest proteins like red meat.

Avoid Processed Foods, Leftovers, and Raw/Cold Foods

Whereas whole foods promote ojas, foods that are overly processed, frozen, canned, and full of additives and sugar are harder for your body to break down efficiently into nutrients. Leftovers fall into this category, too. As a result, it's better to avoid "junk foods" like these and turn your attention to whole foods instead.

Note: RAW FOODS, while technically whole foods, are harder to digest than cooked foods.

For this reason, Ayurveda generally favours well-cooked, lightly spiced veggies over raw salads. Ice-cold foods and drinks are also better avoided, as they dampen the digestive fire and can lead to indigestion (ice water and cold soda, we're looking at you!). Caffeinated beverages and alcohol are best avoided, or consumed in moderation.

Include all Six Tastes in Every Meal

In Ayurveda, taste plays a big role in food selection, because different tastes affect the doshas. The six tastes are: sweet; sour; salty; bitter; astringent; and pungent. Each one has a different effect on the doshas. From the perspective of Ayurveda, a healthy meal includes ALL SIX TASTES, thereby harmonizing the doshas.

Eat Three Meals a Day: Routine is everything in Ayurveda! For this reason, it's helpful to "train" your agni to receive three solid meals per day, rather than grazing and snacking throughout the day (which can overburden the digestive system), or fasting and skipping meals (which can throw your digestive fire out of balance).

Make Lunch Your Biggest Meal and Dinner Your Lightest: As the sun reaches its highest point in the sky, at noon, your digestive fire is at its highest, too.

For this reason, Ayurveda recommends eating your largest meal of the day at noon, when your inner fire is burning brightly and better able to digest and assimilate. EAT A LIGHTER, WELL-COOKED MEAL at least three hours before bed, and try to be in bed around 10:00 p.m. or before. Eating a big, heavy meal late in the evening can tax your body when it's doing its nightly "rest and repair" cycles.

Eat in a Calm, Settled Environment: Balanced health goes beyond physical wellness to well-being in mind, spirit, emotions, and the senses as well. The food we eat can nourish our mind, body, and emotions, not just our body. Cooking and eating in a harmonious atmosphere turns food into nectar. A pleasant, tidy, cheerful environment and the nurturing company of friends or family will actually make mealtimes more nourishing. When eating, try to avoid watching TV, reading, checking your screens, scrolling the news, or discussing stressful topics.

Eat a Balanced Amount: Your mother told you to always clean your plate, but Ayurvedic wisdom advises you to eat until you feel comfortably full, and no more. When you start to burp, that would be about enough! Try to avoid eating to the point of discomfort, or eating rationed portions that leave you feeling hungry and dissatisfied.

Be Spice Wise: Spices not only add flavor and aroma; they also bring therapeutic value to any meal. Spices help BOOST NATURAL IMMUNITY, and most of them can rev up your digestion so your body is able to absorb and assimilate the nutrients from the foods we eat! If you are new to the world of spices and aren't quite sure what to choose, try one of our ready-to-use Churnas.

Stay Well Hydrated: An Ayurvedic diet would be incomplete without a mention of liquids! It's important to stay hydrated throughout the day by drinking pure water (either room-temperature, or warm for cleansing). At lunch, you can also drink lassi, a probiotic Ayurvedic beverage made from yogurt, water, and spices. And don't forget the balancing power of Ayurvedic teas! For Vata and Pitta-predominant types, try a cup of Organic Vata Tea, or boiled milk at bedtime. Try boiling milk with a slice of fresh ginger, or blended with a spoonful of ORGANIC ROSE PETAL SPREAD. Alternatively, try it with our Organic Vata Tea (Vata Milk), or with a pinch of cardamom or nutmeg to aid sleep.

Try Herbal Digestives: Sometimes, your body just needs a little extra help with digestion. Ayurveda offers a wealth of time-tested botanical formulas to help improve digestion comfortably and naturally. For an overall digestive boost to help you curb cravings, try HERBAL DI-GEST, a powerful formula with pomegranate, cumin, and ginger. If occasional acid indigestion crops up,

The bottom line: The Ayurvedic diet is a meal plan based on the principles of Ayurvedic medicine, a form of traditional medicine originating on the Indian subcontinent dating back thousands of years. The diet involves eating or restricting certain foods based on your dosha, or body type, which is claimed to boost weight loss and support mindfulness. However, it can be confusing and restrictive, and it's based on subjective assumptions about your personality and body type. Plus, its theories are not supported by scientific evidence.

Simple Ways to Live Ayurvedically

Lifestyle

1. Schedule a walk with a friend or co-worker Ayurveda considers walking a tridoshic exercise: it balances all three doshas without putting excessive strain on your body. It calms the mind and nourishes the senses.
2. Sit down and close your eyes Take a "just-for-me" break right now, right here. Disconnect from the outer world and tune in to your own self. Even if you do this for a minute, you will feel healed. Practitioners of TRANSCENDENTAL MEDITATION® say their daily 20-minute sadhana helps conquer stress and increase positive energy and a sense of well-being.
3. Call a friend People whose company makes us feel happy and loved are like medicine: they heal and restore us. Keeping in touch with such people nurtures our own hearts.
4. Breathe deep Mindful breathing improves the flow of oxygen and other vital nutrients to the tiniest channels of the body, giving you an instant sense of well-being.
5. Go to bed early Ayurvedic physicians emphasize and re-emphasize the value of good sleep, simply because rest is the basis of dynamic activity.
6. Rise with the sun This will be easy to do if you go to bed before 10:00 p.m. Waking up early gives you time to concentrate on your morning ablutions, and to prepare a good, nourishing breakfast. In addition, it gives you time to enjoy the early morning calm of nature.
7. Bond with nature When you spend time with flowers, butterflies, and trees, you connect in the most intimate way with the earth, of which ayurveda believes we are all an integral part. This sense of connection is tremendously soothing, particularly for those of us who are under stress.

8. See a vaidya At any given time, most of us do have small or big imbalances in our physiology. Even small imbalances can lead to discomfort and malaise. A vaidya will help you understand and correct your imbalances. See one even if you are not feeling particularly unwell.

Nutrition and Digestion

9. Create a fresh lunch Foods that are processed, canned, frozen or packaged are harder to digest, and thus create ama, or toxins. Also, because they are old, denatured by processing, or include harmful ingredients such as chemical preservatives, they no longer contain nature's intelligence. Rather, they create ama and block nature's intelligence from reaching the cells. Just for today, make the effort to eat a fresh, warm lunch. Eat in a settled, quiet atmosphere and focus on your food when you eat.
10. Drink a glass of water Water flushes out accumulated ama, and keeps the digestion smooth. Sipped throughout the day, water is an excellent healer.
11. Drink a glass of milk At the end of a tiring day, when you cannot seem to close your eyes, don't be frustrated: drink a glass of warm milk. Milk should be organic and free of additives, and boiled with a pinch of CARDAMOM before it is drunk in order to make it easier to digest. Drink it alone, away from meals, to avoid indigestion.
12. Sip herb tea All-natural, caffeine-free teas prepared from nature's healing herbs are a perfect way to relax and recharge: choose from among Maharishi AyurVeda's wide range of GOURMET BEVERAGES to pick the flavor and blend that suits your unique dosha type and your needs.
13. Have a good breakfast Skipping breakfast particularly irritates Sadhaka Pitta, a subdosha of PITTA. An imbalanced Sadhaka Pitta can result in irritability and unsettled emotions. Some suggestions for breakfast: COOKED APPLES, eaten first thing in the morning, help to create OJAS-the final and most refined by-product of digestion. Ojas contributes to enhanced vitality, strength, immunity, and overall well-being. Sweet juicy fruits are excellent cleansers-they help to eliminate impurities from the body. According to ayurveda, it is recommended that

fruits be eaten first thing in the morning, 30 minutes before other breakfast items such as hot cereal.

14. From time to time, follow an ama-reducing diet Periodic internal cleansing with a Maharishi Ayurveda detox formulation such as ELIM-TOX or ELIM-TOX-O also helps flush the ama out and prevent more from building up.
15. Decorate your dining table Make each meal a celebration. A pleasant table, set with sparkling cutlery, crisp clean napkins, and appetizing colours whets the appetite and promotes good digestion.
16. Boost your immunity with Amrit AMRIT epitomizes the ayurvedic principles of Sanyog-precise combination; and sanskar-meticulous processing. Thirty-eight rare whole herbs and fruits are combined in precise proportions in this powerful formula to create synergy-a whole that is more powerful than the sum of its parts.
17. Spice up your dinner plate Turmeric, Cumin, Coriander, Fennel, Cardamom-these and other spices used in ayurvedic cooking add not only aroma and flavor, but also healing goodness to your food. Turmeric is an antiseptic, cumin aids digestion, coriander cleanses the system, fennel settles the stomach and cardamom cools the system.

Discover the health benefits of spices: start with Maharishi Ayurveda's CHURNAS-precisely-blended spices that calm the doshas. Spices add good flavor and have a yogavahi property, which means that they support digestion and make the nutrients easily available to the body.

Beauty and Body

18. Massage your body The skin thirsts for your touch and attention. When warm herbalized oil is rubbed gently all over the skin, your body and your mind feel pampered and relaxed. Treat your skin to the magic of self-massage (ABHYANGA) today.
19. Make your own skin pack Ayurvedic healers recommend using totally natural products on your skin: preferably those ingredients that are also safe to eat. Choose from among foods like honey, ORGANIC ROSE WATER, cucumber, oatmeal, ground blanched ALMONDS, milk, and YOGURT to prepare packs that will exfoliate, cleanse, and moisturize your skin.

All-natural actually relates to the ability to protect nature's own intelligence in a product. Not only do we use completely natural ingredients, but we make sure that the techniques used to process those ingredients are such that they do not destroy the natural benefits.

20. Care for your hair When your locks are limp and lifeless, your whole approach to life can turn pessimistic. Counter the problem by paying attention to what you put inside your body. Build small changes into your daily menu. Instead of popcorn, eat fresh fruit. Don't snack on candy-eat soaked blanched almonds instead.

Chapter 6

The Significance of Ayurvedic Medicinal Plants

Introduction

Traditional Indian medicine (ayurveda) is becoming increasingly popular, with many chronic conditions responding to it well. Most patients begin to take conventional medications as soon as their diagnoses are made, so ayurvedic treatments are usually undergone alongside and/or after conventional medical approaches. A detailed knowledge of the action of food, spices, and medicinal plants is needed in order to understand their potential influence fully. While societal use of ayurvedic plants and Indian spices is commonplace, without ill effect, the use of more concentrated products made from single plants, often in the form of teas or tablets, is of more concern. The mechanisms by which polyherbal drugs and their extracts act differ in many respects from the actions of single substances or synthetic drugs. Despite the fact that ayurvedic medicines are based on natural herbal materials, their safety depends on their method of administration, taking into account individuals' needs and their specific disease conditions.

Traditional Indian medicine (or ayurveda) is becoming increasingly popular in Europe, with many chronic conditions responding to it well. While conventional medicine dominates many fields in this market, it does not always outperform traditional ayurvedic approaches. Conventional medicine frequently relies on lifelong medication, on which patients come to depend. Many medications have side-effects, and withdrawal symptoms that, if the medications are later discontinued, can become problematic. In such circumstances, ayurveda has much to offer. Patients generally respond well to ayurvedic treatments, experiencing a reduction, and sometimes even a cessation, of their symptoms. Most patients begin to take conventional medications as soon as their diagnoses are made, so ayurvedic treatments are usually undergone alongside and/or after conventional medical approaches. Patients therefore tend to experience ayurveda once their conditions have progressed. Despite this, much can be done to minimize conditions' symptoms and control their progress. Ayurveda can help improve patients' symptoms by reducing their cortisone and analgesic usage, thereby enhancing their quality of life.

The public constantly seeks out new health care approaches. In this situation, ayurveda is an easy target for bogus health claims. Many of the available books are inauthentic-a product of unqualified authors' ideas and fantasies. Short-term courses similarly vary greatly in the quality of the teaching provided and the qualifications thereby obtained. While ayurveda is becoming increasingly popular, which is a positive development, care must be taken against its mismanagement, especially given the vast array of spurious "ayurvedic" products currently on the market.

Concepts Underpinning Ayurvedic Medicine

Traditional Indian medicine, or ayurveda, is based on a traditional medical system, in the same way as traditional Chinese medicine, with both being developed in their respective geographic regions. Ayurvedic practice is around 3000 years old, with a long history of managing disease. The 3 basic principles, called doshas (vata, pitta, and kapha), are derived from 5 elements of Indian philosophy. Ayurveda's doshas can be identified as regulatory control factors for fundamental physiologic processes in living systems that maintain their identity throughout biologic history: vata and its subdoshas regulating input/output processes and motion; pitta and its subdoshas regulating throughput, turnover, and hence energy; and kapha and its subdoshas regulating storage, structure, and lubrication.

Factors such as food, activity, the climate and stress can, however, disrupt or destroy these functions. Ayurveda seeks to normalize body functions with varied techniques including advice on food and activity, internal herbal preparations, purification treatments (panchakarma), and surgical methods (shalya chikitsa).

Oral administration routes play a major role in influencing individuals' doshas, via the ingestion of food, spices, and medicinal plants. These elements are influencing doshas in different ways: stabilizing, disturbing, and supporting the body's healthy state. A detailed knowledge of the action of food, spices, and medicinal plants is needed in order in to understand their potential influence fully.

Ayurvedic Medicinal Plants

Ayurveda first seeks to diagnose patients' conditions before treating them with internal preparations, diet, and habit restrictions. Plant-based preparations play a major role in the ayurvedic healing process. In broad terms, there is no substance in the world that cannot be used as a potential medicine. Traditional ayurvedic texts warn against the use of substances that are not adequately understood. Any plant, animal, or mineral substance can be incorporated into the ayurvedic pharmacopeia, but only if it is understood fully, in terms of its nomenclature, identity, properties, and applications. The texts also warn against the abuse of well-known medicines, emphasizing the point that even poisons can have medicinal properties when used appropriately, whereas the best of medicines can be harmful if improperly used. Of nearly 10 000 plants used for medicinal purposes in the Indian subcontinent, only 1200 to 1500 have been incorporated into the official ayurvedic pharmacopeia in more than 3000 years. All plants must be studied thoroughly before becoming part of the ayurvedic pharmacopeia.

Actions of Foods, Spices, and Medicinal Plants

The Role of Food

Food plays a major role in ayurvedic practice by supporting the body's healing processes. Metabolic diseases and diseases of the gastrointestinal tract are directly influenced by food. Food can also indirectly affect diseases of the skin, muscles, and joints, as well as neurological, gynecological, and psychological disease.

Infrequent consumption is unlikely to cause a problem, but frequent consumption of inappropriate foods will cause disease or worsen existing disease. Advice on food depends not only on the disease but also on the disease condition and the dosha involved. Because of this, food advice may change throughout the course of a disease, depending on the stage reached. Interactions between foods and medicines are a major issue. The advice given with regard to food must take account of the medicines prescribed, otherwise potential interactions may worsen patients' conditions.

The Action of Indian Spices

The second strongest influence on patients' doshas, after food, is spices. Many spices are strong by nature. Spices are obtained from the roots, flowers, fruits, seeds, or bark of plants or herbs. Spices are native to warm, tropical climates. Coming from woody or herbaceous plants, spices have a different active principle, which gives them specific characters.

These active principles have specific functions within the body. The phytochemicals within spices are secondary metabolites, which serve to protect the plants from damage by insects, animals, fungi, pathogens, and parasites. Before consumption, most spices are dried to degrade these chemicals. Drying also increases the resulting spices' shelf life and potency.

The action of spices within the body differs according to the ways that they are used. Spices are mostly used for their natural flavor and aroma in processing food. In addition to adding taste, some spices (cumin, ginger, coriander) also have preventative effects, aiding digestion through the production of digestive enzymes. When mixed with digestive juices, these substances aid absorption. Such spices have individual effects, their actions depending on the constitution of the person concerned and their disease.

Indian food is becoming increasingly popular and is often seen as healthy. From an ayurvedic perspective, healthy food is food that is used in a healthy way. From this viewpoint, spicy and pungent foods are not necessarily "good" foods. Indian food is not automatically ayurvedic, because the latter insists that individual's health situation be taken into account. People with gastric hyperacidity or gastric or intestinal inflammation may find their health worsened by exposure to some Indian spices.

Ayurvedic Medicinal Plants

Approximately 90% of ayurvedic preparations are plant based. Ayurvedic plants have a stronger action on the body than either food or spices. Such actions enable the plant to reverse pathophysiological processes and stabilize the doshas. For this reason, one should use such plants with caution. Classical ayurvedic preparations, made from such plants, are known as "yoga" in Sanskrit. Yogas have developed following years' of practical experience combining plants to get the optimal effect.

Polyherbal combinations have also proven lastingly effective than single herbs. In ayurveda, most of the classical preparations are polyherbal, with a combination of 3 to 30 plants involved. These constituents are combined accurately, in such a way that the formula is balanced and reproducible. One or two of the plants in these combinations will be active and the others will play a supporting role. The supporting herbs will each have different actions, acting as catalysts to help proper absorption, transportation, and to reduce toxicity. If an ideal combination is delivered, then the result can be excellent, but such outcomes are based on thorough plant knowledge.

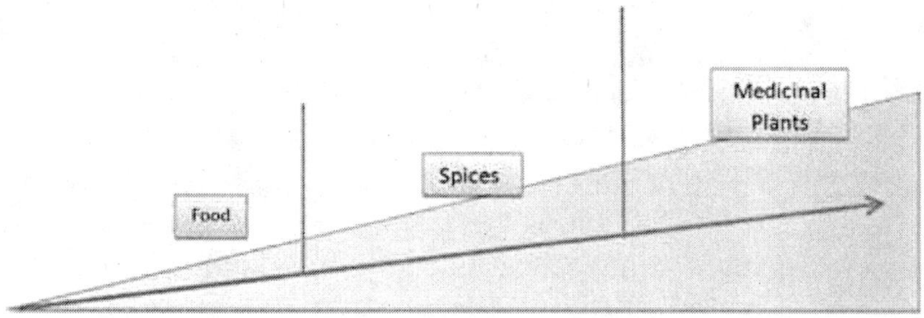

Figure: *Concept of the increasingly intense influence of food, spices, and medicinal plants on the body.*

Ayurvedic Plants: Misuse and Self-Medication

While societal use of ayurvedic plants and Indian spices is commonplace, without ill effect, the use of more concentrated products made from single plants, often in the form of teas or tablets, is of more concern. Ayurvedic plants are generally seen as safe and free from side effects, which is not always true.

Ayurveda Branding as Teas

Classified as vata, pitta, or kapha teas, these products are marketed for their supposed beneficial effects on individuals' corresponding dosha problems. From an ayurvedic perspective, diseases certainly seem to arise from the improper function of these 3 doshas. Ancient texts list 80 vata diseases, 40 pitta diseases, and 20 kapha diseases. The more recent recognition of new diseases should make this number even higher. The complex pathophysiology of modern disease means that the symptoms that individuals experience are always a combination of 2 or 3 doshas. This complexity means that ayurvedic preparations must be equally complex. In the classics, 63 major combinations of doshas have been listed and this complexity needs to be considered to elicit therapeutic effects. For example, migraine, low back pain, or arthritis of the knee can occur from vata imbalance. These diseases have different pathophysiological mechanisms, manifesting themselves in different body regions.

To treat these conditions, drugs that act on the selected region are chosen. Compounds made from groups of plants are then combined in prescribed ways to achieve the desired effects. This means that undifferentiated concepts of vata-, pitta-, and kapha-related teas are nonsensical. Most of the above-mentioned teas contain a variety of nonspecific, commonly used, spices. While these teas can certainly be consumed for refreshment purposes, they will not cure disease.

Herbal Tea

Figure: *Steeping "Hibiscus Delight", made from hibiscus flowers, rose hips, orange peel, green tea, and red raspberry leaf*

Herbal teas, also known as herbal infusions and less commonly called tisanes are beverages made from the infusion or decoction of herbs, spices, or other plant material in hot water. Oftentimes herb tea, or the plain term tea, is used as a reference to all sorts of herbal teas. Many herbs are used in herbal medicine. Some herbal blends contain actual tea (e.g., the Indian classic masala chai).

The term "herbal" tea is often used in contrast to traditionally caffeinated teas (e.g., black, green, white, yellow, oolong), which are prepared from the cured leaves of the tea plant, Camellia sinensis. Unlike true teas (which are also available decaffeinated), most tisanes do not naturally contain caffeine. There are a number of plants, however, that do contain caffeine or another stimulant, like theobromine, cocaine or ephedrine. Some have the opposite effect, acting as a sedative. Some common infusions have specific names such as mate (yerba mate) and rooibos (red bush).

***Figure:** erbal tea in a glass teapot and cup*

Composition: Herbal teas can be made with fresh or dried flowers, fruit, leaves, seeds or roots. They are made by pouring boiling water over the plant parts and letting them steep for a few minutes. The herbal tea is then strained, sweetened if desired, and served. Many companies produce herbal tea bags for such infusions.

Varieties: While varieties of tisanes can be made from any edible plant material, below is a list of those commonly used for such:

- Anise tea, made from either the seeds or the leaves
- Asiatic penny-wort leaf, in South Asia and Southeast Asia
- Artichoke tea
- Bael fruit tea
- Bee balm
- Boldo, used in South America
- Burdock; the seeds, leaves, and roots have been used
- Cannabis tea, used in the preparation of bhang
- Caraway, tea made from the seeds
- Catnip, tea used as a relaxant, sedative, and to calm
- Chamomile

- Che dang, bitter tea made from Ilex causue leaves
- Chinese knotweed tea
- Chrysanthemum tea, made from dried flowers
- Cinnamon
- Clover tea, made from the blossoms
- Coca tea, infusion made from coca leaves. Contains trace amounts of cocaine and similar alkaloids. In some countries where coca is illegal, products marketed as "coca tea" are supposed to be decocainized, i.e., the pharmacologically active components have been removed from the leaf using the same chemicals as manufacturing cocaine.
- Cacao bean tea
- Hot cocoa is not a herbal tea because the plant material is dissolved in water (or milk), but cacao bean can be used to make a tea.
- Coffee-leaf tea, coffee fruit tea, and coffee blossom tea are herbal teas made using the leaves, fruits and flowers of the coffee plant
- Cerasse, bitter Jamaican herb
- Citrus peel, including bergamot, lemon and orange peel
- Dandelion coffee
- Dill tea
- Dried lime tea, made from dried limes common in western Asia
- Echinacea tea
- Elderberry
- European mistletoe (Viscum album), (steep in cold water for 2-6 hours)
- Essiac tea, blended herbal tea
- Fennel
- Gentian
- Ginger root can be made into herbal tea, known in the Philippines as salabat
- Ginseng, a common tea in China and Korea, commonly used as a stimulant and as a caffeine substitute
- Goji

- Guayusa, caffeinated tree of the holly genus, native to the Amazon rainforest.
- Hawthorn
- Hibiscus (often blended with rose hip), a common tea in the Middle East or Asia
- Honeybush, similar to rooibos and grows in a nearby area of South Africa, but tastes slightly sweeter. Has a low tannin content, no caffeine.
- Horehound
- Houttuynia
- Hydrangea tea, dried leaves of hydrangeas; considerable care must be taken because most species contain a toxin. The "safe" hydrangeas belong to the Hydrangea serrata Amacha ("sweet tea") cultivar group.
- Jiaogulan (also known as xiancao or "poor man's ginseng")
- Kapor tea, dried leaves of fireweed
- Kava root, from the South Pacific, can be made into a tea for stomach upsets and other minor illnesses. The traditional form is a water-based suspension of kava roots.
- Kratom, dried leaves of the kratom tree.
- Kuzuyu, a thick white Japanese tea made by adding kudzu flour to hot water
- Labrador tea, made from the shrub by the same name, found in the northern part of North America
- Lemon balm
- Lemon and ginger tea
- Lemongrass
- Luo han guo
- Licorice root
- Lime blossom, dried flowers of the lime tree (tilia in Latin).
- Mate South American caffeinated tea made from yerba mate
- Mint (mint tea), especially peppermint (also mixed with green tea)
- Maghrebi mint tea
- Meadowsweet herb

- Korean mint tea
- Mound of termites tea in Merauke
- Moringa
- Mountain tea, common in the Balkans and other areas of the Mediterranean region. Made from a variety of the Sideritis syriaca plant which grows in warm climates above 3,000 feet. Records of its use date back 2,000 years.
- Neem leaf
- Nettle leaf
- New Jersey tea
- Noni tea
- Oksusu cha, traditional roasted corn tea found in Korea
- Olive leaf tea
- Oregano tea
- Osmanthus tea, dried flowers of the sweet olive tree, are used alone or blended with tea leaves in China.
- Pandan tea
- Patchouli tea
- Pennyroyal leaf, an abortifacient
- Pine tea, or tallstrunt, made from needles of pine trees
- Poppy tea, consumed for its sedative and analgesic properties
- Qishr, Yemeni drink with coffee husks and ginger
- Red clover tea
- Red raspberry leaf
- Barley tea, East Asian drink with roasted barley
- Roasted wheat, used in Postum, a coffee substitute
- Rooibos (red bush), a reddish plant used to make an infusion and grown in South Africa. In the US it is sometimes called red tea. It has many of the antioxidant characteristics of green tea, but because it does not come from tea leaves, it has no caffeine.
- Rose hip (often blended with hibiscus)
- Roselle petals (species of hibiscus; known by other names including bissau and dah), consumed in the Sahel and elsewhere
- Rosemary

- Sagebrush, California sagebrush
- Sage
- Sakurayu, Japanese herbal tea made with pickled cherry blossom petals
- Salvia
- Sassafras roots were steeped to make tea and were used in the flavoring of root beer until being banned by the FDA.
- Scorched rice, known as hyeonmi cha in Korea
- Skullcap
- Shallot peel tea from Kalimantan
- Serendib (tea), tea from Sri Lanka
- Sobacha
- Spearmint
- Spicebush (Lindera benzoin) leaves used to make a tea by some native peoples of eastern North America
- Spruce tea, made from needles of spruce trees
- Staghorn sumac, fruit can be made into a lemonade
- Stevia, can be used to make herbal tea, or as a sweetener in other beverages
- St. John's wort
- Thyme, contains thymol
- Tulsi, or holy basil
- Turmeric tea
- Uncaria tomentosa, commonly known as cat's claw
- Valerian is used as a sedative.
- Verbena (vervain)
- Wax gourd in East Asia and Southeast Asia.
- Wong Lo Kat, a recipe for herbal tea from Guangdong, China since the Qing Dynasty
- Woodruff
- Yarrow

Health risks: While most herbal teas are safe for regular consumption, some herbs have toxic or allergenic effects. Among the greatest causes of concern are:

- Comfrey, which contains alkaloids which may be harmful to the liver from chronic use, and particularly is not recommended during pregnancy or when prescription drugs are used; comfrey is not recommended for oral use.
- Lobelia, which contains alkaloids and has traditional medicine uses for smoking cessation, may cause nausea, vomiting, or dizziness at high doses.

Herbal teas can also have different effects from person to person, and this is further compounded by the problem of potential misidentification. The deadly foxglove, for example, can be mistaken for the much more benign (but still relatively toxic to the liver) comfrey. Care must be taken not to use any poisonous plants.

The US does not require herbal teas to have any evidence concerning their efficacy, but does treat them technically as food products and require that they be safe for consumption.

Fruit or fruit-flavored tea is usually acidic and thus may contribute to erosion of tooth enamel.

Adverse herb drug interactions: Some phytochemicals found in herbs and fruits can adversely interact with others and over the counter or prescription medications, among other ways by affecting their metabolism by the body.

Herbs and fruits that inhibit or induce the body's Cytochrome P450 enzyme complex function can either cause the drug to be dangerously ineffective, or increase its effective absorbed dose to potentially toxic levels, respectively. Best known examples of adverse herb drug interactions are grapefruit or St John's wort, contraindicated for several medications including Paxlovid and oral contraceptives, but other herbs also affect the CYP enzyme family, showing herb drug interactions.

Contamination: Depending on the source of the herbal ingredients, herbal teas, like any crop, may be contaminated with pesticides or heavy metals. According to Naithani & Kakkar (2004), "all herbal preparations should be checked for toxic chemical residues to allay consumer fears of exposure to known neuro-toxicant pesticides and to aid in promoting global acceptance of these products".

During pregnancy: In addition to the issues mentioned above which are toxic to all people, several medicinal herbs are considered abortifacients, and if consumed by a pregnant individual could cause miscarriage. These include common ingredients like nutmeg, mace, papaya, bitter melon, verbena, saffron, slippery elm, and possibly pomegranate. It also includes more obscure herbs, like mugwort, rue, pennyroyal, wild carrot, blue cohosh, tansy, and savin.

The Rationale for Ayurvedic Formulations and Actions

Ayurvedic products are mainly composed of herbal combinations. In certain parts of India, ayurvedic formulations also contain heavy metals. Traditional texts such as Charaka Samhitha, Susrutha Samhitha, and Ashtanga Samgraha do not describe the use of heavy metals-clearly this is a later development. Heavy metals are toxic and are not permitted at any level in modern pharmaceuticals. By contrast, in ayurvedic preparations, metals may be added for their perceived therapeutic effects to form rasausadhies (herbo-bio-mineral metallic preparations). In ayurveda, the use of metals and minerals as medicines have been recommended only after purification (shodhana) and that with recommended low dose, with specific vehicle (anupana), for a particular period and obeying dos and donts in relation to diet, activities, and environment. Ayurveda has also described the toxic effect, complications, and diseases caused due to ingestion of raw or improperly processed metallic preparations. Researches have revealed the metal content in a number of ayurvedic rasausadhies and toxicity cases due to ayurvedic herbal consumptions have been reported throughout the last decade, especially those sold through the Internet. Such metals are not found in pure herbal ayurvedic preparations.

Traditional ayurvedic texts note that quality-assured ayurvedic compounds are strong and potent enough to combat disease. The parts of the plants chosen for use are also important. Depending on the plants concerned, and the medical combinations involved, the leaves, flowers, seeds, bark, roots, or skin of the plant may be chosen. The particular combination chosen results from extensive practical experience of the constituents needed to achieve the maximal effect. The mechanisms by which polyherbal drugs and their extracts act differ in many respects from the actions of single substances or synthetic drugs.

Polyherbalism has its roots in the earliest texts of ayurveda like Caraka Samhita, Susrutha Samhitha, Ashtanga Hrudaya, which systematizes the pharmaceutical procedures. The traditional Ayurvedic text Sarangdhar Samhita, which dates from 1300 AD, highlights the concept of polyherbalism in this ancient medical system. Most ayurvedic formulations are polyherbal. While the active phytochemical constituents of individual plants are well established, they are usually present only in minute amounts and are, thus, insufficient to achieve the desired therapeutic effects. Recent research shows that combining plants of varying potency enhances their effect, both when compared to individual plant use and also to the sum of their individual effect. This phenomenon is known as synergy. Some pharmacological actions, from the active constituents of some herbs, have proven to be significant only when potentiated by those of other plants, but are not evident when used alone. Two mechanisms have been proposed for these actions: pharmacokinetic synergy and pharmacodynamic synergy. The former is based on herbs' perceived ability to facilitate the absorption, distribution, metabolism, and elimination of other herbs. The latter concerns the synergistic effect of active constituents with similar therapeutic actions targeting similar receptors or physiological systems. Most diseases are caused by a multiplicity of factors, leading to both visible and invisible symptoms. A combination of herbs may act on multiple targets at the same time to provide thorough relief.

There is a misconception that ayurvedic preparations, being natural, are always safe. This is untrue. Charaka Samhita notes that ayurvedic medicines have adverse effects when prepared and/or used inappropriately. Ayurvedic Pharmacopoeia of India sets standards of drugs/ingredients mentioned in different formulations of Ayurvedic Formulary of India. There are also 56 referral texts described under the Drugs and Cosmetics Act. Apart from these, there have been several other ayurvedic texts written during 1000 BC to 19th century. The numbers of medicinal plants have gradually increased from the Vedic period to modern era inducting more number of indigenous medicinal plants as well as exotic plants. The Charaka Samhita stresses the factors to be considered when selecting formulations' constituents, including plants' habitat, the season in which they grow, the prevailing harvesting conditions, the selected method of storage, and the chosen method of pharmaceutical processing. However, herbs are natural materials, and their constituents may vary due to differing geographical locations, climatic conditions, environmental hazards, harvesting methods, and collection protocols. Such factors make it difficult to standardize or reproduce the quality of the end product.

The concept of bioavailability is broadly defined as the absorption and utilization of a nutrient. The degree and quantity of penetration of a herbal drug, or its active ingredients, is determined by its bioavailability. Bioavailability can depend on the chemical complexity of an herb, due to the synergistic and antagonistic actions of its constituents, in promoting absorption. A drug's hydrophobic properties determine its ability to cross the luminal wall, as do the gut microflora, patients' liver function, and the chemical modifications made by the herbal constituents. Herbal drugs must cross the blood-brain barrier if they are to affect the central nervous system, but there is a dearth of literature on Indian herbs, especially ones with potential antioxidant-stimulating properties, on this important topic.

The synergistic interactions of herbs can play an important role in their bioavailability. Long pepper, black pepper, and ginger can all increase the bioavailability of some compounds. Person-to-person variation in gut micro flora and hepatic activity also play a role in systemic absorption.

Methods of Drug Administration in Ayurveda

Drug administration methods differ in ayurveda and conventional modern medicine. In the latter, most medications are synthetic; their administration influences the stomach and intestine. Most conventional medications are thus administered after food. Ayurveda has narrated timings of medication according to the patient's nature, disease, and the condition of disease. Ayurvedic preparations are also administered on empty stomach. As the latter preparations are plant-based, they are slow-acting. The absorption of ayurvedic plant preparations occurs as part of normal metabolism.

Ayurvedic preparations must be broken down for digestion in the gastrointestinal tract and has to get digested in the stomach and intestine, before getting into blood circulation and before reaching the target organ and bring about treatment action. For ayurvedic physicians, patients' digestive strength is thus important. Ayurvedic preparations must undergo many digestive processes before being absorbed as part of normal metabolism. Ayurvedic physicians therefore analyze their patients' metabolic state before treatment, as a matter of course, aiming for optimal stability and the least gastrointestinal damage.

Ayurvedic medicines exist in different formats, including decoctions, powders, pastes, fermented products, tablets, and medicinal butters (ghees). The formats used, whether liquids, pastes or tablets, are linked to preparations' efficacy. If the format is changed, then the desired effect may be lost and potential side effects created. The parts of the plants used as ingredients are also very important. Sometimes, ayurvedic preparations are administered alongside other natural products, such as honey, salt, or milk, to get specific actions, according to the disease condition experienced. In Sanskrit, these natural products are termed Anupana. These natural products also help minimize any side effects. The timing of ayurveda preparations also varies according to the specific disease and its condition.

Most Used Ayurvedic Herbs and Their Benefits

As we can not scrub, rub or cleanse our inner body as our outer, we must maintain a healthy nutrition intake. Ayurvedic herbs make one simple yet effective mode of nutrition for optimum health in humans.

Whether one aims at increasing their Ayurvedic antioxidants intake or is trying to tackle concerns such as inflammation of joints, certain Ayurvedic herbs can have a relieving effect against certain health concerns.

In this blog, we will discuss many Ayurvedic herbs that are widely popular, used, and appreciated for their health benefits. Perhaps our readers may find a natural route to a healthier life.

A Brief History of Ayurvedic Herbs and their Significance

Ayurvedic healingis one of the oldest modes of medication and healing. For over 5,000 years, Ayurveda has been helping individuals build and maintain good mental and positive health through various methods such as Yoga, meditation, and a wide range of herbs, offering a wide range of health benefits. Nearly all the herbal recipes and Ayurvedic remedies we use in the present day are an evolution or a revision of the ancient authentic Ayurvedic recipes. For thousands of years, this knowledge of herbs and Ayurveda has enabled Ayurvedic practitioners and doctors (Vaidyas) to help individuals dealing with health co

Ashwagandha

From improving digestion to boosting energy and helping maintain healthy blood sugar levels, Ashwagandha can do it all. Kerala Ayurveda offers several Ashwagandha based products that can help reap the following benefits of Ashwagandha easily:

- Can help enhance memory and cognition.
- Eases stress.

- Supports healthy digestion and metabolism.

***Figure:** f you were raised in the Indian subcontinent, or if your family is Indian, you might have grown up hearing from your grandparents how Ashwagandha can help lead a healthier life.*

- It helps to maintain a healthy immune system and promotes muscle strength to support the comfortable joint movement.
- It is considered as the best herb for calming Vata.

Triphala

***Figure:** riphala is another one of the immensely popular herbs in the Indian subcontinent. For thousands of years, people have been using it for easing constipation, improving gut health and for a bunch of other benefits.*

Here's a list of benefits that one can reap by consuming Triphala, in its bitter natural form, or as an easier and more pleasant Triphala Sparkles or tablets:

- Triphala can help improve the digestion process and improve gut health.
- It is a natural laxative that can help reduce constipation, while improving the consistency of bowel movements
- As Triphala improves metabolism, it can be good for weight management.

- Triphala is a rich source of antioxidants that help fight free radicals and oxidative stress
- It preserves the health and beauty of hair and skin.

Brahmi

***Figure:** rahmi is often known for its benefits on brain health. However, that doesn't explain everything about how it can be helpful. Here's a more comprehensive list of benefits:*

- Brahmi can help enhance memory, increase intelligence, and boost concentration.
- Brahmi can decrease the cortisol levels in the body and reduces stress and anxiety
- Brahmi supplements are cooling and relaxing and can make excellent supplements for optimising Pitta.
- It can help calm the Vata in the mind and can help eliminate excess Kapha in the body.
- It is one of the top Ayurvedic herbs to help reduce stress.

Manjistha

***Figure:** Manjistha is one of the perennial climber Ayurvedic plants offering several health benefits such as purification of the blood, elimination of wastes from the body, regulating the immune system, and more. For a clearer understanding, here's a comprehensive list of Manjistha's sought after benefits:*

- It can help purify the blood.
- It is a natural detox agent that can help cleanse the body by eliminating toxins and waste.
- Manjistha can act as an active lymph mover, which can also help reduce excessive Pitta levels and break up the congested Kapha.
- Manjistha can be one of the best Ayurvedic herbs that can cleanse the liver, ensure healthy kidney function, and clear acne.

Precautions

While Ayurvedic herbs are naturally grown and maintained through organic means, they are safe to consume in prescribed quantities.

Most herbal products you may use or consume may never counter good health. However, excessive consumption/usage is not advised.

For optimum results, and a healthy body, prescribed quantities should not be exceeded, and a professional Ayurvedic doctor's prescription is advisable before starting dosage.

Also, all herbal skincare products and massage oils are composed of various herbs, a few (or more) of which may have an allergic reaction to specific skin types. To rule out the risk of allergy, always start with a patch test, and continue using only if there's no reaction.

Key Takeaways

Here's a look back at what we learned in this blog:

- Ayurvedic healing methods have been helping individuals lead a healthy life for thousands of years
- Various Ayurvedic herbs have frequently been used for preparing effective Ayurvedic recipes and remedies to manage certain health conditions in humans.
- Some of the most powerful Ayurvedic herbs can help manage digestive concerns, hair care problems, weight management challenges, and other healthcare matters.
- Even though Ayurvedic herbs are grown naturally and do not have specific side effects, it's advisable to consume them only in moderation and as prescribed.

Ayurvedic Pharmacopoeia of India

The Ayurvedic Pharmacopoeia of India (API) is a unique book of standards describing the quality, purity and strength of selected drugs that are manufactured, distributed, and sold by the licensed manufacturers in pan India.

It is developed in two parts; the part one comprises of mono-monographs of medicinal substances of natural origin and part two includes selected compound formulations sourced from the schedule - I books under the Drugs and Cosmetics Act, 1940 comprising of popular Ayurvedic classics of different period of times. The first part of the Ayurvedic Formulary of India was published in 1978 and thereafter, the Ayurvedic Pharmacopoeia of India (mono-monograph) Part-I, Vol. I was published in the year 1989 and subsequently, the other volumes were published with their legalized status under Drugs and Cosmetics Act, 1940.

The Ayurvedic Pharmacopoeia of India (API) is a legalized document of the Government of India describing the quality, purity and strength of selected drugs that are manufactured, distributed, and sold by the licensed manufacturers in pan India. Once a Pharmacopoeia, or an article in it, has been approved by the body invested with such authority (The Ayurvedic Pharmacopoeia Committee (APC)) compliance with the quality prescribed therein becomes mandatory under the Drugs and Cosmetics Act 1940 (Anonymous, 1989; Anonymous, 2012).

Since 2010, the scientific body of the Pharmacopoeia Commission of Indian Medicine (PCIM) now Pharmacopoeia Commission of Indian Medicine & Homeopathy (PCIM&H) is an apex body of Ministry of AYUSH, Government of India is guiding APC for quality standards of Ayurvedic drugs.

The API is presented in two parts; the part-I comprise of monographs of selected compound formulations of natural origin find place in the Ayurvedic Formulary of India and part-II includes monographs on single drugs sourced from the schedule-1 books under the Drugs and cosmetics Act, 1940 comprising of popular Ayurvedic classics of different period of time (Malik, 2003). The official formulary of Ayurveda part-I was published in the year 1978 by Government of India, Ministry of Health and Family Planning, Department of Health. Thereafter, the Ayurvedic Pharmacopoeia of India (Mono-Monograph) Part-I, Volume I was published in the year 1989.

Subsequently, through a gazette notification, it was legalized under Drugs and Cosmetics Act, 1940 from 15.09.1964. Up till now 976 compound formulations of Ayurveda and 540 mono-monographs of plant, animal and minerals (including metals) origin has been published with their legalized status. Apart from that upgraded monographs on 15 source plants, their powders, aqueous and hydro-alcoholic extracts for ensuring their quality has been separately published in recent past.

Genesis And Overview : Background The science of Ayurveda has been in vogue in this country from the earliest times and serving the medical needs of most of our people. These systems were developed by ancient scholars on the basis of their own philosophy, oriental methodologies and practices prevalent in that era and have popularised and almost completed it in all aspects as a system of medicine. The advent of foreign invasions and cross cultural interaction had definite impact on these systems. The beginning of twentieth century saw efforts to revive these systems. The members of the Imperial Legislative Council got the resolution of investigations and recognition of these systems was accepted in the year 1916. The Indian National Congress also passed similar resolution in 1920. This led to establishment to number of colleges of Ayurveda.

In the post-independence era, the efforts to develop research gained momentum. As per recommendation of the various Committees, grant-in-aid projects were sanctioned to selected colleges. The Central Council for Ayurvedic Research as an Advisory body was established in 1962 and finally the Central Council for Research in Indian medicine & Homoeopathy (CCRIM&H) was established in 1969. This Council initiated research programmes in the Indian systems of Medicine & Homoeopathy in different parts of the country and started coordination at the National level for the first time.

The Central Council for Research in Ayurveda & Siddha (CCRAS), an apex body for the formulation, coordination and development of research in Ayurveda & Siddha on scientific lines was established in March 1978 after reorganization of CCRIM&H. The Minister of Health & Family Welfare is the President of the Governing Body of the Council while the Joint Secretary chairs the Standing Finance Committee. The Scientific /Research Programmes are supervised by the respective Scientific Advisory Committee chaired by eminent scholars of the system. The Central Council for Research in Ayurvedic Sciences is a Registered Society under Societies Registration Act XXI of 1860 on 29.07.2011 (Formerly Registered as Central Council for Research in Ayurveda and Siddha on 30th March, 1978).

Research areas: The Central Council for Research in Ayurvedic sciences (CCRAS), an autonomous body under Ministry of AYUSH, Govt, of India is apex body in India for undertaking, coordinating, formulating, developing and promoting research on scientific lines in Ayurvedic sciences. The activities are carried out through its 30 Institutes/Centres/Units located all over India and also through collaborative studies with various Universities, Hospitals and Institutes.

The research activities of the Council include Medicinal Plant Research (Medico-ethno Botanical Survey, Pharmacognosy and Tissue Culture), Drug Standardization, Pharmacological Research, Clinical Research, Literary Research & Documentation. Besides this, Council has conducting outreach activities viz. Tribal Health Care Research Programme, Ayurveda Mobile Health Care programme, Swasthya Rakshan Programme and National Programme for Prevention and control of Cancer, Diabetes, Cardiovascular Diseases and Stroke (NPCDCS).

Objectives

1. The formulation of aims and patterns of research on scientific lines in Ayurvedic sciences.
2. To undertake any research or other programmes in Ayurvedic sciences.
3. The prosecution of and assistance in research, the propagation of knowledge and experimental measures generally in connection with the causation, mode of spread and prevention of diseases.
4. To initiate, aid, develop and co-ordinate scientific research in different aspects, fundamental and applied of Ayurvedic sciences and to promote and assist institutions of research for the study of diseases, their prevention, causation and remedy.
5. To finance enquiries and researches for the furtherance of objects of the Central Council.
6. To exchange information with other institutions, associations and societies interested in the objects similar to those of the Central Council and specially in observation and study of diseases in East and in India in particular.

7. To prepare, print, publish and exhibit any papers, posters, pamphlets, periodicals and books for furtherance of the objects of the Central Council and contribute to such literature.
8. To issue appeals and make applications for money and funds in furtherance of the objects of the Central Council and to accept for the aforesaid purpose gifts, donations and subscriptions of cash and securities and of any property whether movable or immovable.
9. To borrow or raise monies with or without security or on security mortgage charge, hypothecation or pledge of all or any of the immovable or movable properties belonging to the Central Council or in any other manner whatsoever.
10. To invest and deal with the funds and monies of the Central Council or entrusted to the Central Council not immediately required in such manner as may from time to time be determined by the Governing Body of the Central Council.
11. To permit the funds of the Central Council to be held by the Government of India.
12. To acquire and hold, whether temporarily or permanently any movable or immovable property necessary or convenient for the furtherance of the objects of the Central Council.
13. To sell, lease, mortgage and exchange, and otherwise transfer any of the properties movable or immovable of the Central Council provided prior approval of the Central Government is obtained for the transfer of immovable property.
14. To purchase, construct, maintain and alter any buildings or works necessary or convenient for the purpose of the Central Council.
15. To undertake and accept the management of any endowment or trust fund for donation, the undertaking or acceptance whereof may seem desirable.
16. To offer prizes and grant of scholarships, including travelling scholarships in furtherance of the objects of the Central Council.
17. To create administrative, technical and ministerial and other posts under the Society and to make appointments thereto in accordance with the rules and regulations of the Society.
18. To establish a provident fund and/or pension fund for the benefit of the Central Council's employees and/or their family members.

19. To do all such other lawful things either alone or in conjunction with others as the Central Council may consider necessary or as being incidental or conducive to the attainment of the above objects.
20. To undertake R & D Consultancy projects and transfer of patents on drugs and process to industry.
21. To undertake R & D projects sponsored by industries in public/ private sector.
22. To undertake international and interagency collaboration.
23. Utilization of results of research conducted and payment of share of royalties/consultancy fees to those who has contributed towards pursuit of such research.
24. To enter into arrangements with scientific agencies of other countries for exchange of scientists, study tours, training in specialized areas, conducting joint projects etc.
25. To provide technical assistance to Govt./Private agencies in matters consistent with the activities of the Council.
26. To assist Medicinal Plants Board, Government of India in achieving its objectives.
27. To constitute small Management Committees consisting of eminent Scientists/ Physicians of local areas to monitor the R & D activities and suggest remedial measures for the improvement of activities of all Central as well as Research Institutes of the Council.

Basic Chemical Research on Photochemistry

Plant produces numerous types of chemical compounds generally to prevent itself from its competitors, predators, or pathogens so phytochemicals are chemical compounds produced by plants. These phytochemicals are generally denoted by secondary metabolites. On the basis of their biosynthetic origins these secondary metabolites may be classified as flavonoids and polyphenolic compounds, terpenoids, alkaloids, glycosides, saponins and steroids etc. The activity of plant is responsible due to these metabolites. Phytochemistry plays a major role for authentication, identification and quality assessment of plant material. For a plant drug, certified reference material is essential to start the research. The preliminary analysis suggests the identification of the plant material by pharmacognostical characters or by testing of these secondary metabolites or by chromatographic procedures.

Other tests which have impact on the quality of drug are physicochemical parameters. The Council has carried out such studies since inception through its peripherial centers located across the country. Presently units located at Chennai, Kolkata, Gwalior, Cheruthuruthy and Patiala are engaged in variour activities related to drug research.

Applied Phytochemicals Research for Drug Development: Various Phytochemical Reference Standards (PRS) and metabolites present in plant ingredients resposible for various therapeutical activities may be utilized for establishing the representation of individual ingrediends in finished formulations.

The identitity and quality of the formulation is essential before taking the drugs for clinical research and other efficacy studies. Various dosages forms required for new drug development may be achieved through pharmaceutical R&D and estimation of suitable markers/ metabolites. The Council has also undertaken the work of establishing the shelf life/stability study of different classical dosages forms under Intramural Research (IMR) scheme. 3. Quality Control and Quality Assurance for Routine Research In view of the controversy in the identification of medicinal plants referred in Classics it has been considered necessary to standardize raw drug materials from plant source by using physico-chemical and phytochemistry studies. Since inception (from 1969 to 2017) multiple samples (2520 samples) of single drugs has been quality accessed for various requirements viz. Pre-clinical and clinical studies. The present trends towads commercialization and mass manufacture, there is no guarantee that the proportion of individual drugs in the required quantities is being maintained.

There is also a need to correlate the transformation of medicinal preparation in different stages by identifying certain charctersitics at particular step. Therefore, standardization of finished product is also of vital necessity to ensure complying of given data in regards to organization characteristics and chemical circumstances. Since inception (from 1969 to 2016) multiple samples (1369 samples) of the formulation/finished products has been standardized along with 356 samples were considered for analytical standardization.

Developmentof Pharmacopoeial Standards: Due to commercialisation of Ayurvedic formulations for manufacture in pharmacies a need for standards of Ayurvedic formulation was felt.

During this period upto 2007, with the publication of First Volume of Ayurvedic Pharmacopoeia of India (API) formulations, Part II the book published by the Council Pharamcopoeial Standards for Ayurvedic Formulations was used as a book of standards. In this book the work done by Captain Srinivasamurthy Research Institute for Ayurvedia, Madras; Department of Pharmaceutical Chemistry, Gujarat Ayurveda University, Jamnagar; Deparments of Dravyaguna, IMS, Banaras Hindu University, Varanasi; Regional Research Institute, Trivendrum and Central Research Institute, New Delhi has been compiled. 431 formulations divided in 21 catagories of dosage forms were arranged in alphabetical order. Each monograph prescribed ingredients of the formulation, description of dosage forms with organo-leptic characters and physico-chemical parameters of the formulations.

Therapeutic indications and uses are also reported in each monograph. Details regarding definition, general method for preparation of different dosage forms and charcteritics were also recorded as a chapter. A small note on guidelines to be followed in the use of the standards and general principle to be followed in prescribing standards were also enclosed in the book. Method followed in standardization the proceedures covering volumateric, gravimetric and other types of determinations were also included in the book. This book is still used by the industry and academics as a guide book of standads because standards of certain number of formulation included in this book are not available in Ayuvedic Pharmacopoeia of India (API).

Contributions to Ayurvedic Pharmacopoeiaand Formulary: Considerable work has been done by CCRAS in evalualution of Pharmacopoeia and Formularies. CCRAS remain members of Ayurvedic Pharmacopoeia of Committee (APC) since its beginning in 1969 to prepare and finalization the main task to bringing out Ayurvedic Pharmacopoeia in convinent instalments on single and compound formulation and Ayurvedic formularies effectively. Later on to speed up the work of development of standards of single drugs and compound formulation, Director General CCRAS was nominated as Member Secretary of APC and CCRAS declared as Secretariat for APC. After holding the position the work of API was speed up and finalized volume of standards of compound formulations (API, Part-II, Vol. I) come out in the year 2007. Presently four volumes on standards of compound formulations are in existence comprising of 202 formulations. Other important publication is the API, Part-I, Vol. VII which provide the standards on 2 1 minerals and metals. Another very precious task done was the publication of standards on extracts included in API, Part-I, Vol. VIII and IX which is highly demandable. 48 Monographs on compound formulations were contributed to Ayurvedic Pharmacopoeia of India. Details at Annexure VI and 8 formulations were developed for Siddha Pharmacopoeia of India (Annexure VII).

Drug Development Programme A. Formulation Developed By the Council

1. Ayush 64: An anti-malarial preparation(Patent No 152863 dated 28.7.1980)
2. Ayush-56 : An anti epileptic preparation (Patent No 141170 dated 28.7.1976)
3. 777 Oil: A medicated oil for Psoriasis((Patent No 166740 dated 11.9.1987)
4. Ksharsutra: A medicated thread for Ano-rectal diseases (Patent No 186243 dated 15.2.2002). 5. Ayush Ghutti: A herbomineral preparation for cough, cold, fever and diarrhoea for children.
6. Balarasayan: A herbomineral preparation for general immunity and strengthening of the body of children.
7. Ayush 82: For management of Diabetes meletaus

B. Reproductive and Child Health Care Programme (RCH):

Various classical and nonclassical formulations were developed under different programme of the Council. Seventeen Ayurvedic formulations have been developed and worked out for quality standards for the project Feasibility of introducing Indian System of Medicine (Ayurveda) in the National Reproductive and Child Health Care Programme (RCH) at the Primary Health Care (PHC) level. The formulations developed are

1. Ayush Candy 2. Ayush Ark Pudina
3. Ayush BL Oil (Bala Taila)
4. Ayush Bala Rasayana Tablet
5. Ayush PK Avleha (Panchakola avaleha)- Ayurvedic herbal compound preparation for post natal care (to enhance the process of recovery after delivery and other complications of puerperal period)
6. Ayush Bala Rakshak Leham: Ayurvedic herbal compound preparation for paediatric care

7. Ayush PG Tablet (Punarnavadi yoga): Ayurvedic herbal compound preparation for Ante natal care
8. Ayush SDM Tablet (Arogya sutika)
9. Ayush SS Granules(Payaswini)- Ayurvedic herbal compound preparation for post natal care (to enhance the quality and quantity of breast milk in mother having deficient lactation)
10. Ayush KVM syrup(Vasadi panak)- For cough and cold.
11. Ayush BC Tablet (Balamrita yoga)
12. Ayush AG Tablet (Shatamuli mandoor)-Ayurvedic herbal compound preparation for Ante natal care
13. Ayush GG Tablet (Gokshura ghanavati)
14. Ayush LND Tablet (Laksha durvadi yoga)
15. Ayush VRG Tablet (Rajahpravartan yoga)
16. Ayush KD ointment (Khadiradi malahara)
17. Ayush UT ointment (Rakshoghni malahara) C. Golden Triangle Project

The Council has Coordinated for procurement of CoA from Maharishi Ayurvedic Pharmaceutical, Noida and chemical characterization data from CSIR(IICT, Hydrabad) of eight Rasaushadhies viz. Arogyavardhini Vati, Vasantkusumakar Ras, Kajjali Yoga, Maha Yogaraja Guggulu, Mahalakshmivilas Ras, Makardhwaja, Rasa Sindoor, Rasa Manikya for preparation of technical report and paper publication.

7. New Drug Development Programme Council has undertaken the following coded/ claim drugs through new drug development for clinical research studies in IMR and collaborative mode Standardization, Pharmaceutical preparation & Shelf life study.
8. Validation of Classical Formulations CCRAS has done plenty of work in the field of validation of classical formulations through quality assurance of a number of the formulations in different dosage forms entering in clinical trials. For the purpose the Quality Control reports submitted by the pharmacy has been examined and compared with API Standards. In case where Quality Standards are not available, in-House standards of pharmacy were considered as standard. The quality standards protocols are as given in API for the dosages with safety data viz. heavy metals, pesticide residues, aflatoxins and microbial

load. Total 13 guggulu, 28 churna/kwath churna, 11 tablets/ vati/gutika, 18 taila/ghrita, 4 arishta/asava, 8 avleha and sveta parpati, apamarga kshara, bhasma has been examined. Details provided in Annexure I.

S. No.	Name of drug	Details
1.	**Ayush- QOL 2Ccapsule**	Drug for cancer patients
2.	**Ayush –Manas tab**	Drug for children with mental retardation
3.	**Ayush- Rasayana-B** capsule and **Ayush- Rasayana-A** (granules)	Drug for ageing/elderly persons.
4.	**Ayush-A tablet**	for bronchial asthama
5.	**Ayush-D tablet**	for Diabetes mellitus
6.	**Ayush-C1Oil**	for wound healing
7.	**Ayush-PJ-7**	for Dengue
8.	**Ayush K1**	(for Kidney disords)
9.	**Ayush CARCTOL-S**	anti-cancer formulation
10.	**Ayush-PE drop**	for conjuctivities
11.	**Ayush-M**	for Migraine
12.	**Ayush-SL**	for Filariasis
13.	**Bhang Leaf Capsule**	In Cancer
14.	**Novel formulation**	Antimalarial
15.	**Ayush SG**	Osteoarthritis

9. ConsultancyServices for DTL through NABL Facility and State Licensing Authority The concept of laboratory accreditation was developed to provide third party certification that a laboratory is competent to perform the specific test or type of tests. Laboartory accredation means to improve customer confidence in the test reports issued by the laboratory so that the customer accept it with confidence. The Council got NABL accredation for Captain Srinivasa Murthy Regional Ayurveda Drug Development Institute, Chennai in 2008. Besides NABL accredation this lab has authority to test drug samples from State Licencing Authority by Government of Tamil Nadu and has been declared as Drug Testing Laboratory (DTL) for ASU(Ayurveda, Siddha and Unani) drugs by Tamil Nadu Government. Since then lot of drug samples were analysed. Major 59 samples listed as table are tested for various parameters(Annexure II).

10. Academic Activities through Doctoral Research Support Captain Srinivasa Murthy Regional Ayurveda Drug Development Institute, Chennai was recognized as a centre for persuing Ph.D.by different Universities viz. > Tamil Nadu M.G.R. Univsersity, > Tamil Universtiy, Tanjavur, > Anna University,

Trichy, > SASTRA University, Tanjavur > Sri Ramachandra University, Chennai > University of Madras Total 39 scholars have been awarded Ph.D by the above mentioned Universities and four candidates are persuing their Ph.D. work. Presently the Institue is recognised by University of Madras as a research centre for Ph.D.

11. Collaboration One of the institutes of the Council- CSMDRIA, Chennai being a pioneer in the field of herbal research the Institute has collaboration with many Institutions. Out side India this Institute has collaborated with Department of Chemistry, University of Glasgow, Scotland, UK; In India the institute collaborated with the University College of Science, Kolkata and Institutions like ICMR, IGCAR, CEERI, CLRI and IIT Madras. Monographs on 95 plant drugs(raw material) have been contributed by this institute to the book "Quality Standards of Indian Medicinal Plants" in different volumes published by Indian Council for Medical Research (ICMR), New Delhi. Details provided in Annexure-IX.
12. Process Patent and Commercialisation Obtained In Chemical Technology Ten patents were granted on isolation of active principles from the plants and Council has occupied seven process patents on formulations. Ninteen process patents have been filed. Twelve technologies transferred to Industry (12)

S Patent Granted = 17 (Annexure III) S Patents Filed = 19 (Annexure IV)

S Technology Transferred to Industry = 12 (Annexure V)

Phyto-Chemical Research

An Overview of CCRAS since Inception Chemical Studies

Phytochemicals has unestablished effects on health and are not scientifically defined as essential nutrients but there presence and absent makes a plant important as medicine for certain extent. Identification of phytochemicals of the plant is imperative part of drug standardization in modem era. In order to concentrate more in standardization to find out efficacy of raw drugs from plant source isolation of compounds were started from 1974 in Drug Standardization Research Unit, Junagadh. Slowly this work was taken up by other units also among them the most important is discovery of vicolides from Vicoa indica carried out by CSMDRIA, Chennai. A number of vicolides have been isolated from this plant through a lead from ethnomedical survey. These phyto-chemistry studies gave lead for development of many combination drugs. Ayush 64, Ayush 56 and Ayush 82 are the successful combination prescribed for malaria, epilepsy and diabetes.

These all products have been commercialized by the Council and first two are Council's patented products. Many new compounds along with active compounds were isolated from 512 samples o f392 Ayuvedic plants. The volume of work undertaken in the field of medicinal plants is too large allocation and personel engaged in this field are minimal and fund is very small. Therefore, the Council has planed time bound programmes and makes co-ordinated efforts with other agencies so that fruitful results can be produced. Council concentrated efforts on the following line

1. To conduct research on those plants which are used in these systems but no significant work has been conducted so far on these plants by any agency.
2. To search and identify those medicinal plants which are not known.
3. To conduct research on those plants which are used in other systems of medicine but not being used in Ayurveda.
4. To work on some of the plants which not at all used as medicinal plants in any systems of medicine but may lead to cure new diseases like AIDS, Cancer etc. and also to explore those plants which are known in folk-lores curing various ailments.

Drug Standardization and Quality Assurance and Contribution to Development of Ayurvedeic Pharmacopeia

Standardization is an essential step to ensure the quality of Ayurvedic drugs. Confirmation of identity, quality, purity, and detection of adulterants are the major objectives of standardization. One of the prime activities of the Council is Quality assessment of the single drugs and compound formulations and their method of preparation (standard operating procedures) through its Drug Standardization units. At present Council has Drug standardization units viz. Captain Srinivasa Murthy Regional Ayurveda Drug Development Institute, Chennai (CSMRADDI) (NABL accredited lab), Central Ayurveda Research Institute for Drug Development, Kolkata (CARIDD), Central Ayurveda Research Institute for Respiratory Disorders, Patiala (CARIRD), Regional Ayurveda Research Institute for Drug

Development, Gwalior (RARIDD) and Central Ayurveda Research Institute for Neuromuscular & Musculoskeletal Disorders, Cheruthuruthy (CARIMNSD) etc. The drugs and formulations required under different projects (Coded drugs, IMR, EMR, Claim etc.) for clinical trials, pharmacological studies etc. have been analyzed for confirmation of identity and quality of drugs as per Pharmacopoeial standards/development of standards.

The quality of herbal medicines has a direct impact on their safety and efficacy. There are many control measures to evaluate the quality of Ayurvedic medicines. Evalualation of quality of Ayurvedic medicine is very complicated and difficult task as it involves many different steps, from microscopic studies to isolation of marker compounds. With the tireless initiatives of the Government of India, Central Council for Research in Ayurvedic Sciences, New Delhi (CCRAS) under the Ministry of AYUSH, has been publishing the Ayurvedic Pharmacopeia of India (API) and Ayurvedic Formulary of India (AFI), from time-to-time.

To cater the need of quality of drug by providing monographs on single drugs and compound formulations where in quality standards of the drugs discussed. In Ayurveda different classical dosages forms of Ayurvdic formulations has been described in AFI. Every dosages form has a separate protocol for evaluation of quality.

Except experts opinion of phyochemists and chemists, chemical and instrumental analysis were routinely used for analyzing drugs to confirm their authenticity. Chemistry division of CCRAS conceded study of drugs in the form of single and compound formulation. Raw materials used as an ingredient in preparation of formulation are treated as single drugs which may be of plant origin, animal origin or mineral origin. There are two types of compound formulations - containing only plant raw material and containing both plant raw drug and mineral, metal called herbo-mineral formulations.

The quality of raw materials and formulations is furnished by regular phytochemical analysis. In schematic standardization of single drugs the following parameters are being covered

1. Physical parameters include colour, appearance, odor, taste and ash. 2. Foreign matters include material linked with drug other than drug. 3. Physicochemical parameters include Total ash, acid insoluble ash, extractive values (alcohol soluble extractives and water soluble extractives), chemical assays and loss on drying etc. 4.

Chromatographic analysis was carried out using TLC/HPTLC. 5. Stability parameters for the formulations which includes physical parameters, chemical parameters, and microbiological parameters or self-life studies. 6. Microbiological parameters include total viable content, total mold count, total enterobacterial and their count. 7. Aflatoxins- B 1, B2, G 1, G2 mixtures (Aflatoxin is a product of the microbial strain Aspergillus flavus). 8. Heavy metals like Cadmium, Lead, Arsenic, Mercury, etc. 9. Pesticide residues.

For mineral and metal, emphasis is given on assay for inorganic radicals as per composition of raw material. Council has NABL accredited laboratory for accreditation work. API(Ayurvedic Pharmacopoeia of India)guidelines were opted for all the standardization work1. For the raw material of mineral & metal orgin/animal origin emphasis has been given to assay for inorganic acid or base radical. They may be either metal or non metal in nature. In these cases TLC has no role in evaluation of quality and microbial studies are to be conducted. Material and Methods: The informations available in the published monographs, technical reports and annual reports of CCRAS as well as achievements have been gathered from compilation of work done by the Council since inception. Observations and physical achievements: Exploration of Ayuvedic drugs for chemical studies and quality assessment was initiated by Central Council for Research in Ayurvedic Sciences (CCRAS) in 1969 in the form of Chemical Research Studies and Standardization Studies with an approach plan to lay down analytical values and to identify the presence or otherwise of main ingredients in the preparation. Meetings of the experts and officials engaged in the field of Standardization Studies have been convened and uniform methodology has been worked out for implementation in the Standardization Research Project of the Council. The Council considers that this approach, in time to come may prove to be full proof method to identify authenticate the single drug and preparations from the spurious and appropriately prepared ones.

The particulars of the single drugs process of manufacture, and finished products taken up under Drug Standardization Research Programme for laying down analytical values of the formulations described in classical texts including the Ayuvedic Formularies (AFIs). At present there are mainly 5 institutes involved in Standardization Studies viz. the Captain Srinivasa Murthy Regional Ayurveda Drug Development Institute, Chennai (CSMRADDI) (NABL accredited lab), Central Ayurveda Research Institute for Drug Development, Kolkata

(CARIDD), Central Ayurveda Research Institute for Respiratory Disorders, Patiala (CARIRD), Regional Ayurveda Research Institute for Drug Development, Gwalior (RARIDD) and Central Ayurveda Research Institute for Neuromuscular & Musculo-Skeletal Disorders, Cheruthuruthy (CARIMNSD) etc.

Chronological Developments: Drug Standardization Research programme has been continued through its 5 peripheral units located at Chennai, Kolkata,Patiala, Gwalior, Cheruthuruthy monitored through CCRAS, New Delhi itself from 1969 to till date. Details of the work carried out may be classified in single drug study (table 2), compound formulation (table 3).

Single Drug Study: The government of India constituted Pharmacopoeial Committee to prepare official formularies of Indian System of Medicine and Homeopathy. In view of the controversy in the identification of medicinal plants referred in Classics it has been considered necessary to standardize raw drug materials from plant source by using physico-chemical studies and decided to publish these studies in the form of monographs in pharmacopoeia. A Phamacopoeia is a book of standards. Since inception (from 1969 to 2016) 2520 samples of single drugs have been assessed for Quality.

Common Medicinal Herbs

For thousands of years, people have used herbs as medicine all over the world. In the U.S., the FDA controls the safe use of herbal supplements. But they are not as strictly controlled as prescription medicines.

It's important to understand the herbs you're using. The quality of herbs also matters. Some companies add fillers. This helps to make their herbal supplements cheaper. But they may not work as well. Or they may cause side effects. Even if something is natural, it may not be safe.

Below are common herbal medicines that research has shown to be safe and work when used right. Always tell your healthcare providers if you use any herbs or supplements. They need to know if they may cause problems when combined with other medicines you take.

Chamomile

(Flower): Chamomile is often used in the U.S. to help with anxiety and relaxation. In Europe, it's used to heal wounds and reduce inflammation and swelling. You can drink chamomile tea. Or you can use it as a compress. It's considered safe by the FDA. But it might make you feel more tired if you're taking other medicines. Be careful, as it could affect how some medicines work in your body.

Chamomile for the skin may be used to treat skin rash from radiation treatments. Chamomile in a capsule may be used to ease vomiting from chemotherapy.

Echinacea

(Leaf, stalk, root): Echinacea is most often used to treat or prevent colds, flu, and infections, and for wound healing. Many studies have looked at how well it works to prevent or shorten a cold. The results have not been clear.

Some studies do show some benefit of echinacea to help with upper respiratory infections.

Studies have shown that long-term use can affect the body's immune system. Because of this, only short-term use is advised. Check with your healthcare provider about any interactions with other medicines that you take. People allergic to plants in the daisy family may have an allergic reaction to echinacea. The daisy family includes ragweed, chrysanthemums, marigolds, and daisies.

Feverfew

(Leaf): Feverfew has been used to treat fevers. Some research has shown that feverfew can prevent migraines. It is also used to treat arthritis. If the leaves are chewed, side effects include mouth ulcers and digestive upset. Stopping feverfew suddenly may cause migraines to come back. Feverfew should not be used with NSAID medicine. These medicines may change how well feverfew works. Feverfew should not be used with warfarin or other medicines that thin the blood.

Garlic

(Cloves, root): Garlic is used in cooking. And it has proven health benefits. Garlic has been shown to fight germs, protect your heart, and reduce inflammation.

It may help lower cholesterol and blood pressure. But the results are mixed. The FDA considers garlic safe. But it can increase your risk of bleeding. It should not be used with warfarin or other medicines that thin the blood. Don't take large amounts before dental procedures or surgery. It may cause too much bleeding.

Ginger

(Root): Ginger is most known for easing nausea and motion sickness. Research suggests it may help the nausea from pregnancy and chemotherapy. Ginger is in research for use in surgery and as an anticancer agent. It has strong anti-inflammatory effects. It is also a strong antioxidant. Side effects may include bloating, gas, heartburn, and nausea.

Ginkgo

(Leaf): Ginkgo leaf extract is used for asthma, bronchitis, fatigue, and tinnitus. It is used to improve memory and to help prevent dementia. Some studies have shown it may work slightly. But how gingko works isn't fully known. Only extract from leaves should be used. Seeds have ginkgo toxin. This toxin can cause seizures. In large amounts, it can lead to death. Ginkgo may increase the risk of bleeding. Do not use it with NSAID medicines or other medicines that thin the blood. Do not use it with anticonvulsant medicines, or tricyclic antidepressants.

Ginseng

(Root): Ginseng is thought to boost energy, sex drive, and balance the body. Research is still unsure about its benefits. Side effects can include high blood pressure and fast heart rate. It's safe according to the FDA, but avoid it with certain medicines. Don't take it with warfarin, heparin, or NSAID medicines. Don't take it with estrogens, corticosteroids, or digoxin. People with diabetes should not use ginseng.

Goldenseal

(Root, rhizome): Goldenseal can help with diarrhea. It can help with eye and skin irritation. It can act as an antiseptic. It's not proven to treat colds. Use it carefully. Too much can cause irritation of the skin, mouth, and stomach. Always follow a healthcare provider's instructions. Goldenseal can be poisonous in high doses.

Milk Thistle

(Fruit): Milk thistle is used for liver problems and high cholesterol. It is also used to reduce the growth of cancer cells. Study results are not clear about its real benefits for liver disease.

Saint John's wort

(Flower, leaf): Saint John's wort can help with mild to moderate depression. Results for severe depression are not clear. It can make your skin sensitive to light in high doses. It can interact with other medicines in dangerous ways. Make sure to talk to your healthcare provider before using this herb.

Saw Palmetto

(Fruit): Saw palmetto is used to treat urine problems from an enlarged prostate. But recent studies have found it not to work for this. It can cause mild upset stomach or headaches.

Valerian

(Root) Valerian is used to treat sleep problems and to reduce anxiety. Research shows it may work as a sleep aid, but the results are mixed. Talk with your healthcare provider before taking it.

Triphala Churna

Three medicinal herbs make up Triphala (in Sanskrit, "tri" means "three" and "phala" means "fruits"). It is an antioxidant-rich herbal preparation described as a Rasayana (rejuvenator) medicine by Ayurvedic practitioners. Combining the three fruits is said to be responsible for triphala's numerous health benefits.

Triphala is made from dried fruits of three different plants: Terminalia chebula (black myrobalan), Terminalia bellerica (bastard myrobalan), and Phyllantus emblica (emblic myrobalan or Indian gooseberry). The spring-harvested fruits of Terminalia chebula are high in tannins such as gallic acid, ellagic acid, chebulic acid, chebulinic acid, chebulagic acid, neochebulinic acid, corilagin, terchebin, punicalagin, and terfavin, flavonoids (rutins, luteolin and quercetin), starches, amino acids (glutamic acid, aspartic acid, lysine, arginine and proline), Î^{2}-sitosterol, succinic acid, fructose and fatty acids.

Figure: *Chemical Composition*

The fruits of Terminalia bellerica consist of proteins and oils that include omega-3 and omega-6 fatty acids (linoleic acid). Because of its high fatty acid content, this plant can impact cholesterol levels, increasing high-density lipoprotein levels (good cholesterol) while decreasing low-density lipoprotein levels (bad cholesterol), making it effective in treating coronary artery disease. Phyllanthus emblica (amla) fruits are high in ascorbic acid i.e. vitamin C.

The high density of tannins may contribute to the overall bitterness of amla. These fruits also include punicafolin and phyllanemblinin A, phyllemblin, and other polyphenols such as gallic acid, ellagic acid, flavonoids, kaempferol.

Uses of Triphala: It is described as a tridoshic Rasayana in Ayurveda, capable of balancing and rejuvenating the three doshas that regulate human life: Vata, pitta, and Kapha. It is widely used in several disease conditions owing to its following properties:

- laxative
- anti-inflammatory
- antiviral
- Blood purifying
- analgesic
- anti-arthritic
- hypoglycemic
- anti-ageing
- antibacterial

Triphala is used to treat fatigue, oxidative stress, and infectious disorders like tuberculosis, pneumonia, AIDS, and periodontal disease, among others for headaches, dyspepsia, ascites, and leukorrhea.

Benefits of Triphala

1. Benefits of Triphala for Infections:

- Triphala and its components have demonstrated potent antimicrobial properties against a variety of microorganisms.
- Triphala churna has proven action against the human immunodeficiency virus (HIV).
- Triphala churna and triphala mashi have shown antibacterial properties against a variety of bacteria like E. coli and S. aureus.

2. Benefits of Triphala for Dental Care:

- Triphala reduced levels of chemicals which are implicated in the destruction of tissue during periodontitis.
- Triphala mouthwash was tested clinically and found to be as effective as chlorhexidine in lowering plaque scores and inhibiting Lactobacillus bacteria microbial levels.

3. Benefits of Triphala for Stress:

- Triphala supplementation has been shown to alleviate stress.
- Triphala treatment can prevent cold stress-induced behavioural and biochemical abnormalities by increasing lipid peroxidation and corticosterone levels.
- In rats, triphala protects against noise-induced alterations in antioxidant and cell-mediated immune response.

4. Benefits of Triphala for Joint:

- Triphala prevented monosodium urate crystal-induced arthritis in mice (gouty arthritis) by reducing various parameters like paw volume, lysosomal enzymes, Î²-glucuronidase lactate dehydrogenase lipid peroxidation, and the proinflammatory cytokine tumour necrosis factor-alpha, according to research.
- It might have potential use in the treatment of gout in humans, however, more studies are needed for the same.

5. Benefits of Triphala for Digestive Tract:

- Castor oil-induced diarrhoea was prevented by extracts of triphala churna powder and triphala mashi.
- The extracts had a strong antidiarrheal effect, as demonstrated by increased first defecation time, cumulative faecal weight, intestinal transit time, improved stool volume, stool frequency, stool consistency, decreased mucus level in stool, and flatulence.

6. Benefits of Triphala for Liver:

- In mice, triphala was found to be beneficial against acetaminophen-induced liver damage, but with less efficacy than silymarin.
- Triphala lowered the levels of proinflammatory cytokines and lipid peroxides while also restoring the levels of many antioxidant enzymes and reducing liver damage as seen by lower liver enzyme values.

7. Benefits of Triphala for Diabetes:

- Animal studies have demonstrated that giving the same amount of triphala and its separate ingredients to normal and alloxan-induced diabetic rats lowered serum glucose levels.
- Thus, with more research, triphala might be useful in treating diabetes in humans.

Did You Know

- Triphala has been shown to improve oral health by reducing plaque and gingivitis. source: pubmed.ncbi.nlm.nih.gov
- Triphala may help lower cholesterol levels and improve heart health. source: heart.org
- Triphala has been used in traditional medicine to treat skin conditions and promote healthy skin. source: aad.org
- Triphala has been shown to have anti-diabetic effects and may help regulate blood sugar levels. source: diabetes.org
- Triphala may help reduce inflammation in the body and alleviate symptoms of inflammatory conditions. source: arthritis.org

8. Benefits of Triphala for Obesity:

- After the treatment of mice with triphala in an anti-obesity study, their body weight was observed to be lower when compared to control animals.
- Gallic acid is a phenolic molecule found in triphala that was chosen as the bioactive marker because of its anti-obesity activity.

9. Benefits of Triphala for Heart:

- Triphala has been found to have a lipid-lowering impact on rats, with significant reductions in total cholesterol, low-density lipoprotein, very low-density lipoprotein, and free fatty acid, indicating hypocholesteremic condition.
- These properties make it cardio-protective.

10. Benefits of Triphala for Skin:

- The topical application of triphala extract aided wound healing in rats infected with a variety of bacteria, according to a study.
- Experiments revealed that the triphala ointment reduced bacterial count and promoted wound closure by increasing collagen, hexosamine, and uronic acid levels.

11. Benefits of Triphala for Radioprotective activity:

- Triphala has been proven in preclinical trials to have radioprotective properties when taken orally.
- The most effective action of triphala was seen when given before irradiation, lowering DNA damage in both blood white blood cells and spleen cells, the normalizing activity of certain enzymes like xanthine oxidase and super oxidase dismutase found in the intestine.
- This indicates that the observed effects were mediated through inhibition of oxidative damage in the cells and organs.

12. Benefits of Triphala for Immunity:

- Triphala has been shown to have potent immunomodulatory properties in a variety of animal models.
- Flavonoids, tannins, alkaloids, glycosides, saponins, and phenolic substances are thought to have immunomodulatory properties.
- Triphala treatment increased antioxidant activity and lowered corticosterone levels in animals exposed to noise stress, according to research.

13. Benefits of Triphala for Antioxidant activity:

- According to research, taking triphala boosts the activity of antioxidant enzymes which may have resulted in a considerable reduction in stomach cancers in mice.
- When rats were given triphala and were subjected to noise stress, similar results were reported.
- Such findings point to triphala's ability to act as an antioxidant and to protect against a variety of stressors and illnesses.

14. Benefits of Triphala for Eyes:

- Triphala was found to be beneficial in preventing and reducing selenite-induced cataract formation, according to a study.
- In animal trials, triphala restored antioxidant enzyme levels, resulting in a reduction in nuclear cataracts. As per Ayurveda, triphala can also help prevent blindness and near-sightedness.

15. Benefits of Triphala for Cancer:

- In cancer studies, triphala has shown killing activity on cancer cells.

- Its main component gallic acid may be responsible for stopping cancer cell growth.
- An increased concentration of triphala was found to reduce the viability of breast cancer cells while having no effect on normal breast cells.
- In breast cancer cells, triphala caused an increase in intracellular reactive oxygen species.

16. Benefits of Triphala for Aging:

- On human skin cells, triphala extract has a strong antiaging effect.
- It stimulates collagen-1 and elastin-synthesizing genes and antioxidant genes responsible for cellular antioxidants in human skin cells.
- Due to the presence of protective phytochemicals, it suppresses melanin synthesis and hyperpigmentation.

How to Use Triphala

1. Triphala churna (Powder): Haritaki, bibitaki, and amlaki are powdered to make triphala churna (powder). As per research, it is advisable to take it with ghee, honey, or milk.
2. Triphala kwatha (Decoction):It is made by combining the powder with water and boiling it. The decoction is then filtered through a clean cloth, and the filtrate can be used to treat skin conditions like erysipelas, eruptions; scrotal enlargement, colic pain, worm infestation, and urinary diseases. It is applied directly to open wounds and eyes, as well as gargled during pharyngitis.
3. Triphala taila (Oil): It is made by boiling triphala powder with oil. It is used as a gargle, snuff, an enema, and orally to treat obesity and itching.
4. Triphala masi (Ash): It's made by heating triphala powder for a long time at a low temperature in a controlled setting. Mashi/ Masi is an intermediate product containing organic and inorganic ingredients. The mashi is black and has a high carbon and oxide content. Triphala mashi, when mixed with honey, can be used to treat soft chancres and wounds.
5. Triphala gritha (in ghee or clarified butter): It is made by cooking the paste of triphala, trikatu (a herbal compound of Indian Long Pepper (Piper longum), Black Pepper (Piper

nigrum), and Ginger (Zingiber officinale) in ghee and milk, as well as grapes (Vitis vinifera), Yestamadhu (Glycyrrhiza glabra), Kutki (Picrorhiza korroa), and cardamom (Elettaria cardamom). It is frequently used to treat eye conditions like conjunctivitis, blindness, and cataracts. Triphala gritha is also used to treat jaundice, leucorrhoea, tumours, greying, and hair loss.

Precautions to Take with Triphala: Terminalia chebula: It should not be used if you have an acute cough, diarrhoea, or early-stage dysentery.

Chyavanaprash

Chyawanprash (CP) is an Ayurvedic health supplement which is made up of a super-concentrated blend of nutrient-rich herbs and minerals. It is meant to restore drained reserves of life force (ojas) and to preserve strength, stamina, and vitality, while stalling the course of aging. Chyawanprash is formulated by processing around 50 medicinal herbs and their extracts, including the prime ingredient, Amla (Indian gooseberry), which is the world's richest source of vitamin C. Chyawanprash preparation involves preparing a decoction of herbs, followed by dried extract preparation, subsequent mixture with honey, and addition of aromatic herb powders (namely clove, cardamom, and cinnamon) as standard.

The finished product has a fruit jam-like consistency, and a sweet, sour, and spicy flavor. Scientific exploration of CP is warranted to understand its therapeutic efficacy. Scattered information exploring the therapeutic potential of CP is available, and there is a need to assemble it. Thus, an effort was made to compile the scattered information from ancient Ayurvedic texts and treatises, along with ethnobotanical, ethnopharmacological, and scientifically validated literature, that highlight the role of CP in therapeutics. Citations relevant to the topic were screened.

Chyawanprash (CP) (also known as chyavanaprasha, chyavanaprash, chyavanaprasam, and chyawanaprash) comprises two lexes, "Chyawan" and "Prasha". The word Chyawan is the name of a sage, and also symbolizes 'degenerative change'. Prasha denotes a drug or foodstuff that is suitable for consumption. Indeed, CP is a comprehensive 'metabolic' tonic; it contains a variety of herbs and is used to promote health and prevent diseases. Chyawanprash is an ancient Indian formulation (a polyherbal jam), prepared according to a traditional Ayurvedic recipe, enriched with several herbs, herbal extracts, and processed minerals. Regarded by many experts as an essential health supplement, CP has been around for centuries. Chyawanprash possesses multiple health benefits and has been widely used since ancient times as a health supplement and as a medicine for enhancing immunity and longevity. Chyawanprash has been a part of every Indian's life from the day it was introduced, irrespective of sociocultural, political, and scientific factors. It was one of the most appreciated foods for its antiaging effects long before vitamins, minerals, and antioxidant supplements came into existence.

Asayana, a branch of Ayurveda, includes a number of specialized approaches aimed at prolonging life, preventing aging and diseases, eliminating degenerative processes, and promoting excellent health. Of all the Rasayana formulations enumerated during the classical and medieval periods, CP undoubtedly stands out as the most important. This formulation has made major strides as an over-the-counter product since it entered the consumer market in the 1950s. It is highly appreciated for possessing multiple health benefits and addressing the preventive, promotive, and curative aspects of health.

Chyawanprash consists of Amla/Amalaki (Phyllanthus emblica/ Indian gooseberry) pulp as a base, and this is considered to be the most effective Rasayana for sustaining homeostasis. Chyawanprash that contains Amla has a mixed taste, combining sweet, sour, bitter, pungent, and astringent qualities. On regular intake, it maintains physiological functions and rejuvenates the whole body system.

Composition: Chyawanprash is a potent antioxidant paste, prepared through the synergistic blending of around 50 herbs and spices. Chyawanprash falls, by virtue of its consistency and form of dosage, under the category of Awaleha (electuaries/herbal jams), a group of Ayurvedic formulations. Typically, CP includes four classes of herbal drugs: The Dashmula class (ten roots); the Chaturjata class (four aromatic plants); Ashtavarga (threatened medicinal herbs from the Northwest Himalayas, which are not commercially available in the modern era); and a general class (materials not belonging to the former classes). The Chyawanprash formula is described in the ancient Ayurvedic texts, namely, Ashtanga Hridayam, Charaka Samhita, Sangandhara Samhita, which are dedicated to clinical management. The dominant ingredient is Amla, a citrus fruit that is a highly renowned and potent botanical in Ayurveda.

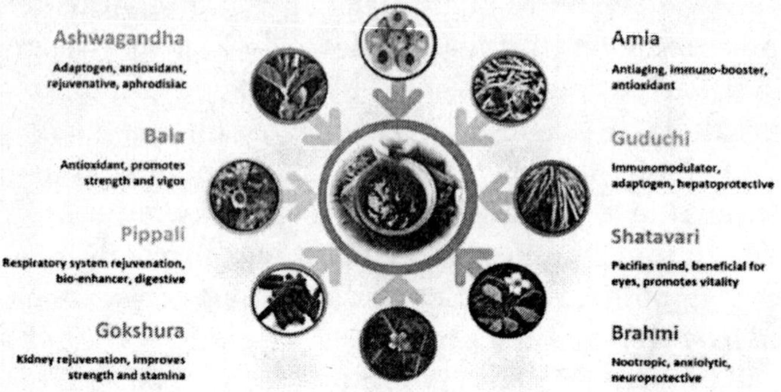

***Figure:** Each ingredient of CP is scientifically validated for its nutritive and therapeutic efficacy. All these nutrients are blended in specific quantities and subjected to unique pharmaceutical processes in such a fashion that builds a potent synergy for optimal health virtues. However, noncompliance with ancient manufacturing guidelines and deviation from the original recipe is a common malpractice in the pharma sector. The original formula is wiped out in between the practices of preparation and immoral marketing tactics to make it more presentable and appealing than the competitors' product. It will no longer be called CP if there is any change in the ingredients of the traditional formula.*

The "Missing" 8 Ingredients of Chyawanprash: The Government of India has already framed policies for the preservation, cultivation, and sustainable extraction of rare and endangered medicinal plants. Out of these, eight rare herbs that are ingredients of the "original" ancient recipe for CP are missing in commercial formulations of this traditional medicine. Commercial formulations now use substitute herbs. Among these eight, four belong to the orchid family, three are from the lily family, and one belongs to the house of gingers. These are conjointly called Ashtavarga and are said to augment the antioxidant role of Amla. Non-availability of authentic plants, confusion in vernacular names, and lack of chemical markers lead to substitution/ adulteration of Ashtavarga plants.

***Table:** Eight "missing" ingredients of CP-the Ashtavarga.*

Botanical Name	Folk Name	Family	Substitutes Used in Commercial CP
Crepidium acuminatum	*Jeevak*	Orchidaceae	*Vidaarikand* (*Ipomoea digitata*)
Malaxis muscifera	*Rishbhak*	Orchidaceae	
Habenaria intermedia	*Riddhi*	Orchidaceae	*Varahikand (Dioscorea bulbifera)*
Habenaria edgeworthii	*Vriddhi*	Orchidaceae	
Roscoea purpurea	*Kakoli*	Zingiberaceae	*Ashwagandha* (*Withania somnifera*)
Lilium polyphyllum	*Kshirkakoli*	Liliaceae	
Polygonatum verticillatum	*Meda*	Liliaceae	*Shatavari* (*Asparagus racemosus*)
Polygonatum cerhifolium	*Mahameda*	Liliaceae	

Manufacturing Process of Chyawanprash: Since the standard operating procedure (SOP) for CP preparation is not clearly narrated in ancient literature, at present, the modus operandi differs for each manufacturer. Current authoritative books of the Indian system of medicine mention the use of 500 numbers of Amla in a single lot. However, variation in Amla size and the quantity of the obtained pulp is the major limiting factor for the SOP and standardization. In historical times, Amla was mainly collected from forests. It was observed that Amla fruit collected from forests has more concentration of vitamin C than that coming from cultivated fruit [60]. The weight of 500 fresh Amla varies from 2.5-25.25 kg, as cultivated hybrid Amla has a bigger size than wild collected Amla. The Ayurvedic Formulary of India (AFI) considers the use of 2.5 kg of fresh Amla for 500 numbers and 2.4 kg sugar for its preparation [10]. If cultivated hybrid Amla is available, 500 such fruits would weigh approximately 6.5 kg.

The standard method of preparation of CP is: 50 g of each of medicinal herbs, such as Bael, Agnimanth, Kashmarya, Shyonak, Paatla, Gokshur, Sarivan, Barikateri, Kantakaari, Kakdasingi, Draaksha, Haritaki, Guduchi, Bala, Bhumyamalaki, Vasa, Jivanti, Kachur, Pushkarmul, Musta, Mudagparni, Mashaparni, Shalparni, Pithawan, Pipali, Kaknasa, Varahi, Vidaarikand, Punarnava, Neelkamal, Aguru, Chandan, Shatavar, and Asgandh, are suspended in 16 L potable water. Five-hundred Amla fruits (each fruit having a weight of around 15-20 g, total weight: 6.5 kg) are swathed in clean cotton cloth to form a bale (pottali) and submerged into the aforementioned combination of herbs.

Thereafter, the admixture is boiled until decoction is reduced to 1/4th. After taking off the pottali, seeds are removed from Amla; the remaining pulpy portion is rubbed on a clean muslin cloth, Amla fibres are separated, and Amlapishthi (wet paste of Amla pulp) is collected. Decoction is then strained, and mare is discarded. After this, Amlapishthi is mixed with Yamakadravyas (lipids: 500 g cow ghee and sesame oil each) in an iron container and fried until it gets brownish-red and the Yamaka (lipids) starts separating. Sugar syrup is then prepared by adding sugar in the herbal decoction. Fried Amlapishthi is added to this decoction syrup and heated until attainment of viscidity of two strings. Then, when the heating is stopped, Prakshepadravya (herbal powders of 150 g Vanshalochan; 100 g Pipali and Nagakesar; Elaichi, Tamalpatra and Dalchini, 10 g each) are added and stirred until a homogeneous mixture is obtained.

After cooling the mixture, 250 g honey (old, natural, pure) is uniformly mixed, and the finished product is obtained and packed in airtight sterile containers. Finally, the prepared CP is of a dark brown colour, having wet paste-like appearance and consistency.

The whole unit operating process of traditional CP preparation is depicted in Figure 2.

Figure: *Unit operating process of traditional Chyawnprash preparation. (A) Raw material collection; (B) fresh Amla taken; (C) Amla boiling in pottali suspended in herbal decoction; (D) Amla pulp separated in muslin cloth; (E) Amla pulp frying in ghee and sesame oil; (F) fried until pulp goes brownish-red and the lipids start separating; (G) Pishthi cooked in decoction syrup until the attainment of two strings viscidity; (H) upon cooling, prakshepa herbal powders and honey added and mixed homogeneously; (I) finally, prepared Chyawanprash packed in airtight sterile containers.*

Boiling of Amla fruits with decoction and the subsequent cooking processes might be inducing pH change, release of acid soluble contents, hydrolysis/cleavage of various bioactive molecules, extraction of soluble chemicals, exchange with intra/extra cellular chemicals of mixture, and several suitable phytochemical interactions to make an ideal blend of this nutraceutical. Some Ayurvedic additives, Shukti Bhasma (pearl oyster calx) 100 g, Abhraka Bhasma (mica calx) 100 g, Shringa Bhasma (deer horn calx) 100 g, Makardhawaja (preparation of red sulphide of mercury and gold) 25 g, clove 25 g and Rajata (silver foil) 75 in number, for special health benefits, are also added by some manufacturers.

Mode of Administration: Chyawanprash can be used by all age groups in every season, as its ingredients nullify the unpleasant effects of intense weather and climate or environmental change [2,61]. Chyawanprash should be taken in a quantity such that it does not interfere with hunger and appetite for food. The general dosage of CP (12-28 g) is to be taken with milk (100-250 ml) on an empty stomach in the morning.

However, it is advocated that individuals suffering from asthma/ respiratory ailments should avoid intake of milk and curd [67]. In such cases, the formulation can be administered with lukewarm water. It is recommended to consume CP within a year from the manufacturing date, as a study has indicated that chemical deterioration may occur during the storage period, resulting in loss of the therapeutic potency of CP.

Phytochemical and Quality Specifications of Chyawanprash: Chyawanprash is a semi-solid sticky paste with a brownish black appearance, chiefly having sweet and spicy odor, with a sweet and astringent feel after taste with aroma of Prakshepadravya (powder of seven herbs). The taste is predominantly governed by the flavors of honey, cow ghee (clarified butter), and Triphala (a mixture of three myrobalans), and the aroma by cow ghee and certain spices viz. sandalwood, cinnamon, and cardamom. Limited studies are available on quality testing of CP. A major part in the composition of CP is Amla, which is rich in vitamin C and polyphenolics, including flavonoids.

The phenolic compounds of CP possess antioxidant principles that are said to contribute to the rejuvenating and tonic attributes of CP. A high-performance liquid chromatography (HPLC) analysis has identified several biologically active phenolics in CP, i.e., gallic acid, protocatechuic acid, catechin, caffeic acid, vanillic acid, chlorogenic acid, syringic acid, rutin, ferulic acid, and quercitrin, which may account for its therapeutic activity. By contrast, individual pharmaceutical companies have their own in-house specifications for the quality of CP, which are not in the public domain.

The Ayurvedic Pharmacopoeia of India (API) has published a monograph on CP along with a brief method of preparation and various physicochemical and assay tests as official quality standards. These include description, identification (such as microscopy, thin layer chromatography (TLC), physicochemical parameters (loss drying, total ash, acid-insoluble ash, alcohol-soluble extractive, water-soluble extractive, pH)), assay, microbial limit, and test for aflatoxin. The Ayurvedic Pharmacopoeia of India mentions that CP should contain no less than 0.5% of gallic acid when assayed, based on the officially stated method.

Chyawanprash: A Nutraceutical and Functional Food The term 'nutraceutical' was coined in 1989 by Stephen De Felice as "a food or part of a food that provides medical or health benefits, including the prevention and/or treatment of disease." Chyawanprash has been a consistent part of Indian tradition both as a functional food and nutraceutical for the past 5000 years, with constant zeal and vivacity, and has survived owing to its peerless health benefits. Chyawanprash is reported to have rich vitamin, protein, dietary fibre, energy contents, carbohydrate, low fat contents (no-trans and zero percent cholesterol), and appreciable levels of major and minor trace elements (mg/100g), such as Fe (21.1), Zn (3.1), Co (3.7), Cu (0.667), Ni (1.4), Pb (2.4), Mn (8.3), vitamin C (0.5), tannic acid (20.2), other vitamins A, E, B1, B2, and carotenoids that act as micronutrients for health-invigorating purposes.

It also provides several essential phytoconstituents, namely, flavonoids, alkaloids, saponins, antioxidants, piperine, phenolic compounds, etc. The synergistic antioxidant effects of vitamin C along with vitamin E and carotenoids are well known. The rich nutritive composition and antioxidant biomolecules of CP act both singly as well as synergistically for immuno-modulation, body building, health restoration, and prevention of oxidative damage (a leading cause of several degenerative diseases).

5 Healing Ayurvedic Recipes Everyday CCF Tea Ghee Golden Milk Vata Kitchari Pitta Kitchari Kapha Kitchari Bok Choy, Tempeh, and Mushroom Stir-Fry Daikon and Tofu Summer Detox Soup Winter-Warming Whole Mung Bean Soup Urad Dal Porridge Easy Breakfast Bowl Chickpea Pick-Me-Up Crunchy Chickpeas

Tongue Scraping

Tongue scraping can help remove debris, bacteria, and dead cells and may have other benefits, including improving your sense of taste.

Tongue scraping is a fast way to remove extra particles - including the ones that cause bad breath - from the surface of your tongue. It's done with a small, slightly rounded tool made from plastic or metal.

Although no amount of scraping can replace a good toothbrushing, its purported benefits have enticed quite a few to add this extra step to their morning and evening routines. Read on to learn more about how tongue scraping can improve your oral health, common misconceptions to keep in mind, and how to get started.

How is tongue scraping beneficial: Debris, bacteria, and dead cells can build up on your tongue over time. This can lead to bad breath and have a negative impact on your overall oral health.

Using a tongue scraper can help remove this buildup, as well as:

- Improve your sense of taste. Older research suggests that using a tongue scraper twice daily can improve your sense of taste. Your tongue may be able to better distinguish between bitter, sweet, salty, and sour sensations.
- Improve the appearance of your tongue. Buildup of excess debris can cause your tongue to take on a white, coated appearance. Daily scraping can help remove this coating and prevent it from returning.
- Remove bacteria. Researchers in one 2005 study found that using a tongue scraper twice a day for seven days reduced the overall incidence of Mutans streptococci and Lactobacilli bacteria in the mouth. These bacteria types are known to cause bad breath and dental decay.
- Improve overall health. Removing bacteria is key to preventing cavities, gum disease, and other conditions affecting the mouth. Tongue scraping can help clear these bacteria from the mouth, improving your tongue's appearance and overall sensation.
- Reduce bad breath. Although tongue scraping can't replace brushing your teeth, scraping may do some things better. Researchers in one 2004 study found that scraping was more effective than brushing at removing odor-causing bacteria.

Is there anything tongue scraping can't do

A common misconception about tongue scraping is that it offers extended benefits in reducing bad breath. Although scraping can help banish bad breath, consistency is key. For example, using a tongue scraper in the morning won't prevent bad breath from developing later in the day. Bacteria will build up as you eat and drink, so if you're concerned about bad breath, you'll need to scrape after every meal.

At a minimum, scrape your tongue when you brush your teeth. This will help prevent long-term buildup that's associated with severe bad breath. Another misconception is that using a toothbrush on your tongue is just as effective as using a tongue scraper. The results of one 2004 study suggest otherwise. Researchers found that tongue scrapers removed 30 percent more volatile sulfur compounds on the tongue than a soft-bristled toothbrush.

Although cleaning your tongue with a toothbrush is better than not cleaning it at all, using a tongue scraper is more effective.

How to perform a tongue scraping: To perform tongue scraping, you'll need the right tool - a tongue scraper. A quick search for tongue scrapers can reveal lots of options. These include ones made from plastic, copper, and stainless steel.

Most will have a slightly rounded shape, much like an inverted spoon. If you're in a pinch, household items like a spoon (clean, of course) or your toothbrush will do. However, they may not remove as much odor-causing bacteria as a dedicated tongue scraper.

To perform tongue scraping, follow these steps:

1. Stand in front of a mirror, open your mouth, and stick out your tongue.
2. Gently set the rounded end of the tongue scraper at the back of your tongue.
3. If you're worried about gagging, you may find it helpful to start at the middle of your tongue. You can gradually start from farther back as you get used to scraping.
4. Gently touch the scraper to your tongue. Slowly pull it forward, toward the tip of your tongue. You should never push the scraper from the tip of your tongue back. Always go from the back of the tongue to the tip.
5. After each scrape, use a washcloth or tissue to remove debris from the scraper.
6. Repeat until you've scraped the entire surface of your tongue. One to two scrapes across the same area is usually enough.
7. Wash the tongue scraper with warm water and soap, dry, and store in a clean, dry area.

The entire process usually takes less than two minutes. Repeat as needed throughout the day.

Are there any side effects or risks to consider: One of the biggest concerns about tongue scraping is stimulating the gag reflex. This could make you vomit while tongue scraping. To avoid this, refrain from placing the scraper too far back on your tongue. When you first start scraping, you may find it helpful to scrape from the middle of your tongue to the tip. You can gradually start from farther back as you get used to the sensation.

It's also possible to accidentally cut the surface of your tongue with the scraper. To prevent this from occurring, make sure your tongue scraper doesn't have any uneven or rough edges. You should inspect your scraper before every use to ensure that it's still safe to use. You should be mindful of how much pressure you're applying. You want to be gentle enough to avoid harming your taste buds or breaking the skin, but firm enough to scrape up excess debris. When in doubt, start soft and gradually increase the pressure.

Products to try Tongue scrapers can be made with plastic or different metals. Which one you choose depends on your personal preference. Metal tongue scrapers are generally thought to last longer. Many are dishwasher-safe, too. Plastic ones are usually cheaper, but may need to be replaced more frequently. Most tongue scrapers cost less than $10.

Other ways to improve your oral health Tongue scraping can be beneficial, but you won't achieve your desired results if you aren't taking a well-rounded approach to oral hygiene.

You can help maintain and even improve your overall oral health if you:

- Use a fluoride-based toothpaste and mouthwash to help fight cavities.
- Brush your teeth and gums at least twice a day.
- Make sure you brush for at least two minutes. Set a timer or play a song on your phone to help ensure that each session is long enough.
- Floss at least once a day to remove tough-to-reach debris between your teeth.
- Drink plenty of water throughout the day to reduce dry mouth, a common cause of bad breath.
- Avoid using tobacco products, which can contribute to buildup on the tongue.

You should also see your dentist for regular checkups and cleanings. Most dentists recommend cleanings twice a year, but you may need to go more frequently depending on your overall dental health. When to see your dentist Although home methods like tongue scraping can help reduce tongue buildup, it isn't a cure-all. See your dentist right away if you're dealing with chronic dry mouth or have a "hairy tongue." They can assess your symptoms and determine whether you'd benefit from more frequent cleanings, special mouthwash, or other treatment options. Sometimes, tongue scraping can reveal symptoms that your dentist should evaluate. This includes white patches in the mouth. Such patches are usually caused by oral thrush or leukoplakia and can be treated under your dentist's supervision.

Oil Pulling (Gandusha)

In Ayurveda, Kavala and Gandusha are the procedures described in Dincharya i.e. the daily regimen and are useful in prevention of the diseases of the mouth, teeth and the gums. Filling the mouth in the morning with oil or medicated water daily and holding for a few minutes without moving it inside the oral cavity is called Gandusha. Oil pulling (Gandusha) has been used to prevent decay, oral mal odor, gum bleeding, dryness of throat, cracked lips and for strengthening the teeth, gums and the jaw.

It is a simple daily regimen, which, when done routinely, enhances the senses, brings about a feeling of freshness and maintains clarity in the voice. After adopting this procedure properly, one feels lightness and clarity in the mouth. It also relieves pain and discomfort. A Gandusha is to be held inside the oral cavity till there is uncontrollable salivation, secretions of tears from the eyes or mucous/watery discharge through the nose.

On the other hand, Kavala is a procedure of holding comparatively small quantity of liquid in the mouth; make it move briskly inside and spitting out quickly. Decoction of Khadira (Acacia catechu L.) or Kshirivrikshas like Nyagrodha (Ficus bengalensis L.), Udumbara (Ficus glomerulata Roxb.), etc. may be used daily for Kavala. It removes loss of appetite, bad taste, dirt and excess salivation from the mouth.

Gandusha - Oil Pulling for Oral Health: Oil pulling has a long-standing tradition in Ayurveda. It is used to purify the organism. In Europe, oil pulling is gaining popularity.

Gandusha, as oil pulling is referred to in Ayurveda, has been used for millennia. In Ayurveda, gandusha not only serves to clean the oral cavity but is also rids the body of and toxins or waste products that arise as a metabolic product. These deposits gather in the body and could lead to an array of discomforts or illness.

Incorporating Gandusha into your morning routine: Oil pulling is best carried out in the morning by swirling a tablespoon of oil in your mouth and pulling it through the interdental spaces and teeth. Spit the oil into a basin after 10 to 20 minutes and rinse the mouth with lukewarm water, and you're done!

Traditionally sesame oil is used in Ayurveda for oil pulling purposes because it is said to be particularly well suited. However, other plant oils such as coconut and olive oils may also be used.

According to Ayurveda, oil pulling is said t have several positive benefits for the whole body. Gandusha can help with:

- migraines
- impure skin
- inflammation of the mouth and throat
- fatigue or dullness
- limb and joint pain
- rheumatic diseases

Unfortunately, very few scientific studies of the above-mentioned holistic effects of this technique have been conducted.

What makes oil pulling so beneficial: Regular oil pulling contributes to oral hygiene because it rids the entire oral cavity of microorganisms. Thus plaque is reduced and as a result also reduces caries, tartar, inflammation and periodontal disease.

Why does it work: Much of the bacteria found in dental plaque have a hydrophobic ell surface. This means that they prefer oil. Bacteria accumulate during oil pulling and can be easily released from the body. They can likely be found as emulsifiers on the boundary between oil and saliva.

Moreover, many plant oils have antibacterial properties which additionally influence dental health.

Can I oil pull instead of brushing my teeth: We simply cannot forgo the good old brushing of teeth. But oil pulling is an excellent complement for those who want to do something extra for dental health, etc.

Products used specifically for oil-pulling: Today you will find numerous products on the market that have been specifically developed for oil pulling. These consist not only of oil but also often contain essential oils that have a specific effect against various bacteria.

This, of course, depends on the raw material of the essential oil. Special oils which have been developed for oil pulling in particular, often have additional benefits. A mixture of plant oil and essential oil is even more effective and can actively prevent inflammation and improve your general oral health.

Positive features are:

- promoting wound healing
- strengthening of the gums
- reduction of plaque
- inhibiting inflammation
- calming the airways

How is Gandusha Kriya Different from Kavala: Oil pulling has been described as Gandusha by the great Ayurveda practitioners Sushruta and Vagbhata. Another legendary Ayurvedic expert Charaka has termed oil pulling as Kavala or Kabala. There is a significant difference between these two practices:

- Both Gandusha and Kavala involve the use of oil, decoction for cleaning oral cavity.
- While Gandusha is done using a larger quantity of oil, Kavala makes use of a smaller quantity of oil.
- In Gandusha, since the oil used is in higher quantity, it cannot be kept in the mouth for a long time. There is no movement of the liquid inside the mouth and needs to be spitted out after a few seconds. In Kavala, a small quantity is kept in the mouth and swished for at least 15 to 20 minutes before spitting it out.
- The main difference apart from the time is that in Gandusha, the oil is swished around the mouth. In Kavala, the oil is kept in the mouth and then gargled before spitting it out.
- Kavala is a single procedure that can be done at home. Gandusha has different types and some of them are done at Ayurvedic centres under supervision.

Gandusha Benefits and Significance: The significance of Gandusha Kriya is that it is a traditional and time tested way of helping to maintain oral health. Your visits to the dentist for teeth whitening and treating decay can be reduced by doing Gandusha. It can become a part of your daily regiment and you can experience multiple benefits by doing it daily.

Gandusha offers multiple benefits when done in the right way:

1. It helps to maintain good oral hygiene. It helps keep the teeth and gum clean. The swishing of the oil helps ensure any food particle debris lodged in the teeth is dislodged and is expelled out when the oil is spit out.
2. The Gandusha oil has antibacterial properties and helps to kill bacteria in the mouth. It is the bacteria that causes decay and various other problems. It works just like mouthwash but instead of using chemicals, it uses a natural plant-based oil that is safe.
3. Gandusha can be more effective than brushing. The brush cannot reach the corners of the teeth. When you practice oil pulling, the oil would reach every corner of the teeth. It is thus more effective and helpful than normal brushing when done in the right way.
4. It helps to strengthen the gums. It also helps to remove plaque.
5. Sinus infections and other bacterial infections cause a sore throat. Gargling is a proven technique to reduce pain. Gargling with an antibacterial oil helps ensure that the symptoms of sore throat can be managed better.
6. The main reason for doing Gandusha is to help reduce toxins from the mouth. When the toxins are removed, it can cause sweating which proves that the procedure is working well.
7. Regularly doing Gandusha can help in strengthening the facial muscles. This helps in preventing flabby cheeks.
8. This helps ensure that toxins do not affect digestion, thus helping in better digestion.
9. Gandusha kriya helps keep your mouth fresh.
10. It is believed that practicing Gandusha can help in whitening teeth. It can work as a helpful natural teeth whitener.

How is the Gandusha Kriya Process Carried Out

There are different Gandusha types that you need to know about:

1. Snigdha or Snehana Gandusha uses herbal oils that help nourish and lubricate the oral cavity.
2. Shamana Gandusha helps to manage various dental problems. It uses herbal oils that can help reduce Dosha imbalance.
3. Shodhana Gandusha uses different substances to help manage the oral cavity.

4. Ropana Gandusha provides a helpful healing effect. Ulcers in the mouth can be helped to be managed with this process.

Gandusha Kriya is done as follows:

1. It is best done early morning before eating or drinking anything.
2. Sesame, mustard, or sunflower oil can be used. One to two tablespoons can be put in the mouth.
3. Swish around the teeth, gums, tongue, and sides of the mouth. Do this for around 5 minutes.
4. Once you are finished spit out the oil. It is very important to spit the oil out and not swallow it.
5. Rinse the mouth with warm water. You can then brush your teeth, floss, and use a tongue cleaner as usual.

Drink Hot Water with Lemon or Lime

Warm lime water on an empty stomach early in the morning helps stimulate the gastrointestinal tract. Digestion improves, heartburn is reduced and it helps in the process of elimination. Lemon juice has citric acid, which helps the enzymes to function better. It also stimulates the liver and aids in detoxification.

Ways Your Body Benefits from Lemon Water: The health benefits of drinking lemon water may include adding vitamin C and antioxidants to your diet, cutting back on sugar-sweetened drinks, and aiding weight loss. You may not want to drink it too often, though.

One glass of lemon water containing one 48-gram lemon, squeezed, contains:

- 10.6 calories
- 21% of the Daily Value (DV) of vitamin C
- 2% of the DV of folate
- 1% of the DV of potassium
- 1% of the DV of vitamin B1
- 1% of the DV of vitamin B5
- 0.5% of the DV of vitamin B2

Here are six ways your body may benefit from drinking lemon water.

1. Promotes hydration Drinking enough water is crucial for your overall health. It's key to preventing dehydration, a condition that may cause a range of symptoms.

Some of these include:

- fatigue
- excess thirst
- dry skin and lips
- headaches
- heart palpitations
- overheating
- constipation

Not everyone likes the taste of plain water, so adding the juice of a lemon to your water may help you drink more.

Healthcare professionals recommend that adults consume six to eight 8-ounce (oz) glasses of water per day, according to the National Institute of Diabetes and Digestive and Kidney Diseases (NIDDK).

2. Good source of Vitamin C Citrus fruits like lemons contain vitamin C, which is an antioxidant. These help protect your cells from free radicals, which are molecules that cause inflammation in your body and may lead to a number of diseases.

Vitamin C may also play a key role in other processes, such as:

- synthesizing collagen and L-carnitine
- protein metabolism
- regenerating other antioxidants
- delaying certain cancers and cardiovascular disease
- absorbing iron
- producing hormones

On the flip side, not consuming enough vitamin C may cause:

- increased susceptibility to infections
- dry mouth, skin, and eyes
- fatigue
- insomnia
- loosening of teeth

3. May support weight loss Drinking lemon water may help you increase your water intake, which is often recommended as a weight loss strategy. However, there's limited evidence to justify this.

In a 2018 study, researchers found that participants who were instructed to drink water before eating a test meal ate less food than when they were instructed to eat the test meal without "pre-loading" with water.

Participants did not feel significantly less satiated when they drank water before eating a test meal, despite eating less food.

The study's authors concluded that pre-meal water consumption may be an effective weight loss strategy, although the mechanism of action is unknown.

4. Easy alternative to sugary drinks Sugar-sweetened beverages like juice, soda, sports drinks, and energy drinks contain the most added sugars in the American diet, according to the Centers for Disease Control and Prevention (CDC).

The Dietary Guidelines for Americans (DGA) suggests that added sugars are used to help with:

- food and drink preservation
- texture, viscosity, and colour maintenance
- making contents more pleasant to consume

That said, the DGA suggests that less than 10% of your caloric intake should come from added sugars.

Regularly drinking sugar-sweetened beverages may increase your risk of developing some health conditions, such as:

- weight gain
- obesity
- type 2 diabetes
- heart disease
- kidney disease
- liver disease
- tooth decay
- cavities
- gout

Lemon water may be a healthy, natural alternative to quench your thirst and sweet tooth.

5. Citric acid helps prevent kidney stones The citric acid in lemons may help prevent kidney stones.

Citrate, a component of citric acid, paradoxically makes urine less acidic and may even break up small stones.

The National Kidney Foundation suggests mixing 4 oz of lemon juice concentrate with water as a complementary dietary remedy alongside other medication for kidney stone prevention.

6. May aid digestion Drinking lemon water before meals may help promote and improve digestion. In a small 2022 study, researchers found that the citric acid in lemon juice helped boost gastric acid secretion. This is a digestive fluid produced in the stomach that helps your body break down and digest food.

In another 2021 study, participants drank 300 millimeters (mL) of either water or lemon water prior to eating meals for 4 weeks. Stool samples were collected before and after the test period and the intestinal microbiota of participants were analyzed.

The study's authors found that pre-meal intake of lemon water appeared to promote digestion and peristalsis.

This refers to the wave-like contractions that help move food through the digestive tract. However, more large-scale studies are needed to fully understand the effects of lemon water on digestion.

How to make lemon water To make lemon water, squeeze half a lemon into 8 oz of warm or cold water.

You can infuse more flavor or a health boost by adding a:

- few springs of mint
- teaspoon of maple syrup or raw honey
- slice of fresh ginger or cucumber
- dash of cinnamon
- sprinkle of turmeric

Lemon ice cubes are another great way to add lemon to your water quickly. Simply squeeze fresh lemon juice into ice cube trays and freeze. Then, drop a few cubes into your water as needed.

You can start your morning with a mug of warm lemon water, and keep a pitcher of water infused with a few sliced lemons in your refrigerator to drink throughout the day.

Side effects of lemon water: Lemon water is generally safe to drink, but there are a few potential side effects to be aware of.

A 2015 study suggests that citric acid, which is found in lemons and lemon juice, may erode tooth enamel over the long term.

To limit the risk, drink lemon water through a straw and rinse your mouth with plain water afterward.

Additionally, citrus fruits may increase gastric acid production and cause heartburn in some people.

Frequently Asked Questions

Does lemon water burn belly fat: Although it's a popular belief, there's no evidence that supports lemon water use for burning belly fat. Drinking lemon water may help with your weight management goals by adding a different way to increase water intake, which may help boost your metabolism. Regular physical activity and a balanced diet are optimal ways to lose weight.

What are the benefits of lemon in water: The benefits of drinking lemon water may include adding vitamin C to your diet, offering an alternative to sugary drinks, preventing kidney stones due to citric acid content, and facilitating digestion. It also helps to keep you hydrated.

What happens if I drink lemon water every day: Drinking too much lemon water may lead to tooth erosion and heartburn over time, due to the acidic content of lemons. However, no side effects have been reported regarding drinking one cup of lemon water every day. You may experience a boost in your immune system due to the vitamin C, and may feel more energetic, because of better hydration. If you also follow a balanced diet and engage in regular physical activity, you may also notice some weight loss.

How much lemon water should you drink a day: One or two glasses or cups of lemon water per day may provide you with some health benefits. For example, squeezing the juice of a 48-gram lemon into a glass of water will provide you with 21% of the DV of vitamin C. Drinking lemon water too frequently, on the other hand, may hurt your tooth enamel and could lead to heartburn.

Takeaway: Lemon water is a refreshing drink and an easy way to add a little extra vitamin C and antioxidants into your diet.

Adding a splash of lemon to your water may make water more appealing to drink, which could help you cut back on drinking sugary sports drinks and juices. While more research is needed, lemon water may help improve digestion and even support weight loss.

Ways to Reduce Water Retention (Edema)

Dietary and lifestyle changes may help reduce water retention and promote fluid balance.

FIgure: *Salt is made up of sodium and chloride.*

You may consider eating more fruits, vegetables, and herbs and limiting processed foods and refined carbs.

Water retention, also known as edema or fluid retention, occurs when excess fluids build up in your body. This may cause swelling in your feet, ankles, hands, and legs (peripheral edema).

Edema could have several causes, such as:

- hormonal changes or pregnancy
- lack of physical activity
- chronic kidney disease
- congestive heart failure
- capillary leak syndrome
- lymphatic dysfunction (lymphedema)
- obesity
- malnutrition
- infections that may trigger inflammation and swelling
- allergies

- certain medications, including:
- oral contraceptives
- corticosteroids
- nonsteroidal anti-inflammatory drugs
- calcium channel blockers
- some diabetes medications

Sometimes, fluid retention may be a symptom of a serious medical condition that could require medical treatment.

But if your swelling is mild and you don't have an underlying health condition, you may be able to reduce water retention with these six methods.

1. Eat less salt

Sodium binds to water in your body and helps maintain the balance of fluids inside and outside your cells. If you often eat foods that are high in salt, such as many packaged foods, your body may retain water. These foods are the biggest dietary source of sodium in most Western diets.

The most common advice for reducing water retention is to decrease sodium intake.

However, the research on this is mixed. Some studies suggest that increased sodium intake leads to increased fluid retention. However, many other factors are also involved in regulating fluid balance, and the effects of salt on water retention may vary from person to person.

2. Increase Magnesium Intake

Magnesium is a key mineral involved in more than 300 enzymatic reactions that keep your body functioning properly.Some research suggests that increasing your magnesium intake may help reduce water retention.

For example, one older study found that taking 250 milligrams of magnesium per day improved several symptoms of premenstrual syndrome (PMS), including water retention and bloating.

However, further studies are necessary to explore magnesium's role in decreasing water retention. Good sources of magnesium include nuts, whole grains, and leafy green vegetables. It's also available as a supplement.

3. Get More Vitamin B6

Vitamin B6, also known as pyridoxine, is a water-soluble vitamin that plays a central role in:

- red blood cell formation
- protein metabolism
- brain function
- immune health

It also regulates fluid balance and may help reduce water retention.

One 2012 study suggests that vitamin B6 may decrease bloating and fluid buildup in women with PMS.

The authors of a 2016 study describe similar findings, adding that vitamin B6 may be even more effective when combined with calcium supplements.

However, research on vitamin B6's fluid-retention effects outside of PMS is lacking. If you want to increase your vitamin B6 intake, you can do so by eating foods such as:

- bananas
- potatoes
- chickpeas
- walnuts
- tuna

4. Eat More Potassium-Rich Foods

Potassium serves several important functions, especially regarding heart health, muscle contractions, and nerve function.

It's also essential for maintaining blood volume and fluid balance to help decrease water retention. It works by counteracting the effects of sodium to prevent fluid buildup and swelling, as well as by increasing urine production.

Low potassium levels may also increase:

- blood pressure
- risk for kidney stones
- bone turnover
- urinary calcium excretion
- salt sensitivity

Foods that are high in potassium, such as bananas, avocados, and tomatoes, can help support healthy fluid balance.

5. Try Dandelion

Dandelion (Taraxacum officinale) has long been used as a natural diuretic in folk medicine. It may help reduce water retention by increasing urine production.

In a small older study, 17 people took 3 doses of dandelion leaf extract over 24 hours, which led to a significant increase in urine production. Other studies in test tubes and animals suggest that the diuretic properties of dandelion leaf extract may also help protect against conditions such as kidney stones.

Additionally, dandelion may have antiviral, antifungal, and antioxidant benefits. However, larger, more recent studies are necessary to support these benefits. Speak with a healthcare professional before adding dandelion supplements to your routine.

6. Limit Your Refined Carb Intake

Refined carb sources such as white bread and pasta are typically high in carbs or added sugar and low in fibre. As a result, consuming these foods may lead to rapid spikes in blood sugar and insulin levels.

High insulin levels may cause more sodium retention by increasing sodium reabsorption in your kidneys. In turn, this may lead to more fluid volume in your body and increased water retention.

Additionally, your liver and muscles store carbs as glycogen, a form of sugar that is bound to water. Each gram of glycogen is stored with at least 3 grams of water, so following a high carb diet could increase water retention.

Fibre-rich whole grains, such as oats, brown rice, and whole wheat bread, are better food sources than refined carbohydrates.

Other Remedies to Reduce Water Retention

Certain natural remedies may also help reduce water retention by increasing urine production and decreasing inflammation. These might include drinking more water, increasing your physical activity, or consuming foods or supplements such as:

- horsetail
- parsley
- hibiscus

- fennel
- corn silk
- nettle

However, some of these tips are supported only by anecdotal evidence, not by research. Speak with a healthcare professional before adding supplements to your diet, especially if you have underlying health conditions or are taking medications.

Frequently Asked Questions

What are the signs of water retention: Water retention, also known as edema or fluid retention, occurs when excess fluid builds up in your body.

Swelling in your ankles, feet, hands, or legs is a common symptom.

If dietary or lifestyle changes don't help reduce inflammation, speak with a doctor. Water retention may be a symptom of a serious condition.

What causes me to retain water: Several conditions, diseases, and dietary or lifestyle habits may cause water retention. Examples include:

- hormonal changes or pregnancy
- lack of physical activity
- chronic kidney disease
- congestive heart failure
- capillary leak syndrome
- lymphatic dysfunction (lymphedema)
- obesity
- malnutrition
- allergies
- infections
- certain medications, such as oral contraceptives and corticosteroids

How does water retention go away: You may be able to help reduce water retention and promote fluid balance by making certain dietary and lifestyle changes, such as:

- reducing sodium and refined carb intake
- increasing potassium, vitamin B6, or magnesium intake
- trying certain herbs such as dandelion, horsetail, or parsley

Takeaway

Many factors could contribute to water retention. Though medical treatments may be necessary depending on the cause, several simple dietary and lifestyle changes may help reduce water retention and promote fluid balance.

Following a balanced diet and limiting processed foods and refined carbs may be especially beneficial.

If water retention persists even after you've made changes to your diet or lifestyle, consult a healthcare professional to determine the best course of treatment.

Dry Brushing

Dry brushing, also known as Garshana, is an Ayurvedic practice that involves dry massaging the body gently with a brush made of natural-fibre bristles.

It's purported to offer several health benefits, such as refreshing and stimulating the skin and lymphatic system and releasing accumulated toxins.

Dry skin brushing benefits may include stimulating the lymphatic system, exfoliating the skin, removing toxins, increasing circulation and energy, and reducing cellulite.

Dry brushing is an Ayurvedic medicine that has been around for centuries.

It's believed to have many health benefits and works by exfoliating the skin. Practitioners of dry brushing rub a brush with coarse, natural-fibre bristles over their bodies in a particular pattern.

The idea is that the coarse fibres will help to remove dead skin and improve the skin's ability to eliminate toxins through the pores.

What are the benefits of dry brushing

Benefits of Dry Brushing

1. Dry brushing may help your body release toxins. It may also help you relax. There's little data to support the benefits of dry brushing, but for most people there's also little harm in practicing dry brushing.

Was this helpful: There is little scientific evidence to support the benefits of dry brushing. There is anecdotal evidence, however. The possible benefits include the following:

Lymphatic system and the removal of toxins: The lymphatic system helps your body fight off infections. Fluids flow through the system and are filtered through the lymph nodes. If you're sick or exposed to a lot of toxins, the system may become backed up and clogged. That is why your lymph nodes often become swollen when you have a cold.

Dry brushing is thought to help the body release toxins through sweat. The course bristles on the brush stimulate the pores and open them up.

This makes it easier for the body to sweat, which in turns reduces the amount of toxins flowing through the lymphatic system. There is little research to support this claim.

Exfoliation: The coarse bristles can brush away dry, dead cells from the skin. This can leave your skin more smooth and soft.

Relaxation: Similar to a massage, dry brushing may make you feel relaxed. To make the most of this benefit, practice dry brushing in a dark, quiet space.

Cellulite: Cellulite is a condition that mostly affects women. Areas affected by cellulite have a rippled or "cottage cheese" appearance. The cause is not fully known.

Massage has been shown to temporarily reduce the appearance of cellulite. Some claim that dry brushing can reduce the appearance of cellulite because it has similar effects on the body as massage. There's no scientific data to support this theory, and it's not a recognized treatment by most doctors.

"[Dry brushing] does exfoliate, which is fine if not done too vigorously," says Dr. Carolyn Jacobs, a board-certified dermatologist and director at Chicago Cosmetic Surgery and Dermatology. "But it won't help cellulite as that is due to fat and collagen bands in women."

What are the Risks of Dry Brushing?

Risks of Dry Brushing

1. Dry brushing may not be for everyone. If you have sensitive skin or a skin condition, such as psoriasis, speak with your doctor before dry brushing.

Some people should avoid dry brushing or proceed with caution. People with open or inflamed skin, including people with eczema and psoriasis, should avoid dry brushing over the inflamed area. You should also avoid dry brushing over an open wound. You could introduce bacteria to the wound, which could lead to infection.

How to practice dry brushing: To dry brush, use a natural fibre brush with a long handle. The long handle will help you reach all areas of your body. Follow these steps:

1. Start at your feet and move up your body.
2. Brush your skin using wide, circular, clockwise motions.
3. Use light pressure in areas where your skin is thin and harder pressure on thicker skin, like the soles of your feet.
4. Brush your arms after you have brushed your feet, legs, and mid-section. You should brush upward towards your armpits.
5. After dry brushing, take a cool shower to help remove the dry skin.
6. After your shower, dry off and then consider adding natural plant oil, such as olive or coconut oil, to moisturize your skin.

When you first start dry brushing, it's best to begin with light brushing. As you get used to it, you can increase the pressure.

Avoid sensitive areas and anywhere the skin is broken. These include areas with:

- rashes
- wounds
- cuts
- infections

Also, never brush an area affected by poison oak, poison ivy, or psoriasis. Don't dry brush your face unless you're using a softer brush made for that purpose.

What supplies do I need: All you need to dry brush at home is a brush with natural fibre bristles. You should also look for one with a long handle to help you reach every part of your body.

You may want to dry brush in the shower so that you can easily clean the area once you're done. You may also want to have a moisturizer on hand, such as natural oil.

You should be able to find a brush for less than $10. Dry brushing kits are also available, though these are more expensive. Dry brushes are available at health food stores or online.

If you don't want to dry brush yourself, you may be able to find a local spa that offers dry brushing. If you have a treatment done at a spa, ask them how they clean the brushes and let them know about any areas they should avoid.

Brush maintenance: Make sure you rinse your brush after you have completed your brushing routine. Dry it in an open, sunny area to prevent mildew. Clean your brush once a week using soap and water. You should also avoid sharing your brush with anyone. This can help prevent the risk for infection.

Takeaway: There's little scientific evidence to support the benefits of dry brushing. For most people, however, there's little risk. If you're interested in dry brushing, you can purchase a brush and try it at home. If you have a skin condition, such as psoriasis, you should speak with your doctor before dry brushing. Be sure to avoid brushing over or around an open wound or infection.

Chapter 7

Oil Massage (Abhyanga)

Introduction

Abhyanga is a massage that's done with warm oil. The oil is applied on the entire body, from the scalp to the soles of your feet. It's the most popular massage in Ayurveda, a traditional system of medicine from India. Ayurveda focuses on maintaining health through natural practices like massage and what you eat.

Abhyanga is a massage technique done with oil that you perform on yourself or receive as therapy from a licensed practitioner. It's a practice rooted in traditional ayurvedic medicine from ancient India, and the purpose is to soothe and balance the body. Nowadays, abhyanga can be used for stress relief and skin health.

The necessity of self-care emerged in an all new way during the pandemic. Why? Because suddenly, almost overnight, many people had more time for it. Some meditated, baked, exercised, took bubble baths, spent time with loved ones in socially distanced circles, and slowed the pace of life.

Hopefully, any reframing that healthier habits brought in 2020-2022 hasn't disintegrated. But if it has and you've once again stepped into the overwhelm of a packed schedule, the ayurvedic practice of abhyanga may help you reconnect with yourself - and improve your overall wellness in the process. Here's a look at what abhyanga is, the potential benefits, how to practice it, and more.

Definition of Abhyanga

Abhyanga is a type of massage performed with oil, often warmed between the palms before application that you practice on yourself or receive as a therapy. It's derived from the Sanskrit words anga (movement) and abhi (different, against, or contrary), according to a review in the July 2017 Journal of Ayurveda and Integrated Medical Sciences.

The California College of Ayurveda notes that abhyanga is also called snehana, which means "to nurture or love." This seems fitting, because that's exactly what you're doing when you take the time to mindfully, slowly massage warm oil into your skin.

"Abhyanga is something that [may help] us overcome daily mental and physical wear-and-tear," says Salila Sukumaran, an ayurvedic educator in Los Altos, California. "Where I come from, in the South of India, abhyanga is performed every day [by many people]," she says.

History of Abhyanga: Abhyanga is a practice in ayurvedic medicine from India, one of the oldest medical systems in the world, according to the National Center for Complementary and Integrative Health (NCCIH). This traditional medical system approaches health in a holistic way, such as through a seasonal ayurvedic diet, yoga and meditation practices, herbal remedies, oil pulling, and dry brushing.

Traditionally, abhyanga is one of the dinacharya, or daily practices, for maintaining health, or as part of the pretreatment procedure of panchakarma (a more intensive "detox" treatment regimen), per the aforementioned published review.

How Abhyanga Works: In ayurveda, abhyanga may work in several ways. "Skin is one of the biggest organs in the body. It plays a role in elimination and immunity," says Sukumaran. Both the oil and massage may improve health in different ways.

Massage itself can be de-stressing, and the oil may act as a moisturizer for the skin to keep it supple and hydrated. Properly hydrated skin allows the skin's barrier to stay intact, which is important because the skin is your immune system's first line of defense, notes a review on skin, immunity, and aging.

According to Banyan Botanicals, ayurveda practitioners believe that oil self-massage may also lead to:

- Better circulation (of blood and lymph fluid)
- Improvement in sleep
- Healthy vision
- Increased longevity

The practice encourages you to put yourself first by carving out time and ritualizing self-care; in theory, this has a positive ripple effect on your wellness. "Abhyanga is one of the most important self-care rituals. When we care for our most precious thing - our bodies - it leads to higher self-esteem and self-respect," says Sukumaran, from her personal experience.

Possible Health Benefits of Abhyanga

Note that more research is still needed to better understand the possible perks of abhyanga. To date, most Western, aka conventional, research examines the general health benefits of ayurveda and its applications for specific populations, and research on abhyanga, specifically, is lacking. If you're looking to incorporate a low-risk, self-care practice (or traditional form of massage therapy) into your new routine, here are some potential benefits of abhyanga.

May Help Relieve Stress: Anyone who's visited a spa for a massage or asked a partner or friend for a simple shoulder rub knows just how stress-relieving a massage might be.

"Abhyanga helps soothe and calm the nervous system," says Katie Silcox, an ayurvedic teacher and author of Glow Worthy, based in Charlottesville, Virginia. She refers back to the state of being a baby, where most people receive lots of skin-to-skin contact - something that happens rarely outside of intimacy today. As you practice self-massage, "you're taking yourself back to that time, reminding yourself through your physiology that you are loved, safe, and valued for who you are. This is a deep spiritual ritual you can do for yourself," she explains, from her personal experience.

Some research corroborates this potential benefit, showing that healthy people who received abhyanga massage from a therapist for an hour reported lower perceived stress levels. It's important to note, however, that studies on the self-massage form of abhyanga are lacking.

May Improve Circulation: The touch in massage stimulates your circulation, and conventional massage therapy has been shown to lower blood pressure levels, according to an earlier study. That research looked at 10-15 minutes of Swedish massage (a different massage technique) and found that these blood pressure benefits persisted for at least three days after the massage.

Though there is no research yet on abhyanga specifically for improved circulation, this may be a possible benefit scientists will explore someday.

This review on abhyanga massage therapy did find participants had a reduction in heart rate and blood pressure, yet given the sample size, more research is needed.

May Promote Better Sleep: Massage therapy, in general, has been shown to improve sleep, including for people with insomnia or those who have pain conditions, according to the American Massage Therapy Association (AMTA).

For many people, a popular time to practice abhyanga is before bedtime. Having soothing pre-bed rituals free of technology and other stressors and distractions may help your body wind down in preparation for sleep. "[Some] people report that abhyanga before bed helps their sleep," says Silcox, of her teaching experience. As you'll learn below, abhyanga can be done in just 15 minutes, but busy people may benefit from performing a light massage in the shower for just a minute or two, she adds.

May Aid Skin and Hair Health: During abhyanga, you'll likely massage both your skin and scalp, which means you may apply the oil to your hair as well. One review noted that the oil may nourish your skin to make it soft, elastic, and strong. Likewise, regular applications of oil to your scalp may boost the health of the skin here, as well as the hair follicles, improving scalp dryness, itching, and even dandruff.

The act of massaging this oil onto skin is believed to dilate small blood vessels to increase circulation, which may deliver nutrients to skin and hair follicles, per past research. Finally, rubbing your hands on your skin exfoliates it by removing dead skin cells, which is another reason why your body may feel softer when you're done.

Abhyanga Safety and Side Effects: The good news? A self-massage practice is usually safe. "Abhyanga is something that does really help almost everyone," says Silcox, in her experience. Research suggests there are certain health conditions that may make abhyanga inappropriate for certain groups. Those can include people with osteoporosis, skin disease, fractures, varicose veins, atherosclerosis, cancer, and an open wound, among others. Talk to your doctor first to determine if abhyanga oil massage on yourself or as a therapy is right for you.

Who Might Want to Try (and Avoid) Abhyanga: Most people can safely practice oil self-massage; it's used in India by both adults and children, says Sukumaran. Of course, if self-massage hurts in any way, you should avoid areas of pain. By performing a light, stroking self-massage, you're able to control the pressure and areas of focus.

Editor's Picks In Wellness: What Are Alternative, Complementary, and Integrative Health Approaches?

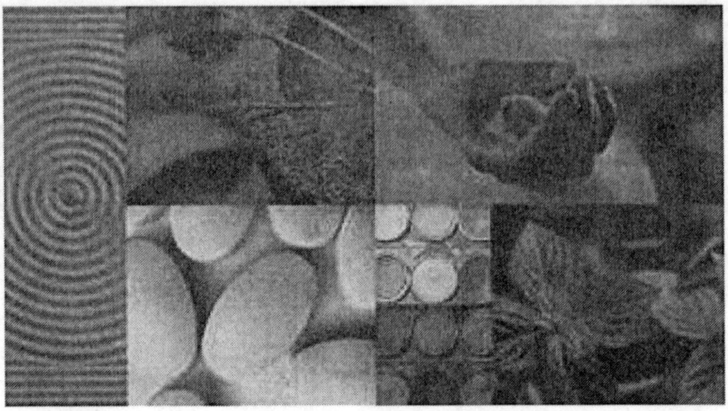

Figure: What Is an Ayurvedic Diet? A Detailed Scientific Guide to Cooking and Eating According to Ayurveda

4 Potential Health Benefits of Oil Pulling

5 Potential Health Benefits of Dry Brushing

Tips for Getting Started with Abhyanga

Consult an Ayurvedic Practitioner

Ideally, before you start a new ayurvedic practice, especially if you're planning to use it longer term, you'll seek guidance from an ayurvedic practitioner. Ayurvedic medicine is not regulated in the United States by the federal government, and no state has a licensure requirement, but the National Ayurvedic Medical Association offers a tool to locate a certified professional near you, who can help you identify your individual constitution to formulate an ayurvedic wellness routine, including establishing an abhyanga practice that's designed for your specific needs.

If you desire to explore abhyanga on your own, here is some introductory information for the self-massage form of this practice, from our discussions with Silcox and Sukumaran.

Identify Your Dosha, or Constitution: In ayurveda, your constitution is the balance of the three doshas in your body, according to the California College of Ayurveda.

A dosha is believed to be an energy that makes up your unique mind and body, based on air, fire, water, earth, and space elements.

According to ayurveda, the three doshas are pitta (fire), vata (air and space), and kapha (earth and water).

Consulting an ayurvedic practitioner can help you identify which ayurvedic practices and applications work best for you and your constitution. Silcox, who is also the founder of the Shakti School, provides a free dosha quiz if you want to learn more about your dosha (or doshas, as some people have dominant combinations of two or all three).

Other quizzes can be found elsewhere online, too, to help you learn more about your doshic constitution or to learn more before you see a formal practitioner. For example, the Kripalu Center for Yoga and Health and the Chopra Center both offer similar free tools.

Choose Your Oil: The oil component of abhyanga is believed to be especially important. "[Most] organic food-grade oils will work great," says Sukumaran. In particular, sesame oil is generally considered one of the better oils for the body, she says, especially if you have drier skin or live in an arid climate.

Coconut oil can be another option, especially during times of heat, as it's a cooling oil, per ayurvedic philosophy. You can use coconut oil in the summer, for example, or if you have a "fire" constitution, also known as a pitta dosha.

Kapha dosha types may be prone to oily skin, notes Sukumaran, and in this case a lighter oil like almond or jojoba, or dry brushing, may be better. The oil is also often paired with spices in an effort to balance your dosha. You can create your own by steeping oil along with food-grade spices, such as cinnamon, clove, cardamom, or bay leaf, says Sukumaran. Seek guidance from an ayurvedic practitioner about which spices or herbal preparations will balance your dosha.

A simpler route, says Silcox, is to purchase a ready-to-use herbal massage oil designed for your dosha. Companies like Banyan Botanicals sell formulations for vata, pitta, and kapha.

Begin by Massaging the Limbs: Warm up the oil with your own body temperature by rubbing it in between your hands. Do not heat up the oil on the stove or with any electric device, to avoid the risk of burning the skin.

To get started with the massage, Sukumaran suggests beginning with your limbs. For example, take your left hand and sweep your hand from your shoulder on your right arm down to your wrist. (The idea is to start closer to the heart and move away from the heart.) Repeat on your left arm and then on your legs.

Employ just enough pressure to massage the oil into your body, similar to the way you'd moisturize with lotion.

Use Circular Strokes on Tender Spots: As you approach a joint, like knees or elbows, move your hand in a soft circular motion around the joint.

Apply a gentle rounded motion to your belly, butt, and breasts or chest as well. Don't forget the top of your head, feet, inside of your navel, and inside your ears. "All of these parts of the body are connected to vital organs [according to ayurvedic philosophy]. Applying oil here [may bring] calm, rest, and peace," Sukumaran says.

Wipe Down and Rinse Off: Let the oil sit on your body for at least five minutes. "Traditionally, next you would walk into a pond or shower to wash yourself off," says Sukumaran. Instead you can wipe yourself off with a towel and then rinse yourself in lukewarm water. Since oil will be in your hair, you may shampoo your hair as well.

This entire process can be completed in under 15 minutes, Sukumaran says. What to Expect Before, During, and After Abhyanga

Here's what you may experience in the time it takes to perform an abhyanga self-massage.

Before: If you're practicing abhyanga at the end of the day, you may approach it feeling stressed or frazzled, depending on how busy you were. If you incorporate it into your morning routine, you may feel sleepy and more relaxed. Either way, if abhyanga becomes part of your regular routine, you may find that you start to de-stress in anticipation of this me-time.

During: As you massage your limbs, your touch may increase your circulation and help stimulate your lymph fluid throughout your body, says Silcox. One study noted this effect. (Lymph fluid is the clear fluid that travels through your body carrying cells that fight infection, according to the National Cancer Institute.) You may also start to feel a general ease or relaxation as your massage progresses.

After: The oil used in abhyanga will likely leave your skin moisturized, soft, and supple. Some people may notice that the oil completely absorbs into their skin - a possible sign that their skin was parched and in need of nourishment, Silcox says.

Beyond how your skin feels, it's believed that there's an overall benefit to this ritualistic practice for many people in need of dedicated time to destress. "The oiling, massaging, and washing has a transformative effect [for some]. You may find that you start to face life feeling less overwhelmed and with a better attitude and less anxiety," adds Sukumaran.

While abhyanga can't do it all - it's not an antidote to a diagnosed mental health condition or meant to be a replacement for conventional medical care - you may find that it helps you feel better overall.

All of these self-care techniques - especially self-massage - are in service of knowing your lovability. "If you add this to your to-do list, it will defeat the purpose. Instead, you can make it a body prayer, or a spiritual practice," she says, of her own practice and experience.

Ayurvedic Self-Massage

Massage. When we hear that word, many of us picture a luxurious spa treatment reserved for special occasions. In Ayurveda, however, the practice of abhyanga (Ayurvedic massage with oil) is recommended daily. Fortunately, there is a more accessible alternative to professional massage therapy when it comes to enjoying the nourishing benefits of abhyanga every day-massaging yourself.

Oil massage may sound like a messy and complicated process best left to the spa, but once you've learned the basics, self-massage with oil starts to become second-nature and well worth the effort.

In this article, we'll discuss the benefits of abhyanga, which oils to use, and how you can tailor your self-massage practice to balance each dosha. If you don't yet know your own unique Ayurvedic body type and current state of balance, take our free dosha quiz to learn more about what type of massage will most benefit you.

Why Is Massage Recommended in Ayurveda: The act of massage itself melts away tension and stress from the muscles. Ayurveda believes that these inherent Ayurvedic massage benefits are further enhanced with the addition of an Ayurvedic massage oil. Health benefits from implementing a daily oil rub into your morning or evening routine include:

- Musculoskeletal and nervous system health
- Proper circulation and lymph drainage
- Improved sleep patterns
- Softer, stronger skin

- Healthy vision
- Graceful aging
- Lustrous hair
- Firm, strong limbs
- Tone and vigor for the body's tissues
- Increased longevity
- Nourishment for the whole body

In Sanskrit, the word sneha can be translated as both "oil" and "love." So in Ayurveda, there is an inherent connection between enveloping the body in oil and enveloping it in love. Both experiences can give a deep feeling of stability, warmth, and comfort. Sneha-oil and love-is sukshma, or "subtle." This allows it to pass through minute channels in the body and penetrate deep layers of tissue (dhatus).

What Is Self-Massage: Self-massage, just as its name suggests, is the act of massaging yourself. However, it is important to note that performing abhyanga on yourself is a more involved process than simply slathering some oil on your neck or back for a few minutes. (For something to address a specific muscle or joint in particular, you might consider applying Muscle Balm or Joint Balm a few times a day in addition to your abhyanga practice.)

Ayurveda recommends spending a minimum of fifteen minutes on self-massage each time you practice it, devoting love and attention to each of the tissue layers as you nourish them with a warm Ayurvedic oil.

Benefits of Self-Massage: Although receiving a massage from a professional massage therapist is sometimes advised, there is a lot to be gained by learning and practicing Ayurvedic self-massage techniques. With self-massage, the fantastic benefits of abhyanga become readily available to you in the comfort of your own home.

In fact, in a recent clinical trial studying the effects of self-massage, abhyanga proved to be an effective way to decrease stress levels, improve quality of sleep, and enhance one's overall quality of life.

Over time, self-massage becomes a regular act of self-love you can look forward to every day.

Choosing the Right Abhyanga Oil: First of all, you may be wondering why to use oil in the first place, rather than a massage lotion. While lotion can be moisturizing, it is not as nourishing for the tissues and does not promote circulation in the same way that oil does.

Oil has long been recognized in Ayurveda as being the go-to substance for self-massage, not just for moisture but for one's overall wellbeing. Ayurveda teaches us that like increases like and that opposites balance, so when it comes to choosing the right oil, your decision should take into account the doshas: vata, pitta, and kapha, and how the qualities of the doshas impact the following:

- Your current state of balance (vikriti). If you currently have a dosha that is high, it is beneficial to follow a dosha-pacifying abhyanga for that dosha. For example, if you are nervous, anxious, and you feel cold and dry, vata is likely to be high in your vikriti and using a vata-pacifying oil for your abhyanga would be most beneficial.
- Your Ayurvedic constitution (prakriti). If none of your doshas are currently out of balance, it is good to consider the dominant doshas in your constitution, or prakriti, to maintain balance. For example, if you are feeling healthy and pitta is your dominant dosha, and if the weather is hot and humid (which tends to aggravate pitta) it would generally be best to choose a pitta-pacifying oil. This brings us to the next factor to keep in mind.
- Your environment. The doshas have an impact on the current season and weather. Fall through early winter is considered vata season, late winter through spring is considered kapha season, and pitta season occurs in the summertime. There are many steps you can take to maintain balance according to the seasons, and selecting a massage oil that will keep you in balance is one of them.

List of Ayurvedic Oils

Because there are so many different ways that the act of massaging with oil can support the body, mind, and spirit, we created an entire organic line of specialized herbal oil blends you can choose from. Using a plain carrier oil is also an option, but using herbal oils created for specific dosha-balancing intentions are especially good choices for full body self-massage.

Oils for Vata: The primary qualities of vata are dry, light, cool, rough, subtle, and mobile. Most of these qualities are opposite to those of oil, so there are quite a few oils that can help counteract vata's qualities. Plain, untoasted Sesame Oil is considered the traditional abhyanga oil for vata dosha. (Ayurveda considers it to be "the king of oils," in fact.) While it is fine to use an unrefined or refined version of this oil on its own, inherently warming nature makes it the perfect base oil for the following herbal oil blends.

Vata Massage Oil: Vata Massage Oil is an excellent abhyanga oil for vata, especially when the dosha is high or elevated. This oil is particularly grounding and calming. The synergistic blend of nine herbs, such as ashwagandha, bala, and shatavari, come together to offer their strengthening, nourishing, and revitalizing properties, enhancing the vata-pacifying qualities of the organic sesame and olive oils used as its base. This oil is the perfect choice for the fall and winter seasons, when vata is most likely to become imbalanced.

Ashwagandha/Bala Oil: If your goal is to increase strength and stamina, Ashwagandha/Bala Oil may be the best choice for you. Ashwagandha and bala are both known for promoting strong, healthy muscles, and bring out the nourishing qualities of the organic sesame oil at this blend's base. Thanks to its potential to help build healthy muscle mass, this herbal oil is often recommended to support an active lifestyle or to strengthen developing or weakened muscles.

Mahanarayan Oil: Featuring over twenty Ayurvedic herbs, Mahanarayan Oil is traditionally used to support comfortable movement in the joints. If you warm the oil, massage it into the affected joints or muscles, and proceed with your regular abhyanga, it can be fabulously beneficial. Following this with a warm bath with 1/3 cup each baking soda and ginger powder (provided there is no skin irritation) can enhance the effects even further.

Vata Oil Alternatives

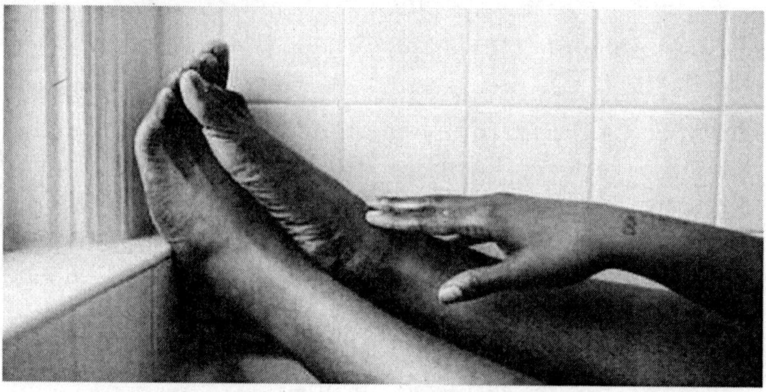

For small, localized areas, ghee is deeply nourishing and hydrating, and it is especially suitable for dry skin. For a formula that adds in herbal support to promote radiant skin and natural beauty, consider using Beauty Balm. This replenishing formula uses ghee as a base, adding in herbal ingredients to support radiant natural beauty. It can be used as a skin cream, eye cream, lip balm, and general moisturizer for the whole body.

Oils for Pitta: The primary qualities of pitta are oily, sharp, hot, light, fleshy-smelling, spreading, and liquid. Traditionally, light, cooling oils have been considered best for balancing pitta, such as Sunflower Oil or Coconut Oil. Cooling effect aside, the addition of herbs can greatly enhance the pitta-pacifying properties of these oils, especially since the concept of oil and the pitta dosha share a number of qualities. The following are some of our favourite herbal oils for keeping the pitta dosha balanced.

Pitta Massage Oil: Pitta Massage Oil is an excellent choice if you have a little more heat in your system and would like to keep pitta balanced or would like cooling support during the summer season. It combines herbs like manjistha, brahmi/gotu kola, shatavari, guduchi, and licorice to cool, soothe, and relax the body and mind.

Bhringaraj Oil: Infused with bhringaraj, known in Ayurveda as the "ruler of hair," Bhringaraj Oil is a great choice for a relaxing scalp massage with added hair benefits.

Brahmi Oil: We offer two varieties of this classic Ayurvedic oil. Also known as gotu kola, brahmi is considered to be one of the best Ayurvedic herbs for the mind. Try Brahmi Oil with Sesame if you want to retain some warmth, or Brahmi Oil with Coconut for maximum coolness.

Neem Oil: For skin that is showing the signs of excess pitta, Neem Oil is an excellent choice. Neem is an intensely cooling herb, which is why our Neem Oil uses a base of warming sesame oil.

Oils for Kapha: The main qualities of kapha are oily, cool, heavy, slow, smooth, soft, and static. Kapha and oil share most qualities. Because like increases like, using oil, especially cool oil, may increase kapha rather than decrease it. However, because oil has the ability to absorb the qualities of substances it is prepared with, appropriate herbal oils can actually decrease kapha. Oil combinations that feature heating, invigorating herbs and a lighter carrier oil are best advised for this dosha.

Kapha Massage Oil: A warming and revitalizing blend, Kapha Massage Oil includes herbs like punarnava, chitrak, calamus, and rosemary. Together, the herbs work together to create an energizing, activating, and mobilizing oil. It is a fantastic choice for the spring season or any time kapha is elevated.

Used with a more vigorous massage, this oil helps to stimulate circulation and lymphatic movement, bringing energy to the body and mind.

Sesame Oil, Almond Oil, or Corn Oil: These plain oils are considered warming and therefore good choices for kapha when used with a vigorous, energizing self-massage. If using Sesame Oil, opt for untoasted varieties that have a lighter scent. Our Refined Sesame Oil is an option you might consider.

Tridoshic Massage Oil: Daily Massage Oil is your tridoshic go-to oil for all doshas and can be used anytime, anywhere.

It combines powerful Ayurvedic herbs like guduchi to soothe and rejuvenate, bala to strengthen, and arjuna and tulsi to invigorate, promote circulation, and support the lymphatic system. Brahmi/gotu kola and bhringaraj are added to further support and steady the mind.

Dusting Powders for Abhyanga-Optional: Dusting is an optional step to abhyanga, but some people find it to be highly beneficial. For vata and kapha individuals, if dusting powder does not irritate your skin, you may enjoy using chickpea flour in the place of soap. Make a paste with the flour and water, gently apply a small amount to the body in the shower, and let it rinse off with the oil.

Dusting powder best accents the positive effects of abhyanga for kapha-types. Vigorously rub an appropriate kapha dusting powder into the body before or after performing abhyanga, either while working in or rinsing off the oil. You can use chickpea flour, but organic calamus powder (vacha) is also nice.

How to do Abhyanga

Taking the first steps to do a self-massage with oil may seem daunting, so if you're trying it for the first time, choose a more leisurely day.

Ayurveda recommends practicing abhyanga for a minimum of fifteen minutes in order for the effects of the oil to reach the seven dhatus, or tissue layers in the body.

Here is a wonderful self-massage routine offered by Dr. Claudia Welch that covers the key abhyanga massage steps. Try doing this routine in the morning for a vital day, or before bed for a more restful sleep.

1. Put about 1/4-1/2 cup oil in an 8-ounce squeeze bottle.
2. Place the bottle of oil in a pan of hot water until the oil is pleasantly warm. You can also try some alternative methods to heating massage oil if you'd prefer.
3. Sit or stand comfortably in a warm room, on a towel that you don't mind ruining with oil accumulation. Make sure you are protected from any drafts.
4. Apply oil generously to your entire body.
5. Massage the oil into your body, beginning at the extremities and working toward the middle of your body. Use long strokes on the limbs and circular strokes on the joints. Massage the abdomen and chest in broad, clockwise, circular motions. On the abdomen, follow the path of the large intestine, moving up on the right side of the abdomen, then across, then down on the left side.
6. Massage the body for 5-20 minutes, with love and patience.
7. Give a little extra time and attention to massaging the oil into your scalp, ears, and feet, at least once a week. Apply oil to the crown of your head (adhipati marma) and work slowly outward in circular strokes. Oil applied to the head should be warm but not hot.
8. Put a couple drops of warm Ear Oil on the tip of your little finger or on a cotton ball and apply to the opening of the ear canal. (If there is any current or chronic discomfort in the ears don't do this without the recommendation of your health care practitioner).
9. When you massage your feet, be sure to wash them first when you shower, so you don't slip.
10. Enjoy a warm bath or shower. A vata, pitta, or kapha dusting powder can help rinse off the oil without drying out the skin. You can use a mild soap on the "strategic" areas.
11. When you get out of the bath, towel dry. Keep a special towel for drying off after your abhyanga because it will eventually get ruined due to the accumulation of oil.

12. Put on a pair of cotton socks (organic, if you can find them) to protect your environment from the residual oil on your feet.
13. Applying a high-quality essential oil to your wrists and neck can further support balance. If you are not familiar with which essential oils are balancing for each dosha, try rose or mitti for vata, rose or khus for pitta, and hina or myrrh for kapha.
14. Enjoy.

Dosha-Specific Abhyanga

- Vata. Practicing abhyanga daily can be highly beneficial, even life-changing, for balancing vata. This dosha benefits from a warm oil massage in a warm environment. Avoid getting chilled afterwards.
- Pitta. Coolness is key. It is important to only gently heat the oil you choose for your abhyanga. Oil applied to the head should be cool in the summer and slightly warm in the winter.
- Kapha. It is usually best to use less oil for kapha abhyanga than for vata or pitta balancing self-massage practices, and use faster, more invigorating strokes.

Other Types of Self-Massage: Ancient Ayurvedic texts describe the benefits of massage for the whole body, but specifically outline the benefits of applying oil to the scalp, the ears, and the feet. Because Ayurveda considers the scalp, the ears, and the feet to be maps representing the whole body, massaging these areas can positively impact other bodily parts and systems.

Scalp Massage: Giving yourself a relaxing scalp massage (also known as murdha taila) is a deeply relaxing experience that has many benefits, including:

- Luxurious, thick, soft, and glossy hair
- Soothing and invigorating the sense organs
- Naturally and gently reducing facial wrinkles

Bhringaraj Oil, Brahmi Oil, and Healthy Hair Oil are especially well suited for scalp massage.

If your hair tends to remain oily after a scalp massage, apply shampoo before getting your hair wet and wash your hair in the shower as you normally would. If your hair is on the drier side, feel free to leave the oil in for a conditioning effect or simply rinse well with warm water.

Ear Massage: Due to their constant intake of sounds and stimuli, ears can become easily imbalanced by the vata dosha. Ear oiling (known in Sanskrit as karna pratisaranam) offers the following benefits:

- Balancing all three doshas (especially vata) in the ears for enhanced tranquility
- Promoting comfort in the neck and jaw muscles
- Helping the body produce and maintain a healthy amount of earwax

Our Ear Oil is a good choice when applying oil to the ears.

For a deeper grounding effect, you can try karna purana. This involves using more oil in each ear, about 3-6 drops, and resting with your head tilted for about 10 minutes before draining out the oil. Practice this monthly or as directed by an Ayurvedic practitioner.

Foot Massage: Massaging your feet (a practice known traditionally as padaghata) can be a deeply relaxing experience, especially when performed along with a scalp massage at night before bed. Some of the benefits of foot massage include:

- Providing comfort to sore, aching feet
- Strengthening the feet
- Enhancing vision
- Balancing vata
- Promoting healthy local tissues, veins and ligaments

Bhringaraj Oil and Brahmi Oil are especially well suited for foot massage. Sleep Easy Oil is a great choice for winding down for the evening as well.

Face Massage with Marma Points: Massaging your face with oil can help relieve tension in the face and promote a healthy complexion. To take your self-care practice even further, consider paying attention to the marma points of your face when practicing abhyanga.

Spending some extra time massaging the marma points of the face can help you maintain natural beauty in a healthy and rewarding way.

Dry Massage: While it doesn't include the application of oil, it's worth mentioning the Ayurvedic practice of garshana, or dry brushing. This is an invigorating and enlivening practice that is most balancing for kapha dosha, and it can be combined with oil massage for a more extended self-care ritual.

When NOT to Do Abhyanga: While self-massage is beneficial for most people at most times, abhyanga is not always recommended.

Ayurvedic oil massage can be a safe and beneficial practice while trying to conceive.

It is a great way to support healthy circulation and lymphatic flow, while gently cleansing and strengthening the tissues to prepare for a strong and healthy pregnancy. However, it is generally not recommended during pregnancy.

Abhyanga is also best avoided during the menstrual cycle, during times of great physical discomfort, or by those who have an acute illness or medical condition.

If any of these circumstances apply to you, please consult an Ayurvedic practitioner before trying abhyanga. If you're curious as to why abhyanga is not recommended for these conditions, read our blog article about when not to do abhyanga.

Cleaning and Plumbing Tips: While oil does wonders for the body, its slick texture makes it easy to spill. Oil can strain plumbing and cause the bathtub floor to get sticky. Here are some tips to address these problems.

- Tidy up after your self-massage. Keep a bottle of dish detergent in your shower or tub. When you are done washing, squirt some on the tub or shower floor and spread it around with your feet, sort of mopping the floor. Let the shower flow over it and wash everything down the drain. Doing this every time you wash after abhyanga prevents an accumulation of oil.
- Take care around slippery surfaces. If your balance is poor, the shower floor is slippery, or you fear you might slip, make sure that you hold on tight to something stable while you do this. Or get somebody else to do it or find another way to keep the floor clean. Please don't slip and hurt yourself. That would defeat the health-giving purpose of this practice.
- Clean your drain. Pour a little environmentally friendly drain cleanser down your drain once a month. Cold water used with soap that can dissolve in cold water may cause the oil to bead up and wash along the drain better than hot water, which liquefies the oil, making it more likely to stick to the plumbing.

Taking Care of Your Abhyanga Towels: Another unintended side effect of abhyanga is that the oil can cause towels or sheets to get rancid and ruined over time.

Preventing Oil Stains

- Organize your towels. Keep one towel for sitting on when you apply the oil and one that you use only for drying off after your shower. The first will get ruined the quickest. The second will eventually too, even with the best laundry techniques.
- Protect your bedding. Although it is ideal to practice abhyanga in the morning, some people don't have time then and prefer to do it in the evening before bed to calm themselves down. If you turn out to be one of these people, wear a "special" set of cotton (or other natural fibre) nightclothes for at least an hour after showering. They will absorb most of the remaining oil on your skin. And if you got oil in your hair, put a towel over your pillow to protect it.

Laundering Options for Oil Stains

- Make a DIY laundry detergent. Add a few tablespoons each of vinegar and baking soda to the hot water, once it has filled the washing machine. When combined, they can be a volatile mixture and eat through pipes, as well as oil. Added at the start of the wash cycle, though, this potentially corrosive mixture will be diluted and safe for plumbing by the time the washer drains.
- Use Lestoil. It is also possible to wash the towels with one tablespoon of Lestoil and no other laundry detergent and to spot-clean oily clothes by rubbing Lestoil into the spot and wash later.
- Find a natural detergent. There are also environmentally-friendly detergents and cleaners on the market that may be quite effective.
- Replace your towels and sheets. If you can't get all the oil out, you might plan to replace your sheets or towels about twice a year.
- Take care when drying towels. Oily towels and linens are at risk of catching fire if they become too hot. If a towel is very oily, even after it is washed, it's better to throw it away or hang dry. If you use a clothes dryer, it's better to use low heat. Do not leave oily towels in a hot car.

Nasal Saline Irrigation and Neti Pots

If you're one of the millions of Americans dealing with sinus problems, you know how uncomfortable facial pain and clogged nasal passages can be. In their search for relief, many have turned to nasal saline irrigation, a therapy that uses a saltwater solution to flush out the nasal passages.

Although several methods of nasal irrigation exist, one of the most popular is the neti pot, a ceramic or plastic pot that looks like a cross between a small teapot and Aladdin's magic lamp. Although nasal irrigation using the neti pot has been around for centuries, its use is on the rise in the U.S. The neti pot originally comes from the Ayurvedic/yoga tradition.

Does the Neti Pot Really Work: Some ear, nose, and throat surgeons recommend nasal irrigation for their patients who've had sinus surgery to clear away crusting in the nasal passages. Many people with sinus symptoms due to allergies and irritants in the environment also use neti pots or other nasal irrigation devices, saying they ease congestion and help with facial pain and pressure.

Research backs up these claims, showing that nasal irrigation can be an effective way to relieve sinus symptoms when used along with standard treatments.

For some people, nasal irrigation relieves sinus symptoms without the use of medications.

How does the neti pot work? At its most basic level, it thins mucus and helps flush it out of the nasal passages. A more biological explanation has to do with tiny, hair-like structures called cilia that line the inside of your nasal and sinus cavities.

These cilia wave back and forth to push mucus either to the back of the throat where it can be swallowed, or to the nose to be blown out. Saline solution can help increase the speed of the cilia and improve their coordination. This helps them better remove allergens and other irritants that cause sinus problems.

Neti Pot Solution: You can buy premade solutions meant for use in the neti pot or other nasal irrigation devices. But you can also make a saline solution at home.

Mix 3 teaspoons of iodide- and preservative-free salt with 1 teaspoon of baking soda. Store in a small, clean container.

When you're ready to use the neti pot, mix 1 teaspoon of this mixture into 8 ounces of distilled, sterile, or boiled and cooled water. For children, use a half-teaspoon of salt with 4 ounces of water.

Using a Neti Pot

Neti pots usually come with an insert that explains how to use them. Be sure to follow these directions carefully. You might want to ask your primary care doctor or an ear, nose, and throat specialist to talk you through the process before trying a neti pot on your own.

Fill the neti pot with the saline solution. Tilt your head over a sink at about a 45-degree angle. Place the spout into your top nostril, and gently pour the solution into that nostril. The fluid will flow through your nasal cavity and out the other nostril. It may also run into your throat. If this happens, just spit it out.

Blow your nose to get rid of any remaining liquid, then refill the neti pot and repeat the process on the other side. Always rinse your Neti pot or other irrigation device after each use, and leave it open to air dry. If you notice burning or stinging when you use the saline solution, cut the amounts of dry ingredients to make it weaker.

Figure: *A neti pot works by thinning mucus and helping to flush it out of your nasal passages.*

Sinus Rinse Dangers

Research has found that the neti pot, used as directed, is generally safe. A few regular users have mild side effects, such as nasal irritation and stinging.

You can also get nosebleeds, but they're rare. Reducing the amount of salt in your solution, using the neti pot less often, and changing the temperature of the water may help reduce side effects.

But it's possible to get a potentially serious infection from nasal irrigation. To prevent this, take these precautions:

Never use unboiled tap water for nasal irrigation. Some tap water contains bacteria or other harmful organisms. It's safe to drink since your stomach acid kills them. But they can live in your nasal passages.

Take proper care of your device. Nasal irrigation devices can harbor bacteria, too. Before you use it, wash your hands and make sure the device is clean and dry. After using it, always wash it thoroughly. You can wash it by hand or put it in the dishwasher if it's dishwasher-safe. Let your device air-dry completely between uses. Replace your neti pot every few months or as its directions recommend.

If you have side effects from using a neti pot or develop an infection, talk to your doctor.

How Often Do You Need to Use the Neti Pot?

In studies, people with daily sinus symptoms got relief from using a neti pot or other nasal irrigation system daily. Three times a week was often enough once their symptoms eased.

But using it too often can irritate your nasal passages. And it might be counterproductive to use it daily for a long time.

The mucus in our nasal passages helps to protect us against infection. It captures germs and irritants before they enter our bodies and can even kill some bacteria. Some experts think that when you flush out mucus with nasal irrigation, you lose some of that protection.

That's why it might not be a good idea to use nasal irrigation as a preventive when you don't have any sinus symptoms. Some experts say you should use it for no more than 1-3 weeks at a time.

If your symptoms don't improve, see your doctor. They can figure out what's causing the problem and find the right treatment.

Where Can I Find a Neti Pot?

Research has found that the Neti pot is generally safe. A small number of regular users experience mild side effects, such as nasal irritation and stinging. Nosebleeds can also occur, but they are rare. Reducing the amount of salt in the solution, adjusting the frequency of Neti pot use, and changing the temperature of the water may help to reduce side effects.

To help prevent infection, always use distilled, sterile, or previously boiled water. Also, it's important to properly care for your nasal irrigation device. Either wash the device thoroughly by hand, or put it in the dishwasher if it's dishwasher-safe. Follow by drying the device completely after each use. If you experience side effects or develop an infection, talk to your doctor.Neti pots are available over-the-counter at many drugstores, health food stores, and online retailers.

Nasya Oil

As always with our Ayurvedic practice, our focus, intentions and habits center around Prana, the vital life force that enters through the breath. Cleansing breath is the foundation of all health, and the nose, with its passages that lead directly to the brain, our consciousness, is the doorway where Prana enters our bodies.

Just like we sweep and clean the entryway of our home before guests arrive, we should cleanse and nourish our nasal passages to restore and balance our Prana. This offers multitudes of beneficial side effects for our overall health.

In Ayurveda, we use Nasya oil to perform this inner cleansing. Nasya treatment involves applying medicinal herbs, decoctions and oils to our nasal passages to support the sinus, nose, throat, and head. While different substances can be used depending on the ailment, we recommend adding one to your daily routine no matter what: Ayurvedic nose oil, or nasya oil.

Nasal oil in Ayurveda is infused with herbs to balance all Doshas, but especially Vata. This healing therapy involves anointing the nose in order to lubricate the nasal passages, provide subtle moisture to our breath, and nurture the higher cerebral faculties and sensory organs.

Nasya Oil Benefits - What is Nasya Oil Good For: Nasya oil supports our inner wellbeing and overall health. When you begin regular Nasya treatment, you'll see the benefits right away. Nasya oil can be used to increase mental function, as a preventative medicine, for better breathing, and for stress relief. Nasya soothes Vata dosha, Pitta dosha and Kapha dosha. What oil is best for you, depends on what is happening.

Nasya Oil Benefits: For Seasonal Transition Support: ubricating the nostrils with herbalized oil is especially supportive during seasonal transitions. During the shift from one season to the next, Vata, Pitta and Kapha are more in flux leaving us more vulnerable to stress and illnesses. There are many types of nasya oil. Which type of nasya oil is most beneficial depends on one's prakruti (constitution) and vikruti (current state) as well as location, stage of life and the season.

Nasya Oil Benefits - For Vata, Pitta and Kapha Dosha: For Vata dosha, the correct nasya oil can soothe anxiety, improve sleep, and improve focus. For Pitta dosha, nasya can cool off that hot headedness and may relief migraines when used as part of a comprehensive Ayurveda treatment plan. For Kapha dosha, nasya can invigorate and clear out dullness in the mind.

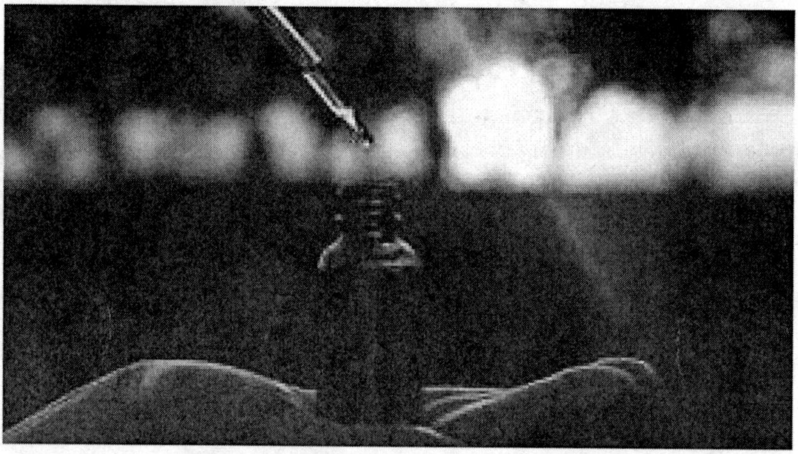

Figure: *hich Oil is Best for Nasya*

The beauty and effectivness of Ayurveda lies in its specificity of treatment.

So it is with nasya treatment. Which oil with which herbs will benefit you the most, depends on your what's going on for you individually, your stage of life, your location and of course your symptoms. There are many formula of nasya, however common base oils are sesame and ghee.

Nasya Oil for Improved Focus: Any medication that is administered through the nasal passages will affect the mind. In the case of Nasya oil, that's exactly what we want. The herb-infused oil will quickly reach your mind to promote concentration, mental clarity and a sharper memory. You'll even feel that you're perceiving the world around you more clearly - both consciously and physically, as nasya oil also supports clear vision.

Being a molecular scientist, it was difficult to grasp the simplistic complexity of Ayurveda, but the changes I experienced with Veena allowed me, not only a general understanding of health, but sparked a lifelong journey to use my knowledge to advance the acceptance of Ayurveda as a needed modality of health. This is a feat, considering I had difficulty focusing and digestive issues only four short years ago.

Nasya Oil as Preventative Herbal Remedy: Since Nasya oil application is a daily practice, it's benefiting our health constantly, in many different ways. Lubricating your nose helps protect you from the pollen, pollutants, and toxins that live in your environment and can slide through dry pathways inside your nose. Nasya oil can be used to prevent and treat allergies. It can also fend off headaches, earaches, sore throats, and other sinus-related symptoms.

Nasya Oil for Better Breathing: The flow of Prana relies on regular, grounded breathing patterns and clear nasal passageways. When all these align, all the vital organs, tissues, and cells are being nourished directly through the bloodstream. Nasya oil relieves mucus and congestion, clears stagnation and improves breathing for enhanced cerebral circulation, longevity, and vitality. It can even provide much-needed soothing for your vocal cords.

Nasya Oil for Stress Relief: When your Prana is cleared through your breath, you'll experience stress and tension melt away in your neck, jaw, head, and shoulders. Any energy that has been blocked will be released, and energy won't be able to stagnate in these areas. Mental and emotional stress and anxious thoughts contribute to fading health and many unnecessary afflictions. Nasya oil can help balance these energies, so you feel energized and revitalized all day long.

Figure: *Nasya Oil for Migraine Relief*

Nasya oil application is a daily practice, and herbalized oil applied to the nostrils is a direct route to soothing and rebalancing doshas in the mind channel. (manovahasrota). Think of it this way. Vata governs movement. Pitta is heat. What does heat do? It rises! When Vata is imbalanced it can push Pitta. In other words, heat goes to the head and migraines are the result. The causes of those doshic imbalances are different for every person, so treatment is customized at Saumya Ayurveda.

How Do I Know If I Have a Dosha Imbalance: Peruse these comprehensive and convenient lists of signs and symptoms of dosha imbalances.

Peruse these comprehensive and convenient lists of signs and symptoms of dosha imbalances. As we are comprised of all Vata, Pitta, and Kapha, there can be an imbalance in any of the doshas, or a combination of dosha imbalances. Read all three lists and see if anything looks familiar.

Nasya Oil Benefits for Hair Loss Treatment: Clearly there are many benefits to nasya treatment including increased focus, happier sinuses, improved energy, and migraine relief. In addition to those significant benefits, according to Ayurveda, nasya treatment can prevent hair loss as well as speed up hair growth. Rejuvenation treatments, which includes nasya oil, overall supports health and wellbeing and therefore slows down the again process. According to the Cleveland Clinic, 30 million women in the United States experience significant hair loss, a total of 80 million people are affected in the US.

Aromatherapy

Aromatherapy, or essential oil therapy, refers to a range of traditional, alternative or complementary therapies that use essential oils and other aromatic plant compounds.

Essential oils have been used for nearly 6,000 years, with the aim of improving a person's health or mood.

The National Association for Holistic Aromatherapy (NAHA) defines aromatherapy as "the therapeutic application or the medicinal use of aromatic substances (essential oils) for holistic healing."

In 1997, the International Standards Organization (ISO) defined an essential oil as a "product obtained from vegetable raw material, either by distillation with water or steam, or from the epicarp of citrus fruits by a mechanical process, or by dry distillation."

A range of essential oils have been found to have various degrees of antimicrobial activity and are believed to have antiviral, nematicidal, antifungal, insecticidal, and antioxidant properties. Aromatherapy applications include massage, topical applications, and inhalation.

However, users should be aware that "natural" products are also chemicals, and they can be hazardous if used in the wrong way. It is important to follow the advice of a trained professional when using essential oils.

Using Aromatherapy

Figure: *range of essential oils may help boost health and wellbeing.*

Aromatherapy is normally used through inhalation or as a topical application. Inhalation: the oils evaporate into the air using a diffuser container, spray, or oil droplets, or breathed in, for example, in a steam bath.

Apart from providing a pleasant smell, aromatherapy oils can provide respiratory disinfection, decongestant, and psychological benefits.

Inhaling essential oils stimulates the olfactory system, the part of the brain connected to smell, including the nose and the brain.

Molecules that enter the nose or mouth pass to the lungs, and from there, to other parts of the body.

As the molecules reach the brain, they affect limbic system, which is linked to the emotions, the heart rate, blood pressure, breathing, memory, stress, and hormone balance. In this way, essential oils can have a subtle, yet holistic effect on the body.

Topical applications: massage oils, and bath and skin care products are absorbed through the skin. Massaging the area where the oil is to be applied can boost circulation and increase absorption. Some argue that areas that are richer in sweat glands and hair follicles, such as the head or the palms of the hand, may absorb the oils more effectively.

Essential oils are never applied directly to the skin. They must always be diluted with a carrier oil. Usually, a few drops of essential oil to an ounce of carrier oil is the concentration. Most common carrier oils are sweet almond oil or olive oil.

To do an allergy test:

- Dilute the essential oil in a carrier oil at twice the concentration you plan to use
- Rub the mixture into an area the size of a quarter on the inside of the forearm

If there is no allergic response within 24 to 48 hours, it should be safe to use.

Some people report developing allergies to essential oils after using them many times before. If a new allergic response appears, the individual should stop using it immediately and avoid its smell.

To achieve a 0.5 to 1 percent dilution, use 3 to 6 drops of essential oil per ounce of carrier. For a 5 percent dilution, add 30 drops to one ounce of carrier.

A maximum concentration of 5 percent is generally considered safe for adults.

Ingesting, or swallowing, essential oils is not recommended. Taken by mouth, the oils can damage the liver or kidneys.

They can also lead to interactions with other drugs, and they can undergo unexpected changes while in the gut.

Benefits

Aromatherapy is a complementary therapy. It does not provide a cure for diseases, rashes or illnesses, but it can support conventional treatment of various conditions.

Figure: *A eucalyptus vapor bath may relieve symptoms of a cold or flu.*

It has been shown to reduce:

- Nausea
- Pain and body aches
- Anxiety, agitation, stress, and depression
- Fatigue and insomnia
- Muscular aches
- Headaches
- Circulatory problems
- Menstrual problems
- Menopausal problems
- Alopecia, or hair loss

Some types of psoriasis may find relief with aromatherapy, but a healthcare professional should advise about use and application.

Digestive problems may benefit from peppermint oil, but it should not be ingested.

Tooth ache and mouth sores can be relieved by clove oil, but this, too, should only be applied topically and not swallowed.

Supporters claim that these and a wide range of other complaints respond well to aromatherapy, but not all of the uses are supported by scientific evidence.

What do Essential Oils do

Different oils have different uses and effects.

- Basil essential oil is used to sharpen concentration and alleviate some of the symptoms of depression. It may relieve headaches and migraines. It should be avoided during pregnancy.
- Bergamot essential oil is said to be useful for the urinary tract and digestive tract. When combined with eucalyptus oil it may help relieve skin problems, including those caused by stress and chicken pox.

Figure: *Rosemary essential oil may benefit the nervous and circulatory systems.*

- Black pepper essential oil is commonly used for stimulating the circulation, muscular aches and pains, and bruises. Combined with ginger essential oil, it is used to reduce arthritis pain and improve flexibility.
- Chamomile essential oil can treat eczema
- Citronella essential oil is a relative of lemongrass and acts as an insect repellent
- Clove essential oil is a topical analgesic, or painkiller, that is commonly used for toothache. It is also used as an antispasmodic antiemetic, for preventing vomiting and nausea, and as a carminative, preventing gas in the gut. It has antimicrobial, antioxidant and antifungal properties.

- Eucalyptus essential oil can help relieve the airways during a cold or flu. It is often combined with peppermint. Many people are allergic to eucalyptus, so care should be taken.
- Geranium essential oil can be used for skin problems, to reduce stress, and as a mosquito repellant.
- Jasmine essential oil has been described as an aphrodisiac. While scientific evidence is lacking, research has shown that the odor of jasmine increases beta waves, which are linked to alertness. As a stimulant, it might increase penile blood flow.
- Lavender essential oil is used as an antiseptic for minor cuts and burns and to enhance relaxation and sleep. It is said to relieve headache and migraine symptoms.
- Lemon essential oil is said to improve mood, and to help relieve the symptoms of stress and depression.
- Rosemary essential oil may promote hair growth, boost memory, prevent muscle spasms, and support the circulatory and nervous systems.
- Sandalwood essential oil is believed by some to have aphrodisiac qualities.
- Tea tree essential oil is said to have antimicrobial, antiseptic, and disinfectant qualities. It is commonly used in shampoos and skin care products, to treat acne, burns, and bites. It features in mouth rinses but it should never be swallowed, as it is toxic.
- Thyme essential oil is said to help reduce fatigue, nervousness, and stress.
- Yarrow essential oil is used to treat symptoms of cold and flu, and to help reduce joint inflammation.

Oil for a massage will be mixed with a "carrier oil" that dilutes the oil and provides lubrication.

Visiting an Aromatherapist

The aromatherapist should take a thorough medical history, and a lifestyle, diet, and current health history.

Aromatherapy involves a holistic approach, so it aims to treat the whole person. Treatments will be suited to the individual's physical and mental needs. Based on these needs, the aromatherapist may recommend a single oil or a blend.

Depending on patient needs and preferences, the practitioner may recommend a single oil or a blend.

According to the National Cancer Institute (NCI), aromatherapy products do not need FDA approval as long as there is no claim that they treat a specific disease.

An aromatherapist is not the same as a massage therapist, although a massage therapist may use aromatherapy oils.

Risks

Each essential oil has its own chemical makeup and reason for use, so it is important to speak with a trained aromatherapist, nurse, doctor, physical therapist, massage therapist or pharmacist before applying or using an oil for healing purposes.

A trained professional can recommend and teach how to use each product, giving proper instructions on application or dilution.

Consumers should also be aware that the U.S. Food and Drug Administration does not monitor aromatherapy products, so it can be difficult to know whether or not a product is pure or if it is contaminated or synthetic.

Some beauty and household products, such as lotions, make-up, and candles contain products that may appear to be essential oils, but they are really synthetic fragrances.

Like medications, essential oils must be treated with respect. It is important to seek professional advice and to follow instructions carefully.

Caution when using essential oils: Since essential oils cause reactions in the body, not all the oils will benefit everyone. Chemical compounds in essential oils can produce adverse effects when combined with medications. They may reduce the effectiveness of conventional drugs, or they may exacerbate health conditions in the individual.

A person with high blood pressure, for example, should avoid stimulants, such as rosemary. Some compounds, such as fennel, aniseed, and sage act similarly to estrogen, so a person with an estrogen-dependent breast or ovarian tumor should avoid these.

Concentrated products may be poisonous before dilution and should be handled with care. A maximum concentration of 5 percent is recommended.

Some oils produce toxins which can cause damage to the liver, kidneys, and nervous system, especially if taken internally. Swallowing essential oils can be hazardous, and fatal in some cases.

Individuals with any of the following conditions should be extra careful when using aromatherapy:

- An allergy, or allergies
- Hay fever, a type of allergy
- Asthma
- Skin conditions such as eczema or psoriasis

People with the following conditions must be extremely cautious:

- Epilepsy
- Hypertension, or high blood pressure

If the oil is to be mixed with a carrier, the individual should tell the aromatherapist or massage therapist about any nut allergies, because carrier oils are often obtained from nuts and seeds.

Aromatherapy can have side effects, but these are normally mild and do not last long.

They include:

- Nausea
- Headaches
- Some allergic reactions

Use of aromatherapy by pregnant or nursing mothers has not been proven safe by research, so it is not recommended.

During the first trimester of pregnancy, aromatherapy may pose a risk to the developing fetus. Women who are breastfeeding should avoid peppermint essential oil, as it may be expressed in breast milk.

Essential oils derived from citrus may make the skin more sensitive to ultraviolet light, increasing the risk of sunburn.

Some oils may affect the function of conventional medicines, so people who are using medications of any type should first check with a qualified pharmacist or doctor.

Finally, when storing essential oils, it is important to be aware that light, heat, and oxygen can affect the integrity of the oil. Products should come from a respected and trustworthy source, to be sure of the quality.

Following instructions carefully reduces the risk of compromising the user's health.

In parts of Western Europe aromatherapy is incorporated into mainstream medicine as an antiseptic, antiviral, antifungal and antibacterial therapy. In the United States and Canada, this is less so. In France, some essential oils are regulated as prescription drugs, and they can only be administered or prescribed by a doctor.

Aromatherapy can help alleviate some conditions, but it should be used correctly, under the supervision of a qualified practitioner. The NAHA can advise on aromatherapists in your area, and some are members of a professional association, but until now there are no licensing boards for aromatherapists in the U.S.

Essential Oils

Essential oils are concentrated extracts of various plants. Practitioners use them in natural and alternative health practices, such as aromatherapy and naturopathy.

Many plants contain some potentially helpful compounds. However, in many cases, there is not enough evidence to suggest their use as a treatment or cure for ailments.

Figure: *Cold pressing and water distillation are two ways that manufacturers extract essential oils.*

Essential oils are liquid extracts of various potentially beneficial plants. Manufacturing processes can extract the useful compounds from these plants.

Essential oils often have a much stronger smell than the plants they come from and contain higher levels of active ingredients. This has to do with the amount of plant matter required to make essential oil.

There are different ways that manufacturers extract the essential oils, including:

- Steam or water distillation. This process passes water or hot steam through the plants, pulling the essential compounds away from the plant matter.
- Cold pressing. This process works by mechanically pressing or squeezing plant matter to cause it to release essential juices or oils. A simple example of this would be smelling the fresh scent of lemon after squeezing or zesting a lemon peel.

After extracting the active compounds from the plant matter, some manufacturers may add them to a carrier oil to get more product from the same amount of essential oil. These products would no longer be pure essential oils, but a mixture.

Uses: Manufacturers use essential oils to create a range of products. The cosmetic and makeup industry use essential oils to create perfumes, add fragrance to creams and body washes, and even as sources of natural antioxidants in some beauty care products.

Many natural medicine practitioners, such as aromatherapists, use essential oils. Aromatherapy involves diffusing these essential oils into the air. Aromatherapists believe that breathing in essential oils might allow them to enter the lungs and bloodstream, where some of the potentially helpful compounds may benefit the body.

Anyone who has used a mentholated vapor rub to help clear their sinuses has used a form of aromatherapy. As the authors of a 2013 study note, inhaling menthol in this way can reduce feelings of congestion and shortness of breath. As well as inhaling them, adding essential oils to a carrier oil and massaging them into the skin may also deliver the active compounds to the body. People should never apply essential oils directly to the skin without diluting them, unless under the direct guidance of a healthcare professional.

It is also dangerous to swallow essential oils. Not only are essential oils extremely concentrated, but they can also irritate the sensitive cells inside the body.

In rare cases, some people might take oral capsules containing essential oils. However, people should only do this under the guidance of a healthcare professional.

Typically, however, a person should not put regular commercial essential oils anywhere near their mouth or other places where it may enter the body, such as the eyes, ear, anus, or vagina.

Are they Effective

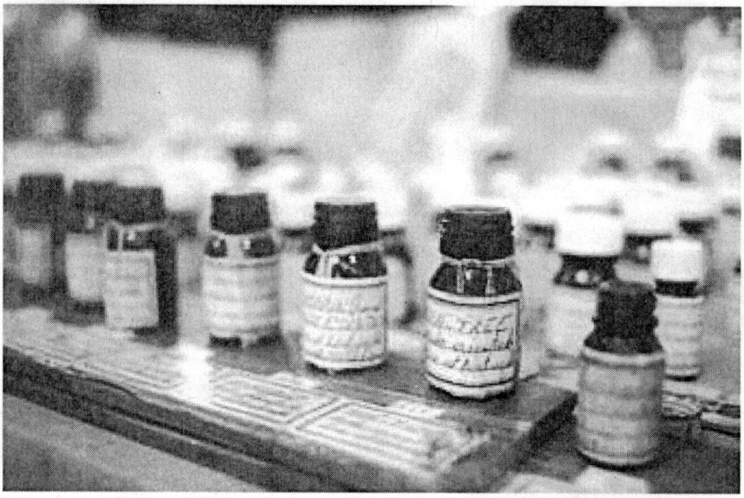

Figure: *Many different plants are available as essential oils.*

Some essential oils can be effective, depending on what a person uses them for. There is a range of plants that contain potentially active compounds. Manufacturers have turned dozens of these plant oils into.

Essential oil products. Some of the most popular essential oils include:

- lavender
- peppermint
- tea tree
- lemon
- sweet orange
- eucalyptus
- orange
- chamomile
- ylang-ylang

The compounds in these oils may have some health effects on the human body. The following articles provide more information on which common health conditions may benefit from the use of essential oils:

- headaches
- constipation
- depression
- cold sores
- sinus infections
- sore muscles
- anxiety

Side effects: Many people think that because essential oils are natural products, they will not cause side effects. This is not true. The potential side effects of essential oils include:

- Irritation and burning: Always dilute oils with a carrier oil before applying it to the skin. Apply a small amount to a small area of skin first to test for any reactions.
- Asthma attacks: While essential oils may be safe for most people to inhale, some people with asthma may react to breathing in the fumes.
- Headaches: Inhaling essential oils may help some people with their headaches, but inhaling too much may lead to a headache in others.

Risks

Accidentally ingesting essential oils can be dangerous and potentially life-threatening.

Figure: *It is important to dilute essential oils to help prevent side effects.*

A 2012 case study looked at a near-fatal case of someone who ingested peppermint oil. While most people do not experience such severe reactions, many oils can act as toxins inside the body.

Keep the bottle on hand to describe it to them. Getting essential oils into the eyes or mucous membranes may also cause burning and damage in the area.

If essential oils come into contact with the eyes, rinse them thoroughly with water and contact a doctor. Store essential oils out of reach of children and keep them apart from other products. Some essential oils can be deadly to pets, even if a person only uses them in a diffuser.

Always research which oils are safe to use around pets, or ask a veterinarian. It is still unclear what effect essential oils have on pregnant or breastfeeding women and their children. While some consider them safe to use, many doctors advise pregnant women to avoid essential oils.

Summary: Essential oils are the liquid extracts of potentially beneficial plants. People are beginning to use essential oils widely for a variety of common conditions, and some research shows they may help relieve symptoms in some cases. Essential oils are generally safe when a person uses them correctly. Always dilute essential oils before applying them to the skin and never ingest them.

Bibliography

Avalon, Arthur and Ellen : *Hymns to the Goddess*, Ganesh and Co., Madras, 1964.

Avalon, Arthur: *Hymn to Kali (Karpuradi-Stotra)*, Ganesh and Co., Madras, 1965.

Beyer, Stephen : *The Cult of Tara: Magic and Ritual in Tibet*, University of California Press, Berkeley, 1973.

Bose, Ram Chandra, *Brahmoism*, Oxford, New York, 1884.

Chattopadhyaya, Sudhakar: *Reflections on the Tantras*, Motilal Banarsidass, New Delhi, 1978.

Chawdhri, L. R. : *Practicals of Mantras Tantras,* Sagar Publications, New Delhi, 1985.

Cozort, Daniel : *Highest Yoga Tantra,* Snow Lion Publications, New York, 1986.

Crawford, Cromwell S.: *Ram Mohan Roy: His Era and Ethics*, Acharya Press, New Delhi, 1984.

Dyczkowski, Mark. S. G. : *The Canon of the Shaivagama and the Kubjika Tantras of the Western Kaula Tradition,* State University of New York Press, Albany, 1988.

Eliade, Mircea: *Rites and Symbols of Initiation*, Harper Torchbook, New York, 1965.

Feuerstein, Georg : *The Philosophy of Classical Yoga,* Inner Traditions, Rochester, 1996.

Guenther, Herbert. V.: *Gampopa's Jewel Ornament of Liberation,* Rider and Co., London, 1970.

Haich, Elisabeth : *Sexual Energy and Yoga*, Aurora Press, New York, 1982.

Karmarkar, R.D.: *Gaudepada Karika*, Bhandarkar Oriental Institute, Poona, 1953.

Kaushalayan, Bhadant Anand: *Swami Vivekananda and the Great Buddha*, Buddha Bhoomi Prakashan, Nagpur 1994.

Krishna, Gopi : *Kundalini: Path to Higher Consciousness,* Orient Paperbacks, New Delhi, 1976.

Majumdar, A. K.: *Caitanya: His Life and Doctrine*, MacMillan, Bombay, 1969.

Munshi, K M.: *Glory that was Gurjaradesa*, Rawat Press, Bombay, 1955.

Natalia V. Isaeva: *Shankara and Indian Philosophy*, SUNY, New York, 1993.

Pratyagatmananda, Swami : *Japasutram*, Ganesh and Co., Madras, 1961

Rajneesh, Bhagwan : *Tantra: The Supreme Understanding,* Chidvilas, Boulder, 1993.

Ranganathananda, Swami: *Science and Religion*, Advaita Ashram, Calcutta, 1978.

Sircar, D. C. : *The Sakta Pithas*, Indological Publishers and Booksellers, Delhi, 1973.

Taylor, A. E.: *Elements Metaphysics*, Methnen & Co., London, 1924.

Trevor Leggett: *Realization of the Supreme Self: the Bhagavad Gita Yogas*, Kegan Paul International, London, 1995.

Vidhushekhara Bhattacharya: *The Agamasastra of Gaudapada*, Motilal Banarsidass, Delhi, 1989.

Wheeler, Robert Eric Mortimer: *Civilization of the Indus Valley and Beyond*, McGraw-Hill, New York, 1966.

Yogananda, Paramahansa, *Autobiography of a Yogi,* Self-Realization Fellowship, Los Angeles, 1946.

Zimmer, Heinrich: *Myths and Symbols in Indian Art and Civilization*, Joseph Campbell, Delhi, 1946.

Index